Subject Leadership and School Improvement

Hugh Busher and Alma Harris
with Christine Wise

Paul Chapman Publishing Ltd
A SAGE Publications Company
6 Bonhill Street
London EC2A 4PU

SAGE Publications Inc
2455 Teller Road
Thousand Oaks, California 91320

SAGE Publications India Pvt Ltd
32, M-Block Market
Greater Kailash - I
New Delhi 110 048

British Library Cataloguing in Publication Data
A catalogue record for this book is available from the British Library

ISBN 0 7619 6620 X
ISBN 0 7619 6621 8 (pbk)

Library of Congress catalog record available

Typeset by Dorwyn Ltd, Rowlands Castle, Hants
Printed in Great Britain by Athenaeum Press Ltd, Gateshead, Tyne & Wear

Contents

iv *Subject Leadership and School Improvement*

Part IV   Efficient and Effective Deployment of Staff and Resources

11 Planning Development and Resource Utilisation to Improve Students' Learning

12 Working with Support and Supply Staff to Improve School Performance

13 Subject Leadership and School Improvement

References

Index
155

169

183

197

211

iv *Subject Leadership and School Improvement*

Part IV   Efficient and Effective Deployment of Staff and Resources

11   Planning Development and Resource Utilisation to Improve Students' Learning   155

12   Working with Support and Supply Staff to Improve School Performance   169

13   Subject Leadership and School Improvement   183

References   197

Index   211

Series Editor's Preface

The importance of subject leadership is now recognised. This book, which explores fully the research on subject leadership, sets an agenda for subject leaders which is challenging but provides guidance on all aspects of the role. It is legitimised because it is so profoundly based on practice with a clear understanding of the different environments in secondary and primary schools and the distinctive subject cultures within those phases.

The authors recognise the unique nature of different subjects, some with clearer accountability processes such as English in the secondary school and others with a more diffuse and complex cross-curricular role such as Special Educational Needs. In primary schools the role is arguably more complex because most teachers have responsibility for subject leadership possibly across Key Stages, but without the authority of responsibility and status. The distinctive role of the subject leader is therefore problematic. This book addresses these issues sensitively.

Hugh Busher and Alma Harris have, for many years, developed a thorough understanding of what actually happens in schools through their own research and through working with teachers. This enormously strengthens the quality of the analysis and guidance that is provided because it is so soundly based on evidence. They have a thorough understanding of international research and current government policy developments in the UK, which embeds their presentation in a broader perspective.

There is clear recognition of the importance of monitoring and evaluation, which is now widely recognised, but here placed in a context which enhances understanding. They have high expectations of subject leaders with the central focus on teaching and learning. There is encouragement of subject leaders to lead and manage staff, including support staff, a complex and difficult role, to understand the department culture, but also to reach outside the narrower school confines to work with parents and to develop professional networks.

Since this book is about subject leadership it will be of immense value not only for subject leaders, but also for all those working with subject leaders, particularly teachers who might aspire to the role, but also senior management. The importance of subject leadership to school improvement is now recognised as central. This is a particularly timely, high quality and significant contribution to the BEMAS Series.

Professor Harry Tomlinson, 2000

Preface

Curriculum and subject leadership in schools has gained substantial attention from both researchers and policy-makers over the last decade as they have come to recognise the centrality of this role in bringing about improvement in teaching and learning to meet the changing needs of students. Since 1998, the Teacher Training Agency (TTA) has reinforced the importance of subject leadership in school improvement, proposing a clearer definition of successful leadership at this level of an education organisation's hierarchy. This is set out in its national subject leader standards (NPQSL) and is reflected in the four main sub-sections of the book.

This book reflects critically on the work of subject and curriculum leaders especially in schools in England and Wales, i.e. within central government's policy framework of the Local Management of Schools, the National Curriculum, nationally directed school inspections, and the Teacher Training Agency. This sets the context for the book in five different dimensions, which all interact:

- a macro level of central and local government policy initiatives;
- a meso level of school policy constructed by senior staff and governors;
- a micro level of subject area activity and interpersonal relationships;
- a personal and interpersonal level of effective practice by subject leaders;
- and a multi-faceted conceptual framework of leadership, management of change and development, educational and social values, and successful professional teacher practice.

Subject leaders are part of the realm of middle management in education organisations, as well as having to be technical experts in their subject specialist fields. As leaders they have to manage the impact of these five dimensions on the work of students and staff in their subject area. As such they are key channels of and hold the keys to lines of communication in the structure of a school organisation. Within their areas they have to enthuse, monitor and develop staff and student performance; plan and sustain curriculum development; make appropriate resource allocations; and represent the views of senior staff to their team colleagues.

Subject leaders also have to manage the external environments of their areas, whether these are internal to a school – for example the actions and policies of senior staff and of colleagues in other subject areas – or located in the local and national communities which a school serves. To perform effectively in these arenas, subject leaders have to engage with the politics of school life as advocates for their areas. They also have to represent their areas to wider constituencies and agencies outside a school, such as parents and the business community. There is also a professional part of the external environment of schools which subject leaders have to monitor. This is the epistemological, pedagogical and professional framework of their subject areas.

As well as maintaining the effective functioning of existing educational and organisational processes, subject leaders have to work with their colleagues to bring about change and improvement to teaching and learning in their subject areas in order to meet an ever changing environment. Changes can be triggered by government legislation, by the changing policies of a headteacher or a school's governors, by demographic variations in a school's pupil intake, or by developments in knowledge in their subject areas.

In order to sustain a process of continual improvement, subject leaders and their colleagues have to engage in a rigorous and continuous monitoring and evaluation of the effectiveness of practice in their area. This involves them considering to what extent existing processes of teaching, learning, assessment, management and resourcing are meeting the needs of students and the educational values of the subject area and the school, and how those needs and values can be met more successfully. Evaluation may be carried out against predefined targets in the manner encouraged in Total Quality Management. However, control of evaluation within this framework tends to lie with those who set the targets, often senior or powerful staff within a school or even based outside it, such as inspectors licensed by the Office for Standards in Education (OFSTED). An alternative approach to evaluation, which locates ownership of the problem solving process with the subject area team, albeit within the organisational framework of the school, is a process of action enquiry or action research. It is this latter approach which is more likely to promote effective social cohesion in a subject area team and coherent and effective team approaches to improving practice.

Two key processes for bringing about change within a subject area are for subject leaders to foster a wide range of knowledge and understanding about teaching and learning, and to moderate the culture of the team

or subject area community towards one of inclusivity and empowerment. An aspect of the former is promoting a wider repertoire of approaches to teaching. Peer observation and mentoring by the subject
leader can help this, encouraging staff and students to reflect critically
on their practice in order to promote development rather than to secure
blame. An aspect of the latter is helping colleagues make public their
shared and disparate professional educational values and beliefs in
order to create an agreed but tolerant collegial culture which encourages
learning by students, staff and parents alike.

What is particular, then, about leading and managing the middle
realm of education organisations is the person-oriented nature of the
subject leader role. At the core of this role is a political process of co-
operation, conflict and compromise based on a tangled web of personal
and professional beliefs and values about the nature of education in a
particular subject area and the appropriateness of particular social relationships between teachers, students, parents, and leaders in educational institutions. People occupying this ground experience structural,
cultural and individual pressures and perspectives from their colleagues,
their students and other members of their role sets which interact with
each other and influence their professional practice as a subject leader.

On account of the many tensions and dimensions to managing in
and from the middle of education organisation hierarchies, Blandford
(1997) suggests that only those people who can handle such tensions
successfully can be effective middle managers. As Busher and Harris
(1999) point out, to sustain effective practice in such circumstances, let
alone bring about relevant change, requires subject leaders to be
adroit politicians in the micro-sphere of the school, wielding a variety
of sources of power and influence effectively, if subtly, to achieve
preferred educational and social values which are believed to meet the
best interests of their students.

The intention of this book is to be of interest not only to subject
leaders and curriculum co-ordinators, to help them reflect rigorously
on their practice, but also to those responsible for supervising them,
such as headteachers and school governors, to whom they are accountable within their institutions. We hope it provides a comprehensive conceptual framework for understanding the work of subject
leaders. However, in writing it we have become aware of the range of
unanswered questions which it has raised and which need further
research before there can be said to be a detailed understanding of the
role of subject leaders and the realm of middle management in primary and secondary schools in England and Wales.

Hugh Busher, 2000

Acknowledgements

We wish to acknowledge the teachers and schools we have worked with over the years and their generosity in co-operating in our various research projects. We are also grateful to Denise White and Val Jones for assisting in the final production of the manuscript. Finally, we are grateful to Marianne Lagrange for having the foresight and enthusiasm for producing a book on this timely and important topic.

1

Introduction

Curriculum and subject leadership in schools has recently gained substantial attention from both researchers and policy-makers in England and Wales as key post-holders for bringing about change and improvement. Work by Harris et al. (1995), Sammons et al. (1997) and Harris (1998) as well as that by Siskin (1994) and by Bell and Ritchie (1999) has pointed to the importance of this role. The Teacher Training Agency (TTA) has reinforced the importance of subject leadership in school improvement in England and Wales in the late 1990s by proposing a new measure of such leadership competence through the creation of national subject leader standards National Professional Qualification for Subject Leaders – NPQSL (TTA, 1998). These have provided a framework for the routine evaluation of the quality of subject leadership and subject areas in schools (OFSTED, 1999).

Research evidence on school improvement underlines the importance of focusing change efforts at different levels within the organisation (Fullan, 1991; Hopkins et al., 1994; 1997a). The importance of school-level, subject-area level and classroom-level change has been shown to be essential in successful school improvement programmes (e.g. Hopkins et al., 1996; Hopkins and Harris, 1997). Similarly empirical evidence in the field of school effectiveness points to the importance of mobilising development at school, departmental and classroom level. Recent research has shown that a substantial proportion of the variation in effectiveness among schools is due to variation within schools and has emphasised the importance of exploring differential effectiveness, particularly at the level of the subject area (Fitzgibbon, 1992; Scheerens, 1992; Creemers, 1994; Sammons et al., 1997).

The largest study of differential school effectiveness in the UK highlighted the importance of differences between departments as explanation for differences in school performance (Sammons et al., 1997). This research provided evidence that both schools and departments are differentially effective with pupils of different abilities and of different social and ethnic backgrounds. Furthermore, the study

1

suggested a need to reconceptualise school leadership more broadly to include leadership at middle-management level. However, as Glover *et al.* (1998) have argued, the distinction between middle and senior management remains blurred and demarcations of leadership functions are still not adequately delineated or defined.

The policy context

Since the mid-1980s in the UK there has been increasing central government control over core aspects of the education process in schools, especially over the curriculum and over teachers' practice. The former can be traced through the implementation of a National Curriculum since 1988, under the Education Reform Act 1988, with various subsequent revisions in the mid-1990s (see, for example, Chitty, 1993; Simkins *et al.*, 1992). This control has been strengthened by the introduction of national tests for students in schools in England and Wales, the results of which have been published as national league tables since the mid-1990s.

This policy thrust has to be understood in its international contexts. Since the early 1980s there has been an emerging international orthodoxy about the importance of the relationships between education and economic growth that is enshrined in statements and policies put in place by, amongst other institutions, the World Bank, the IMF and the OECD (Ball, 1999). This orthodoxy emphasises the centrality of the human factor in processes of production, viewing the skills and qualifications of workers as critical to the effective performance of businesses and countries (Taylor *et al.*, 1997, quoted in Ball, 1999). In this framework, schools and colleges are perceived by governments as the key agencies for creating an adequately skilled workforce to boost national economic performance, with all the social consequences that that implies. In Britain it has led central governments during the last decade of the twentieth century to want to create a 'world class education system' (Barber and Sebba, 1999: 184) – whatever other agenda they have been pursuing coincidentally to impose greater control over public sector professional workers, either through the 'discipline' of market economics or through tightening central government regulation.

The increase in central government control over education in England and Wales is also perceptible in its approach to teachers' practice. This can be traced through the enactment of different legislation in England and Wales since the mid-1980s. Since then central government has asserted ever tighter control over the standards of training for new teachers, gradually taking power away from provider institutions such as universities and colleges of education. The introduction of teacher appraisal in principle in 1986, and in practice in 1991, shows a growing concern by central government to define effective teaching and to shape teachers' professional development to meet these precepts. The introduction of OFSTED inspections of schools since 1993 in England and Wales, with their emphasis on evaluating classroom practice and school management, confirmed central government's intention to be the key definer of standards for teacher practice and for school organisational practice.

As part of this attempt to define standards of practice, the TTA, a central government agency, has, since 1995, set out to define not only the curriculum for the initial training of teachers, but the standards for serving teachers too. In 1997 it launched the national standards for headteachers, building on an earlier initiative for training newly appointed headteachers, the HEADLAMP scheme (see, for example, Busher and Paxton, 1997). In the Standards and Framework Education Act 1998 it was made clear that all teachers who wished to be appointed as headteachers after 2002 would have to achieve a nationally validated qualification based on these standards, the National Professional Qualification for Headteachers (NPQH). Both Ouston (1998) and Gunter (1999) interpret this as evidence of a strong centralist tendency by the UK government to assert its definition of effective teachers over previously held professional definitions.

In 1998, to complement the national standards for headteachers, the TTA launched, but did not immediately implement, National Standards for Subject Leaders (NPQSL) and National Standards for Advanced Skills Teachers. The purpose of these standards is to encourage headteachers and subject leaders to become effective by raising the performance of student achievement and learning to levels prescribed by central government. Fielding (1999a) points out how such an approach emphasises the importance of organisational structures rather than the needs of students and teachers working in them. He questions the impact such a depersonalised approach – with its emphasis on control (performance to standards set by distant authorities) – is likely to have on students trying to develop themselves as part of a process of education, especially those from socially disadvantaged backgrounds who are already questioning the power imbalances in society.

These standards assume that schools, like commercial businesses, can be run largely on rational technicist lines. As Ball (1999: 197) explains: 'What is happening within [central government's] ensemble of policies is the modelling of the internal and external relations of schooling and public service provision more generally upon those of commercial, market institutions.' Fielding (1999b) doubts the extent to which practices can be transferred without modification from commercial business to public sector service industries such as education. He also questions the extent to which the particular model of commercial leadership and management being presented to the public services can actually be considered effective even within a commercial milieu. Work by authors such as Hodgkinson (1991) and Sergiovanni (1994a) suggests that a much stronger attention to the moral and value dimensions of leadership is necessary than this technicist model suggests if organisations are to be run successfully. Blase and Anderson (1995), among others, suggest that a closer understanding of political processes within organisations is necessary, which this model largely ignores.

On the other hand, early evaluations of the National Headteacher Qualification (NPQH) scheme, a parallel and implemented model of leadership standards to that of NPQSL, suggest that it may meet the generic needs of headteachers in a variety of schools (Gunter, 1999), but leave unresolved some key issues. For example, Cubillo (1998) raises questions about the extent to which the assessment processes acknowledge the gendered nature of experience which male and female headteacher applicants have. Johnson and Castelli (1998) express concern that the qualification processes pay little attention to the spiritual and moral values that some headteachers may hold. Gunter (1999) herself suggests that the assessment processes for the qualification fail to take account of the political, moral and cultural dimensions which lie at the core of headteacher leadership in practice.

The national standards for subject leaders outline what the TTA (1998) perceived as the role and function of these office-holders in primary and secondary schools. These were categorised into four sections:

1) Strategic direction and development of the subject.
2) Teaching and learning.
3) Leading and managing staff.
4) Efficient and effective deployment of staff and resources.

These categories reflect much of the work that curriculum co-ordinators in primary schools and heads of department in secondary schools might have been expected to carry out since the Education Reform Act 1988, and the implementation of teacher appraisal in 1991 and regular school inspections since 1994. They reflect a considerable shift in focus in the role of such office-holders from that of a leading professional amongst colleagues to middle-ranking manager. Wise (1999) developed Hughes' (1976) model for headteachers and applied it to subject leaders. This draws on the distinction between subject leaders being chief executives, emphasising their managerial role, or leading professionals, emphasising the curriculum, staff development and pupil care aspects of their role. The emphasis on one or other has considerable implications for the cultures which subject leaders might construct with their subject area colleagues. Only the latter has so far been shown to be consonant with effective departments (Harris, 1998) and effective schools (Stoll and Fink, 1998).

Leadership from the middle

One of the fundamental findings of research in school effectiveness and school improvement is the powerful impact of leadership on processes of successful organisational practice. Research findings from diverse countries and different school contexts draw similar conclusions (e.g. Van Velzen *et al.*, 1985; Ainscow *et al.*, 1994; Hopkins *et al.*, 1994; Stoll and Fink, 1996). Essentially, schools that are effective and have the capacity to improve are led by headteachers who make a significant and measurable contribution to the effectiveness of their staff.

The work of UK researchers, such as Harris *et al.* (1996), Sammons *et al.* (1997) and Harris (1998), suggests that subject leaders can make a difference to performance in their subject areas in much the same way as headteachers contribute to overall school performance. This subject area sphere of influence has been termed the 'realm of knowledge' because of the importance of the subject boundary (Siskin, 1994). At this level too there is a major possibility of influencing whole-school development. Huberman (1990: 5) states: 'From the artisan's logic, I would rather look to the department as the unit of collaborative planning and execution. In a secondary school this is where people have concrete things to tell one another and where the contexts of instruction actually overlap.' These subject areas and, in secondary schools, subject departments are shaped by the cultures which subject leaders create.

An important insight from political and cultural perspectives on school improvement is that individual people matter. This acknowledges the humanity of people as they struggle to improve schools in complex sociopolitical contexts. Greenfield and Ribbins (1993) describe such individual perspectives as phenomenological. School organisations, like communities (Sergiovanni, 1994b), are made up of individual people who each have their particular agenda. It becomes the job of leaders and managers in schools and colleges to combine the individual agenda of staff and students in the service of the agreed common aims and goals of the institution. The teacher does this in the classroom with students, as much as a school's site supervisor does it with cleaning staff, or a subject leader or headteacher does it with the staff of a subject area or the staff of a whole school.

Creating social cohesion is not an easy job for subject leaders. Although different leadership styles are likely to affect colleagues' performances, the influences of leadership will be mediated by other factors, not least those values and perspectives held by other members of a subject area.

People create their own individual meanings for each social event or action in which they engage. Thus for every aspect of teaching or learning or involvement in school organisational activity each person, staff or students, governors or parents, will have a different interpretation. Although people may be willing to work in certain groups for much of the time, be it in a subject area, or key stage area in primary school, or in a class, their choice of membership is provisional and conditional. It is based on each person's willingness to remain part of that group, even when the formal opportunities for leaving it are limited. At those points when people (students or staff) cannot leave a group physically, perhaps for reasons of legal contract or social pressure, they may find other ways of resisting being part of its actions (see, for example, Wolcott, 1977; Plant, 1987) or becoming disaffected (e.g. Willis, 1977).

At the interface of student and teacher values, conflicts and homogeneities emerge as teachers struggle to implement national policies for schooling and students try to implement what they perceive as their learning needs. Teachers use a variety of strategies that try to take account of the students involved and the attitudes they hold, including trying to take account of the influence of the social and home backgrounds from which students come. This raises questions about how the values promoted by senior staff to staff and parents are translated into relationships in the classrooms between teachers and students.

Subject leaders stand crucially at this interface between the whole-school domain and that of the classroom. How they work with their colleagues and with the students in their subject areas will strongly help to shape the cultures of those areas. If the cultures they construct are dysfunctional, people in the subject area will not be helped to meet its purposes or those of the school. Staff in such cultures may be isolated from each other, not working as effective teams. Senior and middle-ranking staff are unlikely to be successful in helping their colleagues meet the challenges of the shifting external environment. Power is likely to be used to stifle initiatives, rather than to support and encourage change. Staff, parents and governors are likely to hold negative views of each other and staff are likely to undertake whatever strategies they can to minimise the other parties' influences on school processes. Consequently staff, pupils and parents are likely to be pursuing their own individual educational interests, values and beliefs rather than trying to discover common ones that address the needs of the students.

On the other hand people in effective schools and subject areas are likely to be part of, and help to generate, a very different culture (Sammons *et al.*, 1997; Harris, 1998; Stoll and Fink, 1998). In creating these cultures leaders at whole-school and middle level, including subject leaders, play a key role.

A conceptual framework

In hierarchical terms subject leaders are middle managers in schools and colleges. They are not part of the senior management team, responsible for the overall strategic development of a school, but are responsible for the operational work of others, namely, classroom teachers. Site supervisors and senior office administrators might, along with heads of academic and pastoral departments in secondary schools, also be classed as middle managers. These, too, are operationally responsible for overseeing and developing the work of their colleagues.

In schools these organisational hierarchical distinctions are not neatly delineated. Many staff will be involved in a complex switching of roles and lines of accountability between different aspects of their work. For example, in secondary schools most teachers will be responsible to both academic and pastoral heads of department for different aspects of their work. The demands of these two arenas can, potentially, be in conflict. Heads of academic departments will also be classroom teachers in their own or other subject areas. Heads of pastoral departments will work in subject areas and be accountable to academic heads of department. Indeed, senior staff will also work in classrooms and be accountable for this aspect of their work to middle managers.

Within this complex matrix of leadership and accountability, subject leaders are increasingly acknowledged to be key figures. Early research into the role of heads of department (e.g. Bailey, 1973; Busher, 1988; Earley and Fletcher-Campbell, 1989) was concerned with the responsibilities and time pressures upon them. Busher (1988) discussed how delegation of responsibilities led to staff development within a department. Most recently, attention has turned towards the leadership role of the head of department and relationship between departmental leadership and the differential performance of departments (Bennett, 1995; Harris *et al.*, 1995; Sammons *et al.*, 1997; Harris, 1998).

Busher and Harris (1999) identified five dimensions of the subject leader's work. These are represented in Table 1.1

Table 1.1   Dimensions of a subject leader's role

Role	Responsibilities
Bridging or brokering	Transactional leadership with senior staff and colleagues
Creating social cohesion	Transformational leadership to create a shared vision and collegial culture
Mentoring	Improving staff and student performance
Creating professional networks	Liaison with public examination and subject knowledge associations; knowledge of changing government policy; liaison with local authority support and parents
Using power	Expert; referent; reward; coercion; legitimate

The first dimension emphasises negotiation. It concerns the way in which subject leaders translate the perspectives and policies of senior staff into the practices of individual classrooms, as well as representing the views of their subject colleagues to senior staff and other colleagues (Busher, 1992). This bridging or brokering function, although perceived by the TTA (1998) and OFSTED as only one of the functions of subject leaders, remains a central responsibility. It implies a transactional leadership role for the subject leader. In this role, subject leaders make use of power – usually power over others (Blase and Anderson, 1995) – to attempt to secure working agreements with colleagues about how to achieve school and subject area goals and practices. Part of this role is the managing and allocating of resources available to a subject area, which in England and Wales is largely determined by the number of students taught a particular subject.

The second dimension emphasises group social processes. It focuses on how subject leaders encourage a group of staff to develop a group identity. This relates to the culture subject leaders create in their areas. The area, or areas, of subject knowledge the staff share usually defines the boundaries of the group in a secondary school. In primary schools it is more complex since every class teacher usually teaches every subject. There, the unit of social cohesion is likely to be the key stage area of the National Curriculum within which a teacher's class is situated. Glover *et al.* (1998) and Harris (1998) suggested that more effective subject areas have a sense of collegiality fostered by subject leaders helping colleagues in the area to shape and establish a shared vision of successful practice. This necessarily implies a leadership style that is people orientated and empowers others. It involves subject leaders using power with or power through other people to generate collaborative departmental cultures (Blase and Anderson, 1995). This style of leadership is termed 'transformational' and helps other people to alter their feelings, attitudes and beliefs, as well as coping with the organisational structures within which they work.

A third dimension focuses on individual people: on how subject leaders bring about the improvement of staff and student performances. At one level this implies a transactional leadership role for subject leaders, monitoring the attainment of school goals and helping staff and students meet particular prescribed levels of curriculum performance. On the other hand, as Glover *et al.* (1998) note, it suggests an important mentoring, or supervisory leadership role in supporting colleagues' development and the development of students academically and socially. In part this requires subject leaders to develop their skills in helping staff to reflect critically and communally on their practice (Smyth, 1991; Hopkins *et al.*, 1997b; Moyles *et al.*, 1998). In part it requires subject leaders to draw on their expert knowledge as well as their referent power to bring about improvement in practice (French and Raven, 1968).

A fourth dimension is oriented to the professional environment. It requires subject leaders to be in touch with a variety of actors and agencies in the external environment of a school and to negotiate, where necessary, on behalf of the other members of the department (Busher, 1988; 1992). For example, subject leaders need to keep in touch with the changing demands of National Curriculum and assessment policies in order to help their colleagues to be aware of these. In secondary schools this will include being aware of changes and guidance in public examination board syllabuses for Year 11 students. Other aspects of liaison might be with local curriculum development groups of teachers (Busher and Hodgkinson, 1996); with national professional associations for particular subjects to be aware of changing thinking on particular topics; or with local business for a variety of resources to enhance the learning opportunities of students.

These four dimensions of the leadership role of subject leaders are both complementary and potentially competing in their demands. They are linked together through a fifth dimension: the way in which subject leaders use power within and through particular organisational structures. They are made more complex because subject areas vary in size, configuration, status, resource power and staff expertise making the job of each subject leader contextually different from that of every other one. The different possible organisational structures for subject areas within schools are summarised in Table 1.2 and are discussed in more detail in subsequent chapters.

Table 1.2 Five different structures of subject areas – a typology

Area	Characteristics
Federal	Multi-subject; large (numbers of staff, rooms, budget); strong centre with integrated subdomains (e.g. science faculty in a secondary school; key stage area in a primary school)
Confederate	Similar to federal, but a weak centre; subdomains hold key power and collaborate (or not) over resources; 'an administrative convenience'
Unitary	Single subject but large (numbers of staff, rooms, budget); leadership and management functions can be shared corporately by members
Impacted	Single subject; small (numbers of staff, rooms, budget); can form part of federal departments or be free standing
Diffuse	Single subject or focus; taught across subject areas/most classrooms; small/large combination (taught in one room by many teachers or in many rooms, sometimes by one teacher only

Source: Busher and Harris, 1999.

The structure and argument of the book

This book is divided into four parts that reflect the four key areas of subject leaders' work outlined in the National Standards for Subject Leaders (TTA, 1998):

1) Strategic direction and development of the subject.
2) Teaching and learning.
3) Leading and managing staff.
4) Efficient and effective deployment of staff and resources.

Aspects of these four areas are discussed in the subsequent chapters of this book with particular reference to improving primary and secondary schools in England and Wales.

Part I: Strategic direction and development of the subject area

This part considers how subject leaders can bring about change within the context of different organisational structures. Chapters in this part focus upon the different school organisational and subject area of relationship taken and how subject leaders manage their subject areas. The chapters review the implications of the three main types of subject area – unitary, federal, and diffuse – for the work of subject leaders.

A key concept within Chapter 2 by Alma Harris is how change and improvement can be brought about in organisational contexts. The tension for subject leaders between developing their own subject areas and meeting the changing demands of external change is investigated and discussed.

Chapter 3 by Christine Wise continues the theme of tensions by recognising that, in some cases, these can be generated within subject areas because of the different agenda of different members of staff. How these tensions are managed to improve the quality of teaching and learning is addressed through an exploration of federal and confederate departments within secondary schools.

Chapter 4 by Hugh Busher considers the problems subject leaders encounter in trying to develop their subject areas when their subject involves a large number of academic staff in a school. This type of subject area is described as diffuse. In primary schools, where most teachers teach all the subjects in the National Curriculum in England and Wales, this is a particular issue. Within secondary schools the delivery of cross-curriculum skills, such as information and communication technology (ICT), or support, such as special educational needs (SEN), are examples of diffuse subject areas.

Part II: Teaching and learning

At the core of any successful subject area and, therefore, at the heart of the work of subject leaders is how successfully students learn. Part II addresses this challenge by first considering, in Chapter 5 by Christine Wise, how successful subject leaders need, themselves, to be aware of what constitutes effective teaching and learning. This is not merely a matter of knowing technically how to structure a syllabus and assess the learning outcomes from it, but also of understanding how teaching and learning within a subject area can be enhanced and improved.

To deliver a subject successfully to all pupils in a school, subject leaders have to work with other staff. Chapter 6 by Alma Harris discusses this aspect and considers how subject leaders may help their colleagues to evaluate and develop their repertoire of teaching strategies. This process involves extending teachers' classroom skills and contributes to the building of a rigorous reflection on practice.

Chapter 7 by Hugh Busher explores the importance of subject leaders working effectively to build strong and positive links with the parents and local communities from which their students come. The chapter considers the benefits to subject areas of developing such links.

Part III: Leading and managing staff

Just as the core business of any subject area is the effective implementation of teaching to bring about successful student learning, so the key means of achieving that is through the successful leadership and management of staff. This means subject leaders have to develop and help teams of staff to work effectively within their organisational contexts. Chapter 8 by Hugh Busher explores the management of subject areas in relation to general leadership within a school from the senior management team. This is balanced by a consideration of how subject leaders can create and sustain an effective team within their subject area.

An important element in the building and maintenance of teams is the quality of interpersonal relationships subject leaders help to create. Chapter 9 by Hugh Busher discusses how the values and beliefs subject leaders hold as part of their professional identity impinge on the constructed cultures of subject areas. As these cultures are jointly constructed by subject leaders and their colleagues, the chapter also discusses how subject leaders might work with colleagues to create effective or healthy cultures.

Working with academic colleagues successfully also involves subject leaders in helping them to develop their skills as effective teachers. Chapter 10 by Alma Harris considers how subject leaders can use processes of review and observation of practice to help colleagues reflect upon their work and to improve it. The chapter considers action research as a key way of promoting professional development within the subject area.

Part IV: Efficient and effective deployment of staff and resources

In managing their subject areas subject leaders need to bring about change by using physical and financial resources. This part deals with resources, including the support staff of a school as a resource for teachers in supporting the curriculum. It also discusses how subject leaders can use physical and financial resources effectively to sustain a curriculum. Chapter 11 by Hugh Busher considers the processes and pitfalls of development planning and how these are linked to budgetary decisions. Such decisions inevitably involve subject leaders and their colleagues in trying to create the optimum mix of resources to sustain the curriculum of each group of students, at least through time.

Chapter 12 by Hugh Busher discusses how subject leaders can work successfully with cover supply staff and groups of non-teaching staff. The chapter argues that, although in many cases support staff appear to be peripheral to the work of the subject area, they provide essential support. Often their work and its importance go unnoticed by subject leaders and, as a consequence, their contribution to effective teaching and learning may not be managed as effectively as possible.

Chapter 13 by Alma Harris considers how recent evidence concerning school improvement highlights the importance of devolved leadership at different levels within the school organisation. It also points to the contribution of departmental improvement to whole-school improvement. The chapter considers the conditions required for improvement in a subject area and discusses ways in which the subject leader might secure the conditions for improvement at the departmental level. The chapter concludes by outlining the strategies for departmental improvement and illustrates how subject leaders can make a difference to departmental performance.

Part I

Strategic Direction and Development of the Subject Area

2

Managing Change within the Subject Area

This chapter considers the subject leader's role in managing the change process. It is clear that this is an important role if subject areas are to develop and improve. At the core of the change process are two main levers: planning and evaluation. Planning is the main lever for initiating and promoting departmental change, while evaluation is the lever for sustaining change and gauging its impact. Both are required for change to take place and, more importantly, to be effectively implemented.

Yet the process of change will be experienced differently because of the variation in departmental configuration. Within any school there will be a range of departmental types that have distinctive cultures. The task facing the subject leader is to understand the culture of the department and to build collaboration and commitment to change and development.

Introduction

Whether subject teams work collaboratively will largely be dictated by the subject leader. Similarly, the extent to which teachers share common goals and subscribe to a shared vision will be partly dependent upon the subject leader's management style. Essentially, the subject leader is in a position to affect the motivation and performance of other teachers. By implication, if this is well managed it will make a positive impact upon the quality of teaching and will also contribute to whole school improvement.

While the complexity and uniqueness of each school context are acknowledged, research evidence has shown that there are some generic features that effective subject areas share (Harris *et al.*, 1995; Harris, 1999a). These features include a 'climate for change' or 'a climate for improvement'. This essentially means the subject area is committed to improvement and is prepared to change existing practices. Developing this climate has been found to be a necessary prerequisite of effective change at the levels of both the school and the subject area.

A core responsibility of the subject leader is to create a climate for change and to manage the change process. This inevitably involves the management of innovation as subject leaders seek to develop and improve their subject areas. Leadership is essentially about inspiring and enhancing the talents, energies and commitment of others. This necessitates developing and sustaining a shared vision, communicating shared values and motivating those within the team to accept and implement change (Day *et al.*, 2000).

Subject leaders are responsible for formulating and implementing a policy for the subject, for setting subject area targets and for ensuring subject area plans are put into practice. Such activities require the co-operation of all the staff who contribute to the subject area or department (Harris, 1999a). However, such co-operation may not be easily achieved, particularly when the proposed changes or developments imply a greater workload for others. Consequently, in order to manage change effectively, subject leaders needs to understand the nature of change and why barriers to change might occur.

The nature of change

During the 1990s the education system in England and Wales was subject to more regulation, standardisation and school-based change than during any other decade in its history. The net result of such change has been an increased emphasis upon 'improving standards' and 'school performance'. The central theme of the UK government's education policy as outlined in the white paper *Excellence in Schools* (1997) is 'the crusade for higher standards'. This dominant discourse has manifested itself in a whole range of externally imposed changes. These have resulted in schools and teachers feeling both swamped with change and tired of innovation (Hargreaves, 1994).

In considering the nature of change, Fullan (1991) makes an important distinction between the terms *change* and *progress*. While all progress necessarily involves change it is important to recognise that all change does not necessarily equate with progress. In other words, it may be more of a contribution to progress to resist ill-conceived change and to reject innovation that is politically rather than educationally driven.

Change itself is a complex phenomenon that needs to be understood by those intending to instigate change. Hopkins *et al.* (1996) suggest that change tends to manifest itself in two distinctive ways within a school organisation. The first way is *incremental change* that is a gradual and sometimes subtle transition from one state to another. Here the change process may occur as the result of internal factors such as changes in personnel, or external factors, such as a change in the statutory curriculum requirements. This form of change is gradual, unintended and rarely involves planning. In contrast, the second way in which change manifests itself within a school is in the form of *planned change*. Planned change deliberately seeks to alter and interrupt the natural course of events (Fullan, 1991). It is a conscious intervention that is purposive and that aims to create a new order or to establish a new set of practices. For subject leaders, this second approach to change is more likely to result in improvement but is also likely to incur most resistance (Harris, 1999a). The reason for this resistance may well be directly associated with the type of change proposed but in most cases it occurs as a natural response to the presence and pressures of the change process.

Fullan (1991) suggests that at the crux of change is how individuals understand and experience the proposed change. In the pursuit of change, very rarely do those proposing it or enforcing it think about what it means to others at a *personal* level. Yet, how others feel about the change is a critical determinant of how they will ultimately respond to it. Consequently, the feelings of team members concerning the change need to be pre-empted and considered very carefully by the subject leader.

Marris (1993) argues there is a major difference between voluntary and imposed change and that people's responses to all change is to feel loss, anxiety and struggle. Accepting these responses as a natural and necessary part of the change process is important for the subject leader. Negative responses to change may be viewed by subject leaders as recalcitrance on the part of team members or a general lethargy to undertake more work. However, if the subject leader acts on such an interpretation it can lead to resentment and misunderstanding by team members which, in turn, makes the proposed change even more difficult to put in place.

An alternative response from the subject leader is to try to understand the nature of the resistance. For some team members the proposed change may leave them feeling vulnerable or apprehensive, for others the increased workload involved in the change might leave them feeling pressurised and stressed. Whatever the response and its cause, it is important that subject leaders anticipate there will be some resistance to change and to try to understand the basis for this resistance. Marris (1993) suggests the purpose of change has to be understood by all team members and that the implications of the change are clear and accepted. This requires anticipation of the possible responses from team members prior to introducing the change. It also necessitates the subject leader considering the proposed change in some depth before sharing it more widely with the team.

Subject leaders need to focus upon some key questions prior to introducing changes:

- How convinced am I of the importance of the proposed change?
- How transparent can I make this change to others?
- How necessary is this change at this time?
- How will others view this change and respond to it?
- What will be the main benefits from this change?

By considering these questions in advance of introducing a new development, the subject leader takes control of the change process. This forward planning is essential if the change process is to be introduced and managed effectively.

Managing the change process

A major reason for the failure of change at both school and subject-area level lies in a lack of careful attention to the process of change. While the instigation of change is relatively straightforward, the subsequent interpretation and implementation of any change are much more difficult. As Fullan (1991: 65) has summarised, 'educational change is technically simple and socially complex'. While the rationale for change may be clear and the type of change well defined, its interpretation within a school or subject area may create difficulties because of the social processes involved.

Although the change process itself may be thought of as a linear and logical process, in reality it is iterative and messy. Miles *et al.* (1988) describe the change process as having three major components:

1) initiation
2) implementation
3) institutionalisation.

These three components are not linear but merge into each other as the change process unfolds. Fullan (1993) suggest that an important element of initiation is raising awareness among staff of the need for change and of the possible plans for implementation. Hopkins *et al.* (1994) suggest these three phases are overlapping and are not mutually exclusive. However, in order for subject leaders to manage the change process effectively it is important not only to understand what each phase involves but also to consider how they interact. These three phases are discussed below.

Initiation

The initiation phase is the point at which the proposed change is introduced. There may be various routes to reaching this stage. For example, the proposed change may emerge from a subject area review, be imposed by the senior management team or may result from a problem within the subject area. The origin of the change is important because it will have a direct affect on the way in which the change is introduced and understood (Hopkins *et al.*, 1996). There are many variables influencing both 'if 'and 'how' a change is introduced. Fullan (1991) has identified a range of barriers that affect the initiation of change. There are two barriers of direct relevance to subject leaders.

The first barrier to change is the lack of access to information about the change itself. For many teachers change is simply imposed from above or externally generated (e.g. the National Literacy Strategy). As a result they are rarely given the opportunity to share in the decision-making processes that have led to the change. As a consequence, initiation of that change by subject leaders can be difficult. Where teachers are kept informed of proposed changes and are part of the decision-making process, a greater sense of commitment and support for the change is generated (Fullan, 1991; Hargreaves, 1994). It may not always be possible for subject leaders to keep all team members informed of every discussion or development but where important and major changes are concerned, the primacy of access to information cannot be underestimated.

A second barrier to the initiation of change are the competing pressures and demands upon teachers' time. In recent years, increased curriculum demands upon teachers in the UK have meant they have less time to meet with each other to discuss new ideas (Ball, 1999). The research evidence demonstrates the potency of teachers working together but also indicates that teachers have less and less time to do so (Day, 1999). It is clear that school development and improvement occur when teachers:

- engage in frequent, continuous and concrete talk about teaching practice;
- frequently observe and provide feedback to each other; and
- plan, design and evaluate teaching materials together.

(Little, 1993)

Where such norms of collaborative practice are not in place, innovation and the initiation of change become more difficult to achieve. Consequently, where possible, subject leaders should encourage and plan for teachers to work together. In this way the initiation and implementation of change has a more secure basis and is more likely to succeed.

Implementation

Whether or not a change happens in practice is largely dependent upon the quality of implementation. This is the phase where the change or innovation is put into practice. It is the stage where planning stops and where action commences. For a large number of innovations this is where change flounders and loses momentum. Fullan (1991) suggests there are a range of factors that causally influence implementation and contribute to the process of successful change. Some of these have been mentioned earlier (e.g. quality and practicality of the change, clarity of the proposed change and the effect of the change on individuals).

For subject leaders, the main tasks during the implementation phase are the carrying out of action plans, developing and sustaining commitment, checking progress and overcoming any problems. During this phase there will be a need for a combination of *pressure* on and *support* for teachers from the subject leader. There has to be enough pressure to ensure the momentum of change continues and that action takes place. Conversely, there needs to be technical, emotional and professional support to ensure team members feel equipped to take on the tasks related to the change (Stoll and Fink, 1998). If there is too much pressure, stress will result. If there is too much support, complacency will follow. It is important subject leaders retain a balance between pressure and support in order to move change through the implementation phase.

During the implementation phase there will be a crucial time when the change appears to be making little progress. Fullan (1991) has termed this the 'implementation dip' which is inevitable in most change processes. Subject leaders need to recognise that this is an intrinsic part of the change process and does not mean the change has failed. Instead, it indicates the change is at a critical stage and that additional effort is required to mobilise the change. In some respects, things will get worse before they get better as people grapple with the meaning and skills of bringing about change (Joyce and Showers, 1988).

The key factors for success at this stage are as follows:

● Shared clarity about the purposes and intentions of the change.
● Shared control over implementation (i.e. team responsibility).

- A mix of pressure and support.
- Early feedback on progress made.
- Teacher trust and collegiality.

Clearly, these factors need to be nurtured and developed by the subject leader. With each successive change, subject leaders and their team members will be more skilled in the change process and more able to ensure the changes implemented are sustained and continued.

Institutionalisation

The point at which the innovation is part of the everyday work of the subject area means the change has entered the continuation or institutionalisation phase. This is the phase where the change is not regarded as being anything new because it has been embedded into the systems and culture of the subject area. While it might be assumed this will happen automatically, in practice it requires that the change is monitored and evaluated to ensure it is making the intended impact and that this impact is sustained. The role of the subject leader will be to ensure appropriate monitoring and evaluation mechanisms are put in place to provide feedback not only on the initial impact of the change but also on the extent to which it is still in operation as intended. As Huberman and Miles (1984: 14) note: 'Innovations are highly perishable goods. Taking continuation for granted assuming magically that it will happen by itself, or will necessarily result from a technically mastered, demonstrably effective project – is naïve and usually self defeating.'

The impact and outcomes of change will be dependent upon the quality of the initiation and implementation plus continuous monitoring and evaluation. One common misapprehension about evaluation is that it occurs at the end of a change or new development. While summative evaluation is important it is formative evaluation that contributes most to effective implementation and continuation. This feedback loop ensures the process of change is sustained and that evidence about the impact of the change process at different stages is systematically recorded.

Change can result from a wide variety of sources. It might occur as the result of a policy directive, from feedback or review data or in response to a particular issue or problem within the subject area. Whatever the impetus for change, it necessitates careful planning and systematic evaluation in order to succeed. As strategic planning is outlined in some detail in Chapter 11, the relationship between evaluation and change will be considered next.

Evaluating change

An important dimension of managing change is judging whether, and to what extent, the change has fulfilled its intentions. Gauging the impact of change is difficult without the existence of clear targets and, by association, requires evidence or feedback about progress towards these targets (Fidler, 1996). Hence, evaluation provides a basis upon which the subject leader is able to make judgements and informed decisions. While definitions of evaluation may vary, in essence, evaluation is the process of systematically collecting and analysing information in order to make informed judgements based upon sound evidence (English and Harris, 1987; Hopkins, 1997). Using this definition, it is evident that the validity of the judgements made is highly dependent upon the nature and the provenance of the data collected. Consequently, the evaluation methods and processes require careful planning and scrutiny.

Hardie (1995) suggests that an evaluation needs to be:

- comprehensive
- systematic
- objective
- reliable.

It has to be comprehensive in so far as it collects a range of data on the development or change. It has to be systematic in the way the data are collected and as far as possible to look at the evidence in an impartial and objective way. Finally, the data collected need to be reliable in order to substantiate and validate the subsequent judgements. Subject leaders need to ensure any evaluation process has these four elements and is focused upon a specific stage of the change process.

Prior to the *initiation stage* of any change process evaluative evidence has to be used to judge whether, firstly, change or development is needed; and, secondly, what type of change and development would be most suitable and feasible. There is a close parallel in this phase of the process with the early steps in an action research spiral which is discussed in more depth in Chapter 10. Evaluation at this stage is much like a feasibility study, gauging the level of support, resources and development required for change to take place. This may involve a forcefield analysis or an audit of current strengths and weaknesses within the subject area. Such evaluative work may arise from a perceived problem or issue within the subject area. Alternatively, the subject leader may want to make some particular change but wants to consider the options for and implications of action before moving into the initiation phase. Fullan (1999) has warned against the proliferation of 'Christmas tree change' which means avoiding the adornment of too much change. He suggests moving towards strategic, planned and evaluated change. If subject leaders incorporate evaluation at the outset of any development it is more likely to lead to change that is meaningful and useful within the subject area. Some evaluative questions subject leaders might ask at the initiation stage are as follows:

- Is the proposed change/development necessary at this time?
- Does the proposed change/development build upon the subject team's strengths?
- Can the proposed change/development be properly resourced? Are additional resources required?
- What will be the benefits of the proposed change/development? How will these be monitored and evaluated?

At the *implementation phase* the evaluation process concentrates upon providing evidence of the impact of change and highlighting any barriers or difficulties incurred as the change becomes embedded in an institution. This formative feedback is important because it provides the basis for altering aspects of the change or development as it is taking place. It also provides an early warning system that problems are being encountered and hindering successful implementation. This evaluation feedback allows the subject leader to problem solve and to make decisions about fine tuning or altering aspects of the change/development on the basis of evidence rather than on the basis of intuition. Munn and Drever (1991) suggests the overall aim of evaluation during this phase is to provide some systematic and reliable information that can be used as a basis for action. Some evaluative questions subject leaders might ask at the implementation stage are as follows:

- How well is the change/development being introduced?
- What are the indicators of success to date?
- What are the major barriers? How might these be overcome?
- Are any changes/modifications required? How might these be introduced?
- What balance of pressure and support is now needed to sustain the change/development?

At the *institionalisation phase* the purpose of the evaluation is to make some judgements about the overall impact or effect of the change/development. However it is important not to make the evaluation task overly burdensome by devising and using too many data collection tools. The types of questions that can assist the subject leader in making judgements at the continuation phase are as follows:

- What have been the main outcomes from the change/development?
- Have there been any unintended outcomes?
- To what extent has the change/development improved work within the subject area?
- What further changes should be made?

A cycle of review, planning, action and evaluation lies at the heart of improving schools and subject areas. Therefore, an evidence-based approach to managing change is vital to the development and the continued success of a subject area. Collecting evidence can be time-consuming so it is important that the evidence that is collected provides the basis for making a judgement on the evaluation issue or question. So, for example, in order to evaluate the impact of a scheme of work on the quality of student learning, sources of data might include test scores, student work and classroom observation. There is a range of data collection methods that have various advantages and disadvantages. English and Harris (1987: 39) have provided a summary of data collection methods, which is shown in Table 2.1 on page 27.

Evaluation involves more than attention to inputs, processes and outcomes. It has to be forward looking as well as reactive or summative in order to inform the next development or change. The best managed companies have a few formal evaluations only. Instead, they focus on measuring success criteria and building evaluation into their development and change processes.

The purpose of evaluation is to inform practice. To do this it needs to be an integral part of what happens within subject areas – a positive and encouraging aspect of the work being undertaken. Consequently, it is important that all teachers who are affected by any process or change are involved in all the steps of implementing and evaluating that change. Holly (1987) suggests teachers should own the process of evaluation by being involved in it and learning from it. Subject leaders, therefore, have a role to play in not only ensuring evaluation takes place but that team members are part of the evaluation process. The different ways in which subject areas are configured will affect the way in which that role is played.

Subject areas: diversity and change

The realm of the department in secondary schools presents a considerable range of organisational differentiation. In a secondary school, subject departments range from multidisciplinary departments such as design and technology, or science with many staff in them, to departments staffed by one or two people or even one person (the

Table 2.1 Summary of evaluation tools

Tool	Advantages	Disadvantages	Particular uses
Interview	Allows for an in-depth response from various informants (i.e. pupils, teachers, governors, etc.)	Time-consuming. Analysis can prove difficult	To obtain information which would not be easily obtained from a questionnaire (e.g. sensitive, personal information)
Audio-tape recording	Provides a complete record of a conversation or interview	Can often inhibit individuals from giving certain kinds of information	To obtain complete records and detailed evidence
Video-tape	Provides visual information	Can often be inhibitive. Can prove expensive and difficult to organise	To obtain information which can be used later in a diagrammatic way. A complete visual record
Questionnaire	Can reach large numbers of respondents. Can provide both quantitative and qualitative data	Return rate can often be low and the information collected may be of little value	To obtain specific information and feedback from a potentially large number of people
Survey	Can yield an enormous amount of information in a very economic way	Not very flexible. Time-consuming to conduct	Appropriate when large samples are involved
Observation	Can reveal characteristics of group or individuals that would be difficult to obtain by other means	Time-consuming and subjective	Appropriate for looking at teacher–pupil relationships or interaction in the classroom
Logs, diaries	Quick and easy to produce. Can provide in-depth information	Time-consuming to keep and analyse	For obtaining insight into pupils' views or ideas about an initiative

Source: English and Harris, 1987.

subject leader) and several part-time staff (e.g. a music department or history department). Furthermore, in some of the larger departments there may be several subject leaders, each with a particular subject specialism, responsible for creating an inspiring vision in their area which fits within the overall vision of a faculty area. In such academic departments (e.g. a humanities or science department), the head of faculty may supervise the work of a specialist department and also has responsibility for co-ordinating the work of the other subject leaders in the area (Kemp and Nathan, 1989; Busher and Blease, 2000). This suggests that not only do heads of department face competing demands in managing change but that they also have widely differing arenas in which to exercise their power.

In secondary schools different departmental structures can be easily defined by size, configuration, staff membership and subject expertise. Using these defining features of departmental structure, it is possible to identify five departmental types, as Busher and Harris (1999) argue. The first and largest, containing many members of staff and possessing generous resources, are *federal* departments, such as science faculties or humanities departments. These federal departments are likely to contain and support the teaching of several departments. These usually encompass cognate subjects, such as in science faculties. Alternatively, such large departments may be largely an administrative convenience, as perhaps in the case of some design and technology departments. These departments can be described as *confederate* departments. In this type subject areas are allied together but share little in common with each other. In such departments, the culture is likely to be heterogeneous, with individual departments creating their own identities that are at best in harmony with each other, but have the potential to be conflict.

A third type of large-scale department is the *unitary* department defined by a single subject (e.g. English or Mathematics). In this case, only one subject would be taught within the unitary department. Smaller than unitary departments but also teaching a single subject only are departments which might be described as *impacted*. This fourth type is represented by the departments in secondary schools which have very few staff, some of whom are part time and/or teach other subjects as well. They are likely to have a few rooms only in which to teach, and may have relatively small budgets. These most commonly include departments such as Music, History and Geography.

The fifth type of departmental structure can be termed *diffuse*. For example, in a primary school information technology may have no identifiable base and may be taught by a wide variety of staff under the guidance of a school co-ordinator. It may be very difficult for the subject leader to create a sense of subject identity under these conditions. Consequently, co-ordination may fall into a largely technical, instrumental process with the subject leader creating materials for the other staff to use. Such informal administrative processes are likely to be supplemented by infrequent team meetings focusing on predominantly instrumental matters.

These different departmental structures inevitably affect the leadership approaches of a subject leader and the possibility of change. The extent to which cognate subjects within a *federal* department actually work together in various strategic and operational ways will depend on the quality of leadership both of the whole department and of the semi-autonomous departments within it. Other factors likely to affect this process are the demands made upon it by the senior staff in the school and the wider environment outside. The historical development of the department and the formal and informal distribution of power and authority within it will also affect how it works. An implication, however, in the notion of a federal department is that the 'centre', held by the department or faculty leader, is sufficiently powerful organisationally to ensure that, in key decisions, such as processes of change or resource allocation, the members of the department will work as a unit.

In the *confederate* departments, however, the 'centre' is not sufficiently powerful to ensure the members of the department work together on key decisions. In such departments, leadership is likely to involve a great deal of micropolitical activity between the allied departments. Formal meetings might well be relatively formalised processes of statements of position by leaders of the departments, with the real negotiations taking place informally outside the meetings. The management of joint resources, including staff development, is likely to be a tense process, with the separate departments making their own arrangements as far as possible.

In *unitary* departments, such as an English department, leadership is likely to display less obviously some of the more central characteristics of micropolitical activity found in the first two types of departments described. On the other hand, it will still include complementary formal and informal processes of interacting with and co-ordinating the work of staff and students. The more effective of these departments are likely to display a well developed homogeneous culture.

Departments in secondary schools are realms of particular types of knowledge (Siskin, 1994). However, they are more than simple labels of 'Maths' or 'Science' as the knowledge base defines the status of the department within the school organisation. The professional identity of what Van Maanen (1995) calls 'occupational community' lies not in teaching but in the teaching of a particular subject. Teachers explain who they are, what they do and how they do it according to the nature of the department itself. Similarly, the potential and possibility for introducing and managing change will be influenced by departmental structure and culture.

By virtue of the subject they teach, the teachers within a *unitary* department bring distinctive perspectives, procedures and values to their teaching. As subject specialists they share a sense of who they are and what status they occupy within the school organisation. In managing change within these departments, the subject leader needs to take account of particular cultural norms and values that exist within single departments. For within any department, the main task of the subject leader is the management of people and to do this effectively necessitates an understanding of departmental culture (Busher and Harris, 1999).

Within the *unitary* department the shared subject expertise allows subject-related change to be more easily undertaken than in other departmental types. One English teacher's explanation of a general readiness to try new ideas was 'the subject matter allows us to do that' (Siskin, 1994: 153). Repeatedly the subject plays an active role in influencing teachers' actions and attitudes towards change. Even when teachers do not directly reference the subject matter when considering a change or innovation, their attitude and choice of words reflect the nature and type of department in which they work. As one Maths teacher commented, 'our attitude to change is shaped by our experience of working within the department. In maths we share a vision of the subject and work collaboratively. Therefore, we approach change in exactly the same way' (Harris *et al.*, 1995).

The implications for managing change within a *unitary* department are threefold. Firstly, there is more potential to engage in innovation and change within *unitary* departments because of the greater likelihood of shared values around the subject area. Secondly, these shared values offer a sound basis for building collaboration and teamwork. Subject leaders can seek to exploit the common ground afforded by the subject to generate the momentum and enthusiasm for change amongst staff colleagues. Thirdly, as *unitary* departments tend to be larger than other departments within a school, there is an opportunity for devolved leadership within the department. Highly effective departments have been shown to encompass collaboration and shared leadership roles (Harris, 1999a). Consequently, the subject leader of a *unitary* department is in a good position to delegate responsibilities and to trust other members of the department with leadership tasks.

The subject leader has more opportunity to generate trust and to build interpersonal relationships within the *unitary* department because the teachers not only share the same discipline but, in most schools, also share the same teaching accommodation and resource areas. Research evidence confirms the connection between the type of department and the possibility of positive interpersonal relationships. At the core of the work of *unitary* departments that were effective was a shared philosophy that stressed the importance of making individual connections both with colleagues and with students (Siskin, 1994).

In order to introduce and manage change effectively within a *unitary* department the subject leader has to:

- acknowledge the natural cohesiveness of the department;
- make explicit the shared philosophy of the department;
- build trust and commitment to change;
- delegate leadership tasks; and
- establish shared vision and goals.

While these are not exclusive to the unitary department, the structure and configuration of these departments make these more possible.

3

Managing Federal and Confederate Departments

Christine Wise

The management of federal and confederate subject areas brings with it particular problems related to the often disparate values and practices of the individual subjects. This potentially leaves them in a weakened position, particularly in relation to departmental improvement where collegiality, common values and shared culture are important.

Recognising the different factors which people emphasise in the identity of their department, the social belonging, the politics and the subject congruence, helps to understand where the potential weaknesses in a subject area's culture may arise. Additionally, understanding the basis for authority in a subject area and being able to work with it to better effect, and being able to highlight means by which subject leaders can increase their legitimacy will aid the smooth working of the subject area.

Working as a team provides a forum and mechanism for sharing opinions in an atmosphere of trust and challenge. However, it cannot be assumed a team will naturally form and coalesce. Much of the subject leaders' skill in managing these departments will be in building and maintaining teams.

Introduction

In the previous chapter the management of change was discussed in relation to the unitary type of department which was described as a large single-subject department. However, not all the departments or subject areas in a secondary school fit this description and the subject leader's area of responsibility in a primary school will certainly not fit this simple description.

Busher and Harris (1999: 309) note that: 'In secondary schools the different departmental structures can be easily defined by size, configuration, staff membership and subject expertise. Using these defining features of departmental structure, it is possible to identify five departmental types.' A similar differentiation of subject departments was used by Wise (1999). One of these is the unitary subject department already described. Two further examples of the different types and their associated management are discussed in this chapter, while a third example is considered in the next chapter.

Departments which contain and support the teaching of several subject areas where the work of the areas can be seen to be broadly similar such as science or humanities are called by Busher and Harris (1999) 'federal' departments. These areas may work closely together because their subjects and pedagogies are perceived as having the same roots and, as a result, their cultures are assumed to be analogous.

Although 'confederate' departments are also large, multi-subject departments, they are often formed for administrative convenience rather than educational reasons. Subjects are joined together but share little in common. The culture is likely to be a conglomeration of those of the individual subject areas, each of which creates its own identity.

Subject area culture

School improvement literature emphasises the need for cultural change. It is well documented that in most schools the departmental or subject cultures often differ from those of the school (Huberman, 1990). If the subject leader is actively to change the culture to support improvement better, then there needs to be a move towards the development of a shared culture. This is not a new concept. Indeed, Schein (1992: 5) suggests that 'the only thing of real importance that leaders do is to create and manage culture' and Siskin (1994) argues that leaders have a central role to play in shaping departmental culture.

It is important to be clear about what departmental culture is. It represents what Busher and Harris (1999: 311) call 'the enacted views, values and beliefs of teachers and support staff about what it means to teach students in particular subject areas within particular institutional contexts'.

In unitary departments or subject areas the subject knowledge itself appears to be the unifying focus of identity. However, what it is to be an English teacher goes beyond being a particular part of the curriculum structure or using certain books to teach from. It is also the values, processes of study and underlying epistemologies that shape the teachers' approaches to teaching and learning and which give them a common base on which to develop a departmental culture (Siskin, 1994). This shared understanding may not be as readily apparent in the federal departments as in the unitary departments and may be completely absent for the colleagues in confederate departments.

Not only will the lack of shared culture limit improvement but it might also have a negative effect. Harris (1998), in her research on ineffective departments, found that the dysfunctional staff relationships found in the least effective departments adversely affected departmental performance. Poor communication, for example, can lead to duplication of work or delayed responses to requests. Micropolitical activity between individuals within the area can lead to differential responses to agreed procedures.

In her research on departments in American schools, Siskin (1994: 185) found that teachers talked about their departments in three ways:

> social – as 'we' the department – the colleagues with whom they relate most closely at work;
> political – as 'the department' – whose primary role is in acquiring and distributing resources;
> subject – as 'English' or Science' – the subject matter being central to who they are, what they do, and how they go about doing it.

Socially focused aspects

Federal departments have certain advantages over their confederate counterparts. For example, the teaching of the subjects is often 'integrated' for much of the week, that is, they do not appear on the timetable as separate subjects. This creates greater flexibility of staff deployment.

The level of integration varies. For some, integration means the teaching of the separate subjects in modules by one teacher. The integration is often a timetabling convenience to aid flexibility, although the increased time students spend with the one teacher during the school week aids classroom management. Students do not have to learn three or more different classroom modes of practice. It is common in secondary schools to have an integrated humanities course at least in the lower school, at Key Stage 3. This means that, in most cases, the subject specialists teach material from all the areas and prepare modules of work for others in the department to share. This will enhance the social cohesion of the department by the staff regularly having to liaise over plans, resources and assessments. The resource base and the department library become areas where staff meet, and often become shared social areas for use during non-teaching time. The subject identities, however, are often retained for the upper-school work, which leads to public examinations, and are visible in the different styles of preparation of the modules and the skills that are developed.

For other subject areas 'integration' means the total integration of the subjects into one whole for teaching. Topics cover the various perspectives without making the divisions between the subjects clear; indeed, often a topic will draw on more than one of the individual subject's content. Integrated science is now taught in many secondary schools through to the end of Key Stage 4. Often students cannot tell whether the subject they are studying is biology, chemistry or physics and often they do not even know the subject specialism of the teachers. This level of integration is not usually simply a timetabling convenience – it draws on shared philosophical beliefs about the subject area, its pedagogy and its place in the students' total curricular experience. This shared knowledge and values have other effects too. Students can seek out any teacher to provide assistance outside lesson time; indeed, many science departments organise lunchtime 'clinics' which are covered by a duty rota of teaching staff. This reduces the call on the non-contact time of staff which can then be used more effectively to prepare resources.

This level of integration and sharing of resources is less probable in confederate departments because of the wide differences between the subjects. Whilst the teachers in a design and technology department might all teach to a common National Curriculum and towards a common GCSE syllabus, there is seldom an integrated approach. It is more often a circus of activities drawing on the subject expertise of the resistant materials teacher followed by the food or textiles teacher, for example. Each teacher usually remains within his or her specialist teaching area, maintains his or her own scheme of work and often is responsible for his or her own budget for materials because he or she will have different sources. This isolation from each other on a subject basis often leads to social isolation too.

This lack of dependency and social contact is often the reason confederate-style department leaders create a social area within the subject area's facilities for non-teaching periods and break times to create a social unity. This might be an office where all the catalogues of the various suppliers are kept, or access to the school's administrative computer network can be made which also has a kettle or drinks machine.

Politically focused aspects

Both federal and confederate departments have much to gain from individual subject areas working together politically within the whole-school arena. From this united action when negotiating with senior staff in a school they are likely to gain better resources, such as funding, teaching time on the timetable, more attractive rooms and possibly even curriculum organisation better suited to their subjects. However, once this whole-school level negotiation is settled there is likely to be much micropolitical activity within the department about the internal distribution of the 'winnings'.

Within the federal departments, with their similar subjects, this activity is likely to be less marked than within the confederate ones. Within an 'arts' department which encompasses music, fine art and drama, the specialist rooms are clear but the relative weighting of subjects in financial terms less so.

Federal and confederate departments are often 'blocked' on the timetable and the subject leader has decisions to make about who teaches what, where and when. Where subjects are integrated, the political activity is likely to be reduced but in others the relative position of subjects within the department may seem to determine who has the better rooms, who teaches the less preferred slots on the timetable and so on. Where the federal or confederate departments involve subject areas of different sizes, subject leaders need to take particular care to be seen to be fair to the smaller factions.

Subject-focused aspects

Although federal and confederate departments are regularly treated as single communities by others outside them, within them, at times, it can be very clear that the teachers are from separate subjects. Siskin (1994: 180) noted in her research that: 'By virtue of the subject they teach, these teachers bring the distinct perspectives, procedures, values, and discourses of their fields into the school – and sometimes into conflict. Intellectually and professionally, as well as socially, they inhabit quite different worlds.' A common 'subject' basis is likely to be missing for many of the teachers in these two types of department. For example, the modern linguists may share a common pedagogy but not a common culture base for their language. The humanities teachers may use a variety of sources as the basis of their work but for the geographers the subjective accounts of past events may seem very imprecise.

Within the confederate departments the common subject identity may be more difficult to establish but it is, none the less, important that common ground is found as part of the drive towards a collaborative culture. In design technology departments, they have the 'design process' to focus their work around, in expressive arts faculties, they may have a common understanding of the role of creativity in the teaching and learning within their area.

The establishment of common threads between the individual subjects aids the unity of the department or faculty. This is important because so much of secondary school life is based on the departmental unit. Much of a teacher's ongoing professional development is achieved through the formal and informal processes, the interaction with staff and sharing of experience that goes on in departments. The common thread underlying the work of the subject area provides a basis for discussion of teaching and learning at departmental meetings. If regularly rehearsed it emphasises the similarities rather then the differences between subjects.

Leadership of federal and confederate departments

Busher and Harris (1999: 310) argue that: 'The extent to which cognate subjects within a federal department actually work together in various strategic and operational ways will depend on the quality of leadership both of the whole faculty and of the semi-autonomous subject areas within it.' By implication, leadership should come from the department or faculty leader. They need to have the respect of and authority over their colleagues to be able to have their members work as a unit when there are key decisions, such as those related to the process of change or resource allocation, to be made. The root of that authority is important for a subject leader to understand.

Hales (1993: 18) describes '. . . power as a resource' and 'influence as the process of attempting to modify others' behaviour through the mobilisation of power resources'. He goes on to define 'authority' as '. . . the possession of power resources and attempts at influence which are deemed legitimate and, hence, acceptable by those subject to them' (*ibid*.: 28).

A power resource is considered to be the possession of something the other person lacks, such as physical strength, control over economic or financial resources, knowledge or influential personal beliefs or values (Bennett, 1995: 56). Recognition of the subject leader's expertise as a teacher is an important power resource which the majority of teachers would view as legitimate (Wise, 1999: 50).

It is unlikely that physical strength would be viewed as a legitimate power resource by many teachers but it is easy to see that both the federal and confederate subject leaders are likely to have control over finance and other resources which would be viewed as power. It is also conceivable that in the federal departments the leader may be viewed as possessing knowledge that is valued by the other members, such as subject or pedagogical knowledge.

However, the power resource viewed as most legitimate by teachers is probably that of teaching expertise. Several writers (Marland and Smith, 1981; Donnelly, 1990; Harris *et al.*, 1996) comment on the need for a department head or subject co-ordinator to be a good teacher. They need to be viewed as a leading professional and to have most authority within their area – the leading professional in their subject.

This is likely to be much more difficult in the 'confederate departments' where the broad range of subjects means it is unlikely the faculty leader will be sufficiently proficient to be considered a leading professional in all the areas. Indeed, within some practical areas the subject leader may not be qualified to teach in all the areas of his or her responsibility because of health and safety considerations. The development of a common thread or fundamental shared base of values or pedagogy discussed earlier is likely to help here. The subject leader could be recognised as expert in his or her individual subject which, because of the application of the common base, would give him or her some authority in the teaching and learning of all subjects within his or her area of responsibility.

However, a lack of commonality or a development of shared values in the early stages of creating a department may mean they are not powerful enough to ensure the members of the department work together on key decisions without a considerable effort by the subject leader. Much of the work might involve micropolitical activity between the individual subject areas, but some of it will be developing a team which can work together because the small departments or subject areas will be in a weakened position if they cannot act as a cohesive whole.

Managing through teams

One way of beginning to work together is to develop a system of management that operates through teams. This topic is covered in much more detail in Chapter 8, but will be introduced here in the interests of coherence in understanding the management of federal and confederate departments.

The term 'team' is often used too loosely in schools and colleges. Groups of staff are often referred to as the 'departmental team' or the 'Key Stage 2 team' without any evidence of teamworking.

Teamwork can be said to exist when a group of people work together on the basis of:

- shared perceptions;
- a common purpose;
- agreed procedures;

- commitment;
- co-operation; and
- resolving disagreements openly by discussion.

(Coleman and Bush, 1994)

Within the federal departments much of this will come about because of the shared epistemological basis for the subjects so that the work of the subject leader can concentrate on agreeing procedures, securing commitment and co-operation. The confederate leader may have to overcome hurdles of different perceptions, so the process of negotiating and developing values between the various members of the team may take a long time, but she can do much to reduce the isolation and idiosyncratic ways of the various interest groups within the team. It is not a process that should be rushed: teams do not just happen, they have to be actively built and managed.

Teams need individuals who are willing to adopt different roles within the team. There has been much work on this concept of team roles. Like learning styles, it builds on certain innate preferences. Belbin (1996) and his team developed a series of psychometric tests on personality, mental ability, values and motivations. The outcomes of the tests taken together are said to be able to predict the team role an individual is likely to play. However, an individual's team behaviour is likely to be modified by his or her life experience and by other constraints as well as by the process of training in teamwork (Coleman and Bush, 1994: 270).

Dunham (1995: 54) agrees that successful teams have eight essential roles within them, and factors such as personality, training and experience effect the roles team members prefer to assume. West-Burnham (1992: 128) added a ninth type of team role to Belbin's original eight and offers the following descriptions:

- Implementer – translates ideas into practice; gets on with the job; works with care and thoroughness.
- Co-ordinator – controls and co-ordinates; is driven by objectives; utilises team resources.
- Shaper – pushes to get the job done; inspires; makes things happen.
- Innovator – advances new ideas; synthesises knowledge.
- Resource Investigator – identifies ideas and resources from outside the team; questions and explores.
- Monitor Evaluator – critical thinker; analyses ideas; constantly reviews the team.
- Team Worker – socially orientated; loyal to the team; promotes harmony; perceptive of feelings, needs and concerns.
- Completer Finisher – drives for task completion – on time and according to specification.

- Specialist – [this role added to the original eight] – having pre-existing specialist skills and knowledge.

Applying Belbin's typology of team roles to teams in school or college can provide useful insights as to why some teams appear to be much more effective than others despite both having very able individuals within the team. Too often it is assumed a team's failure is because of lack of a shared epistemology, pedagogy or value system. On the other hand 'a team that contains several shapers and/or chairs will experience internal leadership problems that may lead to the team being unable to operate at all. Similarly, a team that has a large number of team workers and company workers may lack sufficient drive and direction to accomplish much' (Coleman and Bush, 1994: 270).

One design department having recognised that its team did not have a natural 'completer/finisher', decided to allocate the role for each item on a meeting agenda or within a project. At first this appeared a very artificial solution with some individuals feeling very uncomfortable in the role. With time, certain colleagues developed the ability to fulfil the role more than adequately and the natural balance in the team led to them working much more effectively.

There is also an optimum size for teams of between five and seven members. It has been found that teams with more than ten or less than three members function less well. It is fortunate that for many primary schools their staff teams fall within this optimum size. However, it does mean that in very large departments in secondary schools, involvement of the entire staff complement in a team is going to reduce its effectiveness and efficiency. It might be better for the subject leader to consider splitting the work of the area and setting up smaller teams to carry out particular aspects of the work, taking care there is across-subject representation and a balance of roles in each team. This does, however, also allow for other staff within the department to show leadership. These might be from a subject other than that of the subject leader.

Teams and change

With time the team will be working well together but the test will be when the need for change is introduced. Where the planned change is in an area which has traditionally been thought of as being within the subject leader's remit, there is likely to be less of a problem than where the change is more subtle. A move from traditional didactic means of teaching to more flexible learning will potentially lead to conflict between the teacher's right to autonomy within the classroom and the subject leader's right to manage (Wise, 1999: 5). There will be a tendency for the interest groups within the team to start to 'fight their own corner'. As Bell (1992: 150) explained: 'Where the change affects the work of the team it is the responsibility of the team leader to attempt to manage the change in such a way as to minimise the resistance, the conflict and the hostility that will be generated.'

The introduction of change increases the need to monitor the team's performance so that the implementation of the planned change can be evaluated and strategies adjusted as appropriate (Wise, 1999: 5). Having established a team, it is the subject leader's role to work with the team and guide it through the process, to develop the focus and strategies that actualise the potential of the staff. Team leaders need to 'know' their teams, be able to draw on their strengths whilst reducing limitations and marginalising negative attitudes by analysing the strengths and weaknesses within the team (Bell, 1992: 47; Armstrong, 1993: 17).

One way to monitor progress is through the use of meetings. Dunham (1995: 56) points out that:

> Meetings are important as one of the most significant performance indicators of a team's development and effectiveness. They are equally, if not more, important as opportunities to enhance effective and satisfying teamwork. This happens as members share a growing fund of knowledge, experience, feelings and skills in decision making and problem solving . . . Meetings also encourage teamwork by strengthening commitment to the team's objectives, policies, decisions and actions . . . Meetings can achieve the benefits of successful and supportive teamwork by good planning, clearly presented objectives, good organisation of the interaction between members, well formulated decisions and actions, and follow-up procedures to check the effectiveness of decisions.

During research into the role of middle managers in secondary schools, Wise (1999: 262) found that in many departments the regular meeting was abandoned: 'There were no regular department meetings because the department was very disparate, with subjects appearing in different timetable blocks, so, unlike other departments, they could not have meetings built into the timetable.' This had the unfortunate effect of leaving its members feeling isolated. There was a range of evaluation methods in operation and no clear department ethos. Whilst the individual teachers knew they could seek out the subject leader if necessary and that he or she was supportive, they felt very alone for much of their time.

Another important role for the department or subject area meeting is to give the members an official route to influence the decisions of the leader. It will damage the culture of teamworking if micropolitical methods by key interest groups are seen to be successful. In her research, Wise (1999) found a clear majority of middle managers placed their subject team as their most important influence in all areas of decision-making. Likewise, the teachers within the subject areas were aware they had influence, mainly because of their subject affiliations. Very few knew how they exerted that influence. There were various comments about informal conversations in staffrooms and department workrooms. In only a few subject areas were department meetings seen as a suitable forum for exercising influence over the leader's decision-making. The development of trust through teamworking could open the meetings to be forums where this influence can be expressed, where disagreements can be discussed and thus the apparent power of cliques dissolved.

The use of meetings and teams is discussed more fully in Chapter 8.

4

Leading and Co-ordinating Diffuse Subject Areas

Discussion of the role of subject leaders of diffuse types of subject areas shows they have much in common with each other whether they work in primary or secondary schools. The work of such subject leaders is exemplified by an exploration of the work of SENCOs, who have a particularly complex cross-curriculum task to undertake. In doing so it is possible to see how their work touches that of all other subject leaders and teachers through the organisational structures and culture of the school.

Introduction

In all schools there are some subject areas which can be called diffuse. These are areas of knowledge which are often taught by a number of non-specialist teachers in a variety of different classrooms. For example, in a secondary school, information technology, health education or economic awareness may have a limited physically identifiable base and may be taught by a wide variety of staff through their own subject specialist areas. Subject leaders of these diffuse areas have to give leadership to this wide range of staff. In such circumstances, it may be very difficult for the subject leader to create a sense of subject identity.

In primary schools, where most teachers work with one class of students for all those students' lessons, most subject areas are diffuse. Teachers have to teach every subject and can be caught between the competing demands of different subject leaders and subject areas. Teachers look for guidance for each subject from a different colleague, at least in larger schools. In these schools subject leaders are likely to have responsibility for the following:

- Initiating the development of the subject in a school;
- Facilitating the development of teaching and learning in the subject in a school;

- Co-ordinating the teaching and learning of a subject in a school;
- Evaluating the teaching and learning of a subject area;
- Educating others to help them to develop a subject area.

Bell and Ritchie (1999: 15)

In many smaller schools one teacher may be a subject leader for several subject areas (Bell and Ritchie, 1999) and so has the potentially impossible task of performing the above functions and generating a sense of enthusiasm and identity for each subject for which he or she is responsible. Transformational leadership, which is closely associated with effective school and subject leadership (Blase and Blase, 1994; Wallace *et al.*, 1997), is difficult to enact when there is not a clear organisational focus around which a leader can help to build a cultural identity for his or her colleagues. Blase and Anderson (1995) define transformational leadership as a process by which leaders work with and through their colleagues to create and sustain a common vision and set of values.

A major problem facing subject leaders of diffuse areas is they have to compete with the claims of other subject areas for the support and enthusiasm of teachers who are faced with a multiplicity of subject demands on their time and on those of their students.

This tension is heightened in primary schools because for many teachers the main focus of their professional identity is likely to lie with the Key Stage in which they work or even the whole school (Nias *et al.*, 1992). It is with the people in these areas that they will develop their sense of being a close-knit professional team (O'Neill and Kitson, 1996) rather than with other teachers of a particular subject. In part this is because of the organisation of primary schools, with most teachers being generalists who work with a specific group of students throughout the school week for the whole curriculum.

If teaching and learning are at the heart of every school, as Bell and Ritchie (1999) contend, then the main focus for the work of a subject leader is in improving teaching and learning. How students are taught constitutes the pedagogy of a subject area. What is taught in school is the curriculum. However this raises many problems for subject leaders since, despite the efforts of central government to define the school curriculum, that curriculum is made up of many aspects. Armstrong (1998: 49) points out that what constitutes the curriculum of any school system has long been contested, providing a focus for 'political, religious and philosophical debate'. She cites (*ibid.*) Carr's view (1993) that the curriculum is 'not a description of subject matter but a set of proposals indicating how . . . subject matter is to be organised, the educational purposes it serves, the learning outcomes it is intended to achieve and the methods by which such outcomes are to be evaluated.'

As well as the formal or prescribed curriculum of a school, since 1988 enshrined in the National Curriculum in England and Wales there are hidden aspects (Pollard and Tan, 1993) that focus around the social and behavioural norms teachers impart to their students, and unintended aspects. An important aspect of a subject leader's role, especially in diffuse areas, is to ensure that what is actually taught, be that subject knowledge, learning methods or social behaviour, is actually what is intended to be taught and meets agreed subject area policy.

Features of diffuse subject areas

Diffuse subject areas have several features in common which contribute to their relative lack of influence in a school:

- Their lack of adequate accommodation.
- The problematic nature of their identity in a school.
- The expectations of their leaders.
- Their staffing.
- Liaison with senior staff.
- The fragmented or diffuse nature of their teaching base.
- The importance of their links with the external environment of a school.

Diffuse subject areas rarely have a subject base in a school that is sufficiently large for all their teaching needs. For example, subject leaders of diffuse areas are likely to have a limited range of facilities in which they can make their subject visible. These might range from a computer suite for information communication technology (ICT) to one or two small rooms for Special Educational Needs (SEN) for teaching small groups, to a stock-cupboard somewhere in the school for most other areas from which subject leaders can hand out resources to their colleagues. While this situation is common in primary schools for all subject areas where teaching is usually organised on a class, rather than a subject basis, in secondary schools it leads to diffuse subject areas having a lower status than the large unitary subject departments such as English, or federal departments such as science. These latter areas are likely to have their own suite of rooms as well as a considerable budget to disburse for consumables and equipment, through which a subject leader can make his or her influence visible to staff, students, parents, senior staff and governors.

A key role for a subject leader in diffuse areas is to provide help and support to colleagues who may be struggling to deliver a topic with which they themselves are uncomfortable. For example, ICT co-ordinators may be asked to act as trouble-shooters when computer systems crash during other teachers' lessons, unless a school is

fortunate enough to have an ICT technician. Subject leaders in primary schools may be asked to give guidance to their colleagues on the
pedagogy of their subject areas, a matter that might be addressed
through formal curriculum development meetings as well as through
informal discussions in the staffroom (Bell and Ritchie, 1999). In personal and social education, subject leaders, who are often pastoral
team leaders in secondary schools, are likely to be expected by their
colleagues to make a variety of topic and administrative materials
available to facilitate teaching, learning and administration.

Subject leaders of diffuse areas have to compete for resources from
senior staff in schools along with other subject leaders. Expectations
on schools in England and Wales from central government that students perform at particular levels at certain ages in the specified academic subjects of the National Curriculum – literacy, numeracy and
science, in particular – can lead to senior staff according non-
examination subjects lower priorities in a school's budget. It is into
this category of subjects that diffuse subject areas fit. This set of priorities is exacerbated by schools' public examination results being
published in league tables for parents to judge the effectiveness of a
school. It weakens the bargaining power of leaders of diffuse subject
areas both with senior staff, for resources, and with their colleagues,
for time and space in the teaching timetable. To pursue their case,
subject leaders of diffuse areas in particular need to build up coalitions
among enthusiastic staff who will lobby senior staff and speak at staff
meetings on their behalf (Busher, 1992). This may be to urge, for
example, that more money or space be given to ICT facilities.

Leaders of diffuse subject areas can also sometimes engage powerful support from outside a school or from a school's governing body.
For example, in some schools there may be governors who are able to
make available resources or provide support for developing school–
industry links through facilitating experience of work schemes or
curriculum-related materials. ICT subject leaders have, since the early
1980s, been able to draw on central government emphases in education to further the teaching of ICT. That stream of funding was sustained into the late 1990s with the Technology Colleges initiative, for
which schools can bid if they can show that emphasis is given to
technology in their school curriculum.

A particular diffuse subject area

A particular diffuse subject area in every school in England and Wales
is that of SEN. Although lacking a clear subject knowledge identity, its
knowledge base is a range of teaching and diagnostic skills which

allow teachers with support from its subject leader to enhance the learning opportunities of students with learning and behaviour difficulties. Its leader – the Special Educational Needs Co-ordinator (SENCO) – has to work across every other subject area in a school and with every teacher. Although in some small primary schools the SENCO may be the headteacher, in other schools it is usual for the post to be at the middle management level.

Students who have SEN fall into many categories. Some have learning difficulties. Some have physical difficulties. Others have behavioural problems or, at least, behave in ways their schools find difficult to handle. Many students have SEN at some time in their school careers and need support with their learning (Clark *et al.*, 1997). Only a few have learning or behaviour difficulties for long periods of time. Although students with SEN are often difficult to teach successfully, schools are expected to give them the best educational opportunities they can. OFSTED includes evaluation of the provision made for students with learning difficulties in its inspection of schools (OFSTED, 1999).

The legislative framework of SEN has changed considerably in the last 20 years in England and Wales, changing it from a Cinderella subject dealing with marginal students who were offered remedial education to a key subject area helping students, teachers and schools to perform to the best of their abilities (Clarke *et al.*, 1997). This has given a school's SENCO powerful leverage for pressing senior staff and other colleagues to consider equitable solutions to students' learning difficulties that take account of all students' needs. It has made previous practice of merely relegating SEN children to special classes or schools unacceptable (Clark *et al.*, 1995).

In part this change has come about through central government sponsorship. The Education Act 1993 raised the importance of SEN in schools by specifying that each school in England and Wales had to have a SENCO. The subsequent Special Education Code 1994 specified the policies schools had to implement. In part it has come about through a developing awareness that schools have to be inclusive of all students, and not merely incorporate as many as can be into mainstream schooling (Clark *et al.*, 1995). This was given powerful support internationally in 1994 by the Salamanca Declaration (UNESCO, 1994).

Appropriate education for all: the changing role of the SENCO

SENCOs have a powerful bridging and brokering function to perform in schools in persuading senior staff to put adequate resources into the support of students with SEN, some of whom may not have any learning difficulties but may have behavioural problems or physical incapacities. The former category of students are usually not perceived by senior staff to contribute powerfully to the good reputation of a school in its local area. Schools in England and Wales are castigated by school inspectors for high truancy and exclusion rates, which usually focus on disaffected students, many of whom are identified as students with SEN. Yet through the formula for schools by which funds are allocated under the local management of schools (Education Reform Act 1988), each school is given a special allowance to support students with such needs through the LEA. The amount available varies dramatically from LEA to LEA (Fish and Evans, 1995; Bibby and Lunt, 1996). In certain circumstances additional payments can be made to schools if, for example, there is a particular proportion of students in a school who suffer social deprivation or have English as a second language and need additional language support to help them access the mainstream curriculum of a school.

To help different subject areas and a school gain maximum resources, it is important for a SENCO to keep a register of which students are eligible for special needs support of different kinds and to carry out appropriate diagnostic tests to find out how many such students there are in the school. Ainscow (1995) emphasises the importance of accurate record-keeping and monitoring of special education provision in a school to create a rigorous framework within which decisions about support for students with these needs can be evaluated.

In creating such a framework the SENCO has a pivotal function, as well as being required to do this in schools in England and Wales under the Code of Practice for Special Education Needs 1994. The SENCO and other subject leaders can facilitate this by regularly monitoring which students are failing to perform adequately in the academic curriculum or behaving unacceptably in particular lessons. While identifying students in need of help quickly may not lead to extra external funding, it can lead to extra temporary support from learning support assistants or with materials within a school. Such solutions may be sufficient to help a student through a crisis, even if they cannot solve a long-term problem.

A different aspect of the SENCO's search for additional resources for particular students is to establish effective contacts with a wide range of local authority agencies that can provide or permit support. This is a form of professional networking. For example, they have to work with their local Educational Psychology service to establish the level of learning or behavioural support a student requires beyond a specified threshold (Level Three under the SEN Code of Practice in

England and Wales 1994). These links are also needed to provide expert guidance to staff on how to work effectively with such students. Evidence from Osler *et al.*'s (2000) study of school exclusion also suggests that SENCOs have a key function in helping schools to link with education welfare agencies, to tackle student absenteeism; to link with social services (especially for children at risk of abuse or in local authority care); and with health services. Roaf (1998) points out the importance of effective inter-agency working to help students, parents and teachers tackle the learning and behaviour difficulties some students have. As she explains, many teachers are not aware of the range of services that can give students support, and may not have the time to find this out. It is an important service function of the SENCO to have this information and to use it to help students and teachers access it appropriately. In addition, SENCOs may need to co-ordinate information on individual students across local authority services if those services do not do that themselves.

Another aspect of resource acquisition is shown in how SENCOs develop networks of support for themselves (OFSTED, 1998a). Cade and Caffyn (1995) discuss how in Nottinghamshire there has been a move to encourage SENCOs to work with each other across the schools that form an administrative cluster. In doing so SENCOs are able to share and evaluate resources more effectively than if they only do so in a single school. It helps them to refine and reflect critically on their own practice in schools and on their practice in managing classroom assistants to support other teachers. It also helps schools in a community to develop common approaches to working with parents. This may be particularly important for helping students to transfer successfully from primary to secondary school. In some areas where schools worked successfully together to provide sophisticated support to meet students' needs, whether primary school students or students late in their careers in secondary schools, local authorities reported a sharp fall in the levels of permanent and fixed-term exclusions (Osler *et al.*, 2000).

Advocacy and morality: the dilemmas of equity in education

The advocacy function of SENCOs lies at the heart of their work as subject leaders. Through it they endeavour to build up social cohesion in a school around a particular set of social and educational values. More clearly than other subject leaders, perhaps, they have to argue a moral case for a particular approach to education that applies to all students in a school, and not only those with learning difficulties.

They might, for example, press the case for a positive discipline system in a school that will help all students receive clear support for improvements in their behaviour. Bradley and Roaf (1995) argue for the development of a whole-school framework for addressing the learning and behaviour needs of students, especially those who are said to have special needs. In this way the needs of all students will be considered when staff are discussing such matters as resource allocation for students with special needs. In England and Wales, central government expects this whole-school inclusivity to focus as much on behaviour and pastoral care for students as on support for learning difficulties (Farrell, Balshaw and Polat, 1999).

This move towards inclusive education focuses on acknowledging the rights of all young people to education (Clarke *et al.*, 1997). Such a philosophy suggests that no student of an appropriate age should be excluded from a mainstream school, missing the learning opportunities contained in the curriculum. Since the curriculum is a set of aims, objectives and plans which reflect a holistic expression of what society wants its participants to learn, to exclude students from part or most of that is to exclude them from society. As Clough (1998: 7) explains:

> [this] calls for an inclusive teaching organisation which is sensitive to individual learners and learning styles. This in turn means the careful assessment of learners, the critical appraisal of the curricula and the evaluation [by teachers] of [their] own teaching. In this way a more effective matching of the resources and deficiencies of learners and curricula is possible, and the potential for school failure is reduced.

This challenging but equitable view of education faces staff and students with some very difficult issues. For example, SENCOs need to explain to senior staff in schools and other colleagues how such policies can be implemented. This will involve them and other colleagues in finding ways to:

- support students with special learning needs;
- involve parents in supporting their children's learning;
- create staff development; and
- optimise staff deployment.

In the case of the last, although it is particularly about the use of learning support assistants in mainstream classrooms to aid students and staff, it is also about how to create schemes of help and support for parents.

OFSTED (1998a) was very clear about how it thought SENCOs could implement effective practice. Their emphasis was, first, on how SENCOs acting in a mentoring role could give support to individual students with learning and behavioural difficulties through Individual Education Plans (IEPs). These were to set students clear targets that would help them improve their performance and their integration in mainstream classrooms. SENCOs have an important function in monitoring student performance on the IEPs (OFSTED, 1998a) and in reviewing this at regular intervals to ensure there is an appropriate allocation of resources to meet identified needs (Clough, 1998).

A core aspect of an inclusive school policy is that students should perceive themselves as active constructors of the processes of a school. Sergiovanni (1994a) points to the importance of understanding schools as communities to promote senses of participation in and belonging to them by staff and students. Marsh (1997) gives an example of how this works in practice by encouraging students to share in creating a work-orientated culture for a school. OFSTED (1998a) argue that students should be involved in formulating their IEPs in order to have a sense of ownership of them. Armstrong (1995) suggested that students involved in SEN assessments often felt themselves disempowered and victimised. They thought they did not have an opportunity to tell their story from their perspective. Consequently, these students perceived the behaviour and learning demands made on them by teachers and other professional workers as impositions which oppressed them rather than as the means of support for greater social and academic success they were intended to be. It suggests that where SENCOs are able to help students construct their own IEPs to meet required education goals, and where they are able to encourage senior staff and school governors actively to involve students in decision-taking, there is more likely chance of continued improvement in student performances. In turn this is likely to help young people take greater control of their own lives, encouraging them to do so in their social communities outside school.

Working with local communities

OFSTED (1998a) point out a further difficulty with IEPs: that to be effective they need to be easily understood by parents, students and staff. This raises another area of important activity for SENCOs, which can give help and support to colleagues in their schools: that of developing effective liaison between parents and a school. In this, SENCOs perform an important mentoring role, as they do with their colleagues when helping them to work more effectively with students. Unfortunately there is considerable evidence to suggest some parents feel disempowered by school processes, especially those involving the assessment of their children's SEN (Armstrong, 1995). Many parents have difficulty in understanding what is expected of them when schools begin to take action to support their children's learning and behaviour needs (OFSTED, 1998a). This points in part to a difficulty many schools seem to have in involving parents as partners, especially in coping with students' learning difficulties (Busher, 1992; OFSTED, 1998a). Some of these parents are not able to cope with their children's problems themselves (Osler *et al.*, 2000). Others are unsympathetic to the processes of a school, perhaps because of their own difficult experiences as students. Yet others do not understand the work a school is trying to do with its students but would be most willing to help if they knew how to.

One consequence of this is the need for SENCOs to guide their schools to indicate more clearly to parents what is expected of them (OFSTED, 1998a; Roaf, 1998). While it is up to school governors and senior staff to support such policies, it is likely to be one of the functions of the SENCO to implement action which will lead to greater involvement of parents in supporting students. Alongside clearer letters, reports and brochures to parents and carers, drafted in a language that each parent can understand, some schools and local authorities engage in parent education seminars to help parents understand both the school curriculum and how they can help their children (Osler *et al.*, 2000). Yet other schools make great efforts to engage parents in every disciplinary incident in which their children are involved, encouraging them to see themselves as part of the solution to the problem, a view which goes back at least to the Warnock Report (DES, 1978) on special education needs. Armstrong (1995) suggests that SENCOs, other professional staff and school governors also have to make time to understand the parents' and carers' perspectives on the educational problems their children are having, and tailor support strategies to take account of these perspectives and of the needs that might be nested in them.

Developing staff skills to support children with SEN

A third crucial dimension in creating an inclusive school is that of developing staff abilities to improve the quality of learning opportunities students have. This is part of a SENCO's mentoring role. OFSTED (1998a: 16) point out how important it is for the SENCO to 'Improve their communication with other teachers and . . . devise effective ways of involving subject teachers in the planning of work for individual students'. Ainscow (1995) points out how emancipating staff development can be when it is undertaken by teachers working collaboratively to engage with the problematic nature of teaching and learning. To do this effectively, however, certain conditions have to be created, as Ainscow *et al.* (1994) point out:

- effective leadership by the headteacher and throughout a school;
- involvement of staff, students and community in school policy making;
- a commitment to collaborative planning and development;
- effective co-ordination strategies;
- awareness of the potential benefits of enquiry and reflection;
- a policy for staff development.

(quoted in Ainscow, 1995: 66)

Apart from facing SENCOs with the need to persuade senior staff to adopt this approach, it also faces them with the need to create a staff development programme for their colleagues.

SENCOs can construct such a programme through three interlocking approaches. The first is through consultancy with colleagues within a school (Dyson, 1990), responding to colleagues' requests for information or advice on the learning needs of particular students. This provision of expert knowledge to particular situations may take place informally, but it might lead to more formal activity. For example, a SENCO may have to go into a classroom to observe the events a teacher has described, or may have to interview several students as well as the teacher to find out what occurred. Through the use of such expert power, effectively SENCOs can assert influence over the shaping of the outcomes of the events.

A second approach is likely to be more formal but still focused on the needs of individual staff. For example, it could involve SENCOs in discussing with many colleagues what the problems are of implementing appropriate education support for certain pupils or groups of pupils, inviting each teacher to develop solutions that will improve the learning of the pupils in a class. This focus is neither on what might work for the majority of pupils in a class or the few pupils who are pathologised as being special. In this framework, the SENCO and teacher will have to consider the following:

- What support a student is already receiving – taken from the SEN register a school has to keep (Special Education Code of Practice 1994).
- How learning support staff might be used.
- What diagnostic tests or observations the SENCO or teacher might undertake.
- What particular teaching, learning or behaviour support programmes might be implemented.
- How and when those programmes will be monitored and evaluated.

A third approach is the implementation of formal staff development seminars that focus on particular institutional aspects of handling students' learning and behavioural needs, such as a series of seminars on how a school in England and Wales can implement the Special Education Code of Practice 1994. Joyce and Showers (1988) suggest these, to be most effective, should involve practical application and engagement as well as an exploration of theory and the passing on of information.

Like subject leaders of some federal departments in secondary schools, such as science, and like class teachers in primary schools who work with classroom assistants, SENCOs usually have a team of support staff to manage. The management of support staff is discussed in more detail in Chapter 12. What makes the situation more complex for the SENCO is that the management of the support staff has to be in conjunction with the other teachers in whose classes they are likely to work. So the SENCO has to negotiate with class teachers and other subject leaders how these specialist support staff can be deployed in classrooms. This could involve allocating individual support staff to particular students to support their learning. This can have the disadvantage that the class teacher does not work closely with the students identified as having special learning needs and so does not fully engage with the learning problems and opportunities related to them. An alternative strategy is to use support staff with all the students in the class in various ways at various times that have been agreed with the subject teacher, allowing that teacher the opportunity to engage fully with the work of the students identified as having special needs.

As in other subject areas, SEN support staff are likely to be a mixture of school employed part-time teaching staff and learning support assistants (LSAs). In addition they may include specialist counsellors or people who work specifically with ethnic minority communities or students with specific learning difficulties (Bradley and Roaf, 1995). These latter types of support staff may not be employed by the school but by its local authority. Millward and Skidmore (1998) note that local authorities in England and Wales are increasingly encouraging schools to take the initiative in formulating policy for deploying resources and then calling on local authorities for support to deliver these. OFSTED (1998a) note that most learning support staff are on part-time contracts and, at present, there is only limited training opportunities for such staff. It is the responsibility of the SENCO to create a sense of team and community amongst these support staff, which will include providing them with what training opportunities can be generated either within a school or in conjunction with the local authority (Bradley and Roaf, 1995). Busher and Blease (2000) note the importance of training opportunities for support staff to help to make them feel a sense of belonging to the teaching team.

The support staff can be used in a variety of different ways. Use within the classroom has already been discussed, but they also offer wider means of support to teachers in a school. For example, in some local authorities and schools, learning support staff take on major responsibility for developing links with the parents and carers of students with special needs, whether these relate to behaviour or learning difficulties. In doing so they help parents to become involved as partners with the school in tackling students learning difficulties (Osler *et al.*, 2000). In other schools LSAs can become sources of specialist knowledge to subject areas if they attend subject area meetings that are discussing the curriculum (Clarke *et al.*, 1997). They can also be used by SENCOs to monitor changing patterns of student behaviour and learning across a school, pointing to the importance of SENCOs having regular and (probably) formal meetings with their support staff when planning support for students (with special learning and behaviour needs) across a school.

Part II

Teaching and Learning

5

Being a Curriculum Leader: Helping Colleagues to Improve Learning

Christine Wise

This chapter looks at the subject leader's role in supporting and improving the curriculum for the students. It considers the place of the leading professional in demonstrating the core values and best practice within the subject area along with the importance this has for notions of authority within a profession.

Despite the restraints the National Curriculum has placed on the opportunities for curriculum development by subject leaders, there are still many important philosophical issues for curriculum managers to resolve with their teams. The need for a common understanding of the values and skills underpinning this curriculum and for a shared understanding of the pedagogy applicable to the subject is discussed as part of the process in which subject leaders need to engage to gain the willingness of colleagues to commit to the intended curriculum.

After the agreement of policies and documents comes the need to monitor, not only the teaching but also the learning. This should not be considered as a supervisory function only. Monitoring and peer observation are important steps towards a collegial approach to curriculum development and improving classroom practice. They should be used to aid professional reflection. Only through the use of student monitoring can the seven basic tenets of curriculum design be accomplished.

Introduction

The curriculum responsibilities of the subject leader have been well documented (Morris and Dennison, 1982; Chamberlain, 1984). There are many who view the subject leaders' work on the curriculum as being their only or main role above that of the classroom teacher (Wise, 1999). Within the 'National Subject Leader Standards' (NPQSL) this view is reinforced by the expectation that subject leaders will know the following:

- the relationship of the subject to the curriculum as a whole;
- statutory curriculum requirements for the subject and the requirements for assessment, recording and reporting of students' attainment and progress;
- the characteristics of high quality teaching in the subject and the main strategies for improving and sustaining high standards of teaching, learning and achievement for all students;
- how evidence from relevant research and inspection evidence and local, national and international standards of achievement in the subject can be used to inform expectations, targets and teaching approaches;
- how to use comparative data, together with information about students' prior attainment, to establish benchmarks and set targets for improvement;
- how to develop students' literacy, numeracy and information technology skills through the subject;
- how teaching the subject can promote students' spiritual, moral, social, cultural, mental and physical development.

(TTA, 1998)

This chapter will examine these areas of knowledge in order to create a better understanding of how they impact upon the subject leader's role.

Leading professional or professional leader?

Hughes (1976: 58), in writing about the dual role of the head, says: 'The innovating head, it appears, relies partly on exerting influence on staff colleagues as a fellow professional; equally, however, he accepts his position as chief executive, and uses the organisational controls which are available to him to get things moving.' The same is true of the effective subject leader. If they are well informed in their subject area, well qualified and a first-class practitioner, they will be able to lead by example (Earley and Fletcher-Campbell, 1989: 52); they will have respect as a good teacher; and they will be able to attempt to influence their fellow professionals by the use of 'functional authority' based on competence (Lambert, 1972: 9). Of course, if that fails, they can resort to 'pulling rank', using formal authority based on position (Lambert, 1972: 9), but this latter strategy is viewed as non-legitimate by many and the use of such power could result in non-compliance. Therefore, subject leaders should attempt to operate by consent, by gaining commitment to the change rather than coercion (Bennett, 1995: 57–58).

There are strong arguments for a subject leader being a leading professional. Adey (1988: 332) states that:

A leading professional is someone who demonstrates the application of the core values and procedures of the subject area, shows expert knowledge of their subject and of the pedagogy associated with it, becomes a point of reference for busy colleagues who also require visible evidence of a skilled and knowledgeable practice by a post holder and a clearly elaborated enactment of educational values.

Adey (*ibid.*) detects 'widespread belief amongst teachers that the head of department should be a good teacher.' He goes on to show that good teaching is supportive of the managing role because, by setting a personal example of good teaching, demonstrating their subject knowledge and clear philosophy of teaching, the subject leaders are successfully fulfilling the prerequisites for the policy-making role. Likewise, Hughes (1985: 277) expresses a similar view when he says that leaders of professionals have to show themselves to be involved in the actual work if their views are to have any impact. He points out that education managers must . . . aspire to professional authority as educators as much as to positional authority as managers of organisations.

In their work on effective departments in secondary schools, Harris *et al.* (1995: 288) found the subject leaders were acting as leading professionals. In contrast to the effective departments, Harris (1998: 273) found ineffective curriculum areas had a subject leader who, in most cases, was not respected as an expert practitioner. In the vast majority of the departments studied, the subject leader's teaching approaches were far from being exemplars of good practice and in many cases were viewed as outdated.

Hughes (1990: 25–26), in his work about headteachers, describes the other part of the subject leader's role, that of chief executive or professional leader. He claims that a 'more creative and dynamic role is required, preferably in a collaborative framework, which includes involvement in defining and re-assessing goals, facilitating change, motivating staff and students, and external representation. Their professional background should enable the professional-as-administrators . . . to retain credibility as "leading professionals" while also being effective "chief executives" '.

Curriculum selection

Stoll and Fink (1996: 122) argue that 'If teachers taught everything experts and special interest groups recommended, school systems would have to have a retirement plan for students!' There necessarily has to be selection but the basis for the choice must be understood and shared; the role of powerful interest groups from inside and outside the school must be recognised (OFSTED, 1998b). In the words of

Morrison and Ridley (1989: 41): 'The curriculum is value based. It is founded on the principle of protection and neglect of selected values. Curriculum planners need to expose such values before evaluating how they are brought into the planning debate.'

It is perhaps necessary to give a definition of the 'curriculum' so that the object of the discussion is clear, although it must be recognised that this in itself is a selection. Morrison and Ridley (1989: 41) argue that: 'A curriculum is taken to be all those activities designed or encouraged within the school's organisational framework to promote the intellectual, personal, social and physical development of its students.' This definition refers to the whole-school curriculum but could as easily be used to define the subject curriculum, which should go beyond simply the imparting of knowledge. So, decisions about 'whether streaming, setting or mixed ability teaching best serve the interests of the students and make work feasible for the teachers' (Busher and Hodgkinson, 1996:62) are making visible the decision-makers' educational and social values. There are assumptions and beliefs about the conditions under which they think students learn and teachers teach most effectively.

Each teacher will have an educational ideology which is formed of their values, beliefs and assumptions about children, learning, teaching, knowledge and the curriculum (Morrison and Ridley, 1989: 41), but they may not be consciously aware of it despite its enactment in their daily behaviour in the classroom. If this ideology is different from that which underpins the curriculum for the subject area, or the values of the school or subject leader, there is likely to be conflict or a lack of implementation.

The ideology of a subject will usually be closely related to its epistemology – for example, the basic skills and attitudes required to become a historian. Within the secondary school the various subject epistemologies are usually shared by teachers of the subject, they are part of the induction into the subject throughout its study and become a part of the subject culture. As Siskin (1994: 180) states:

> teachers bring the distinct perspectives, procedures, values and discourses of their fields into the school . . . As subject specialists, they share a sense of who they are, what they do and what they need to do . . . Whether they are looking at pedagogical practice, at how courses should be arranged or students assigned to them, or what makes a useful professional development experience, these teachers bring the perspectives of their particular knowledge realms to bear on what they see.

Of course teachers who have changed their teaching subject or taken an unusual route into teaching will not necessarily arrive with the same values. Within the primary school, where usually on꞉ teacher teaches a range of subjects, the epistemology underpinning the intended curriculum is much harder to establish and the subject co-ordinator will need to be aware of the potentially disparate teacher-based ideologies that their colleagues bring to each aspect of the curriculum.

Morrison and Ridley (1989: 41) offer a more detailed treatment of some educational ideologies but they suggest that, as a minimum, the curriculum debate should include the development of the following seven theories:

- A theory of knowledge: its content and structure – what is considered worthwhile or important knowledge, how it is organised and who shall have access to it.
- A theory of learning and the learner's role – an active or a passive style, doing or listening, co-operative or competitive learning, producing or reproducing knowledge, problem-solving or receiving facts.
- A theory of teaching and the teacher's role – formal or informal, authoritarian or democratic, interests in outcomes or processes, narrow or wide.
- A theory of resources appropriate for learning – first hand or second hand.
- A theory of organisation of learning situations – criteria for grouping students.
- A theory of assessment that learning has taken place – diagnostic or attainment testing, written or observational assessment, defining what is to be assessed.
- A theory of aims, objectives and outcomes – a view of what is desirable for society, the child and knowledge.

Curriculum planning

There are traditionally seven founding principles or basic tenets of curriculum planning (Leicestershire LEA, 1989; NCC, 1990). They state that the curriculum should be:

1) broad
2) balanced
3) relevant
4) differentiated
5) coherent
6) progressive
7) participative.

It has been very easy for curriculum planners to lose sight of these with the introduction of the National Curriculum and the raft of curriculum directives that followed it, but they should always be borne in mind and revisited regularly to check the curriculum conforms to these basic principles at all times.

The first of these principles, breadth, means not only breadth of content but also breadth of teaching styles because, as Hirst (1974: 5) notes, a curriculum which is specified by its content becomes restricted in its teaching methods. It also means breadth of learning styles, personal quality requirements or development, skills, knowledge and understanding. The skills may be those required by the actual subject or those generic skills being developed in a cross-curricular way, such as communication, numeracy, study, problem-solving, personal and social, and information technology. The NCC (1990: 6) believed these skills 'can be developed coherently throughout the curriculum provided that teachers adhere to the principle of sharing responsibility.' However, they also believe it is 'absolutely essential that these skills are fostered across the whole curriculum in a measured and planned way'.

Stoll and Fink (1996) draw on the work of others to argue for a new learning paradigm in which teachers function collaboratively to bring coherence to the curriculum and to ensure students succeed in learning the cross-discipline skills of critical thinking, problem-solving and using technology, among others. However, they also add a higher level, the need to develop the 'being' within the student (such attributes as tolerance, caring and responsibility), which, they suggest, requires teachers to think about the principles that underwrite their daily work.

The second principle (that the curriculum should also be balanced) applies to its areas of experience, its teaching strategies and learner activities, as well as its assessment. So, for example, a subject leader might specify how a particular section of the curriculum is to be covered because that will change the teaching strategy from the normal style of teaching for that subject. The use of a computer package that makes graphs from equations might be used to 'discover' what effect the various terms in a quadratic equation have on its curve, making the activity learner centred and encouraging a different style of thinking.

The fact that the curriculum should be relevant, the third principle, implies it should be taught in ways which link with the students' own experiences, in ways which bring out their application and value to their immediate and future life circumstances. This means the subject, leader should encourage the subject team to look for applications for the knowledge and skills outside school and convey these to the student, or use the local community to provide stimulus or content. Where the material is repeatable it should be included in the written scheme of work. A teacher of a low-ability French group had the students design and create leaflets about accommodation in their own town, for use by tourists, written in French.

The fourth principle of differentiation, the matching of the curriculum to individual students' abilities and aptitudes, is widely accepted but not so widely enacted. Too often the differentiated materials for those students with reduced literacy skills also have reduced content or they do not develop a skill the remainder of the class have access to. They may assume a student with weak literacy will enjoy colouring or endless cloze exercises. When differentiation of the curriculum is by outcome it can be very damaging for the self-esteem of students who know they always produce work not thought worthy of being displayed or demonstrated.

Within a subject, the curriculum needs to be coherent as it does across the subjects of the whole-school curriculum. In part, in England and Wales this is created by the National Curriculum but in part it is left to subject leaders and staff colleagues to create this through their pedagogic approaches. This fifth principle, coherence, is about how the various elements link together, whether the result of the learning is the very pleasing fit of a difficult jigsaw or a collection of strange mis-shapen pieces.

The sixth principle is that of continuity and progression. It is part of the coherence from the students' perspective but is more complex than it at first appears. Progression in knowledge or content is relatively easy to plan but the skills associated with the subject and the generic skills of learning are more difficult to plan for. Some students may have better developed problem-solving skills than others but need to study the same subject content. How the curriculum plan allows for them to continue to progress in the area where they have aptitude is an important issue.

The need for active involvement or participation is now a more readily accepted part of most lesson planning. After considering the many theories of learning, Mortimore (1993: 293) lists what he considers is known, or can reasonably be inferred, about effective learning. The first of these is the seventh principle of curriculum planning, the need for active participation. His other requirements for effective learning are that it should be covert rather than overt and complex rather than simple. It is also affected by individual differences amongst learners and influenced by a variety of contexts.

However, there are also other factors which research on effective schools is showing should be borne in mind when planning the curriculum. The research has lessons for curriculum planning at the subject level too. Factors such as high expectations and appropriate challenge, student responsibilities and involvement, rewards and incentives all have a place in the culture and therefore the curriculum of a department aiming to provide an effective experience (Sammons *et al.*, 1994).

Learning and curriculum management

Becher (1989: 60–61) suggests that:

> Those responsible for shaping the curriculum need to remember that their best laid-plans are vulnerable to the non-conformity of individual practice . . . teachers who strongly dissent from existing national or school or departmental policy will retain the professional's scope to do things in their own way. The classroom is a private place not easily invaded by opposing forces. As must always be the case in human affairs, even strongly coercive legislation has its limits.

For this reason it is important that subject leaders should carefully monitor not only the teaching but the learning experienced by students whilst in their areas. It is for the subject leader to ensure the intended curriculum is actually delivered rather than remaining a collection of ideals on paper. This means that not only must teacher delivery be monitored but the receipt of the curriculum by the students must be checked. While students' learning is the responsibility of the subject leader in whose area they are, responsibility for the delivery of the teaching has been devolved to the classroom teacher. The subject leader also needs to monitor both the assessment practices used by the teachers, to check the full range of skills and knowledge are being assessed, and the actual results of assessment.

Remembering that the curriculum is as much about how the students learn, how they construct knowledge, as content, it is important the subject leader provides written guidance on not only *what* is intended to be achieved by each group of students but also *how* it is to be achieved (Mathematical Association, 1988: 19). This means the written curriculum might have particular pieces of work where a selected resource is to be used, a computer package utilised, group work incorporated or team teaching encompassed. Whilst looking at the differences between countries in the Northern Hemisphere and the Southern Hemisphere, a humanities subject leader decided the students should search a CD-rom for facts about a country and then enter them into a class database which was used for a later lesson. In that lesson, the students plotted scatter graphs and interpreted the results. By including it as part of the curriculum and monitoring that all the classes participated, they were covering aspects of the information communication technology (ICT) curriculum they were responsible for as well as extending the students' analytical skills.

The ongoing nature of curriculum development means managing change is a crucial skill for the subject leader (see Chapter 2). Bearing in mind the quotation from Becher's view (1989) at the beginning of this section, it is vital that a subject leader 'takes his colleagues' with him (or her). As was mentioned earlier, coercion does not lead to commitment. It is not simply a matter of demonstrating the change in action. Ball and Bowe (1992: 112) found readiness to change was effected by three factors. The first impediment they suggest is that of 'low capacity'. This is a measure of the experience and skills of the colleagues involved. The provision of appropriate, focused professional development prior to instigating the change is likely to increase the likelihood of commitment to change.

A second impediment was what they termed 'low commitment'. This is best described as the existence of firmly held and well entrenched subject or pedagogical paradigms by subject teachers. The need for subject leaders to help create shared values, beliefs and philosophies was mentioned at the beginning of the section. This is not simply a 'nice' idea a subject team can 'get round to' when it has time. It is crucial to the successful implementation of the intended curriculum.

The third impediment they detail is the lack of a 'history of innovation' which, they suggest, 'results in a high degree of reliance on policy texts, external direction and advice, which in some circumstances verges on panic or leads to high uncertainty and confusion and a sense of threat' (Ball and Bowe, 1992: 112). There is need for support and guidance through the early stages of ongoing curriculum review and development. The development of strategies for coping with change must be shared in a collegial atmosphere which accepts risk-taking and encourages innovation. Within the primary school, where the teacher may be having to face change in a whole range of subject areas simultaneously, careful co-ordination of expectations is necessary.

Monitoring of teaching and learning

Monitoring of teaching and learning is often seen as a human resource issue and it is dealt with in more detail in a later chapter. What needs to be discussed here is the relevance of the issue for curriculum management.

The earlier quotation from Becher (1989) highlights the vulnerability of curriculum plans to the individual response of staff members. If the attitudes and values of the teaching or the process of learning are an essential part of the planned curriculum, then monitoring the teaching and learning in action is as important as checking that the marking of exercise books is in line with the subject area marking policy.

Earley and Fletcher-Campbell's (1989) findings (that subject leaders did not regularly review or monitor the work of members of their team) are supported by comments in more recent OFSTED reports. One report comments that '. . . [there was] no system for monitoring work or evaluating effectiveness of the curriculum' (Glover, 1994: 3). Yet monitoring is essential: 'Research and experience both indicate that they [adults in professional roles] learn through experience, through reflecting on that experience and through receiving constructive criticism about their performance' (McMahon and Bolam, 1987: 2).

However, teachers need help to reflect on their performance, and it is preferable for that to be from someone they can both trust and respect as a competent teacher of that subject (Wise, 1999: 91). The overall aim of the monitoring and evaluating of practice is to empower the individual teacher to 'do the job better' (Leask and Terrell, 1997: 138). This sense of working collegially in an atmosphere of trust for the greater good, rather than because of fear of reprimand, is captured by the Mathematical Association (1988: 17) in their advice to subject leaders: 'If some colleagues are not currently working with the intended breadth of approach then it is fundamental that we should try to help them to do so on the basis of conviction rather than by coercion or through a sense of guilt.' In Harris's (1998) work on ineffective departments it was found that the teachers in these departments had not taught with another colleague from the department nor had they seen their head of department or any other team member teach. This lack of collegial working practice meant they had no idea how another teacher of their subject taught.

It is, however, especially difficult for small primary schools to instigate team teaching and peer observation. Most teachers in these schools have responsibility for co-ordinating more than one subject as well as teaching their own class. It places the teachers under tremendous strain when they have to induct non-specialist colleagues into the working syllabuses and relevant resources and materials they have prepared (Busher and Hodgkinson, 1996). However, by the careful use of the professional development budget it is possible to organise appropriate periods of time when mutual observation may take place.

Mortimore (1993: 296) states that: 'Effective teachers . . . bind together skills and knowledge through the use of their imagination, creativity and sensitivity in order to stimulate, support and encourage learning, using such means as high expectations and modelling behaviour.' Busher and Hodgkinson (1996: 59) comment on the 'micropolitical tensions as teachers' different sets of values co-exist uneasily within a school's organisational framework' and the same can be true within a subject area. Teachers of a subject will not automatically work within the same value system but a common understanding of pedagogy is essential if the curriculum is to be delivered as intended. This means the subject leader will need to lead activities which examine values and their application to lead his or her team to a common understanding.

Harris *et al.* (1995: 288), in their study of effective departments, found 'the real success of these departments lay in their ability to organise key elements of the teaching and learning process'. All the departments 'had detailed and agreed schemes of work that had been collectively approved'. Importantly, these schemes of work 'were consistent with the general vision of the subject . . . were very detailed, with clear guidance'.

Both these extracts highlight the need for the sharing of values to lead to a shared understanding of the pedagogy of the subject. Without this common understanding, students will have different experiences of the curriculum depending on the teacher they have. What is more, some of the educational experiences required for higher-order learning may not take place, which might limit students' learning of the subject in the future.

Improving learning through monitoring and assessment

Hirst (1974: 5) argues that: 'Curriculum planning is not just a question of whether what is learnt is worthwhile, it is a question of whether or not what we wish to be learnt is in fact being learnt.' The chapter so far has concentrated on providing the right things in the curriculum, the planned experiences in line with the agreed values of the school and subject team. It is now pertinent to consider how the efficiency is to be checked.

The responsibility for student's learning remains with the subject leader. As part of their monitoring of this learning they need to be aware of what assessment is taking place and its results. Glover (1994: 3) reported that in some departments a lack of clear guidance led to a situation where '. . . in assessment reporting and recording, each teacher appears to have an individual system'. In addition, even where the records of students' attainment were detailed and well kept, there was a tendency for attainment to be recorded from a narrow range of evidence (Glover, 1994: 7).

Harris *et al.* (1995: 292), in their work on effective departments, found these departments paid great care and attention to the assessment process. They had excellent record-keeping, placed great emphasis on marking consistently within the department, encouraged student involvement in the process of marking or assessing where practicable, gave feedback to the students on a criterion rather than a norm-referenced basis and actively sought opportunities to reward good performance. A significant amount of assessment work was related to homework and these departments consistently set and marked homework in line with a homework policy. It was returned quickly and good work celebrated and displayed.

Many of the practices displayed in these effective departments are in line with what Stoll and Fink (1996: 124) call 'assessment literacy' which, they believe, educators need. They suggest that the answers to questions such as those below begin the process of effective assessment:

- Are these the best assessment practices to assess this learning outcome?
- How well does this assessment sample students' achievement?
- Do the students understand the achievement targets and assessment methods?
- Does this assessment assess outcomes that matter?
- Are assessment strategies fair for all students?
- How are the resulting data to be presented?
- Who will have access to the data?
- How will they be reported and to whom?

They suggest assessment must be seen 'in concert with shifts in curriculum design and teaching strategies'. There is little point in designing radical teaching methods and outstanding learning experiences if the assessment processes cannot assess the learning outcomes generated. They propose that rather than design the 'what' and the 'how' followed by the 'how do we know', there needs to be a paradigm shift in planning. Rather than being based on what the teacher intends, curriculum planning should be based on what the student outcomes should be. This requires a change in thinking about assessment. The standards of performance required need to be determined at the beginning of the teaching–learning process rather than at the end (Stoll and Fink, 1996: 124–25).

Using performance data to improve the subject area

There is growing awareness of the use of performance data to calculate value-added measures, although there is some evidence this is more at senior than middle management level, such as comparisons between subject areas on the basis of their external test or examination scores. In some schools the data are not even disseminated to subject leaders for them to use to make their own comparisons (between examination groups, for example).

The often negative attitude towards the use of performance data is related to the tendency in some schools to use it to 'blame' teachers or subjects for poor results. There is also a concern that it displaces professional judgement if taken in isolation as a predictor of ability and is concerned only with 'who will score what' if nothing changes. Used in this way it can place the emphasis on the students, not on the curriculum.

It is certain that performance data analysis cannot measure everything learnt in schools but what it can do is show if there are trends, it can pose questions, it can help to suggest areas worthy of further investigation. Do boys perform better than girls in the measures possible? Why does one group of students show a wide variation in their performance in one subject but not in another? In much the same way as student assessment can be used formatively or summatively, so can performance data.

The subject leader needs to go beyond the strings of numbers to understand the trends being suggested and think about the implications for his or her curriculum. Might a change in approach to teaching and learning reduce the spread of results? Do the analyses suggest a particular ability band that is being poorly catered for? The inter-subject variation might also be an area for investigation – going to look at good practice in other subject areas.

6

Improving Teaching and Learning within the Subject Area

This chapter focuses upon improving teaching and learning within the subject area. The relationship between teacher development and improving the subject area is shown to be important. The research concerning effective learning and teaching provides clear guidance and direction for improved teaching and learning outcomes. The centrality of the teaching repertoire in improving teacher performance is unequivocal. Consequently, ways to develop and extend individuals' teaching repertoire need to be established and secured within the subject area.

One way of achieving teacher growth and development is through peer observation. Where this is presented to teachers as a means of development rather than a form of accountability, there is evidence that it positively influences teacher performance. The main challenge for the subject leader is to encourage team members to view peer observation as an opportunity to learn about their own teaching practices and a means of improving their teaching. If this achieved, there is evidence to suggest that improved student learning and increased performance within the subject area will ensue.

Introduction

Classroom-level change has a much greater impact upon student performance and achievement than change at whole-school level (Creemers, 1994). From both a theoretical and empirical perspective, the classroom is the predominant place in the school where learning and teaching take place and, as such, is potentially more important than the level of the school. Successive research studies have shown the importance of locating change efforts within the classroom and of focusing attention directly upon teaching and learning (Teddlie *et al.*, 1984; Fullan *et al.*, 1990; Stringfield and Teddlie, 1992; Harris and Hopkins, 1999). These findings point towards the centrality of teacher development in whole-school improvement and improvement within the subject area. Consequently, it is the responsibility of the subject leader to assist colleagues to improve teaching and learning within the subject area.

Whatever the subject area, in order to be most effective, teachers need to develop a wide range of knowledge and understanding about teaching. The national standards for subject leaders (NPQSL) (TTA, 1998: 6) specify this requirement in some detail: 'Knowledge and understanding of curriculum as a process; the concepts and skills in the subject beyond what is required by the National Curriculum; how children learn; the strengths and weaknesses of different teaching approaches and how they may be implemented effectively.' Consequently, subject leaders need to concentrate their efforts upon two important dimensions. They should:

- Seek to organise subject, or team meetings so they always devote some time to teaching and learning issues.
- Find ways of allowing teachers to teach together and to observe each other in the classroom. This way good practice can be shared and departmental collaboration established.

A major challenge for subject leaders is to develop and extend the teaching practices used by colleagues in order to meet a range of student learning needs in the classroom. This inevitably raises tensions. Teachers need to have a sufficiently wide repertoire of teaching strategies and approaches to cope with the wide range of learning and needs students may have (Hopkins *et al.*, 1997a). Conversely, there is a need to give individual teachers sufficient autonomy to work in ways that acknowledge their interests and particular set of personal values (Day, 1999). This potential tension has to be managed but the importance of extending teachers' skills, knowledge and understanding of the teaching process itself has to be recognised by subject leaders (Harris, 1999b).

This is not to ignore the importance of the curriculum within the subject area. Teachers still need to have a sufficiently broad range of skills and knowledge to teach all aspects of the National Curriculum within their subject area. Within the curriculum framework of a school, teachers need to consider how students are grouped for purposes of instruction. This includes considering how different aspects of a syllabus can be most effectively taught to different age and ability groups of students (Mortimore, 1999). It includes considering the different ways to teach a topic, how assessment forms part of the learning process and the role of monitoring in securing optimum student achievement.

Subject mastery is an essential prerequisite of being able to teach well. Thus, it is important teachers not only develop their own under-standing of their subject but that they deliberately take steps to im-prove their range of teaching approaches. This is best achieved in partnership with other colleagues by using peer observation and by discussing teaching with colleagues (Day, 1999). Hence, subject leaders need to have a firm understanding of their curriculum area along with knowledge and understanding of what kinds of teaching result in improved student learning. In order to improve the quality of teaching and learning within the subject area, subject leaders need, first, to be aware of what constitutes effective teaching and learning and, secondly, to know how to develop the teaching expertise and repertoire of team members.

Effective teaching

The essence of being an effective teacher lies in knowing what to do to foster students' learning and implementing that process effectively. Effective teaching is primarily concerned with the process of obtaining some desired student learning outcomes through educational activity. As Kyriacou (1991) points out, effective teaching is primarily con-cerned with setting up a learning activity, task or experience for each student, which is successful in bringing about the type of student learning (knowledge, understanding, skills and attitudes) the teacher intends.

Unlike learning, teaching is an overt activity and should be easier to describe and evaluate. There have been numerous theories of teaching approaches, or styles. However, the effective teacher does not neces-sarily fit neatly into such categories or typologies (e.g. Bennett, 1976). Whatever the relative merits of different teaching approaches or styles, the research findings still reveal little concrete evidence in fa-vour of one approach rather than another (Bennett, 1976; Mortimore *et al.*, 1988). In terms of enhancing teacher effectiveness in the classroom it would appear a mixture of approaches or methods is preferable (Mortimore, 1993). Indeed research on teacher effectiveness is still relatively consistent in emphasising the importance of having a reper-toire of different teaching approaches (Kyriacou, 1986; Creemers, 1994).

Within any single subject area, teachers are likely to have a range of teaching skills, styles, models and approaches that comprise a teach-ing repertoire. Within the subject team some practitioners have dif-ferent sets of teaching skills or abilities from others. Different subjects and aspects of subjects necessitate different types of teaching approaches. To develop their skills and cope with these differences, over time teachers acquire something akin to a map of their discipline which guides their teaching. This is based on their knowledge of the subject, how they perceive it and issues it addresses. Consequently, the challenge facing the subject leader is how to maximise the effectiveness of teachers within his or her team and how to ensure colleagues have the opportunity to extend and develop their individual teaching repertoires.

There have been many different perspectives on the theme of quality teaching and teaching repertoires. Hopkins (1997) has provided a clear framework for describing the teaching repertoire that reflects the diversity and breadth of teaching activities. Hopkins (*ibid.*) suggests there are three broad aspects to teaching which have their own literature and research tradition. These are reproduced in Figure 6.1 and are discussed in more detail in Hopkins (1997), Harris (1999b) and Hopkins and Harris (2000).

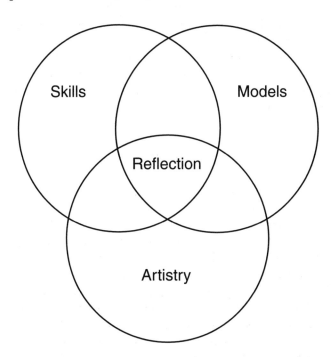

Fig. 6.1   Three ways of thinking about teaching
(*Source*: Hopkins and Harris, 2000)

The first perspective on effective teaching is that of teaching 'effects', which encompasses sets of teaching behaviours or *skills*. Within this extensive literature, consistently high levels of correlation are demonstrated between student achievement scores and classroom processes. Very effective teachers possess a set of generic skills that underpin their work. These skills include organising skills, analysis skills, assessment skills and management skills (Mortimore, 1993). Yet, within subject teams, teachers rarely have the opportunity to talk about or review these skills in any explicit way. While schools tend to be communities consisting of people with wide-ranging teaching skills and abilities, these are rarely articulated or shared. Consequently, a central responsibility of the subject leader should be to create a dialogue around teaching and learning. This has been shown to be a characteristic of effective subject areas (Harris *et al.*, 1995).

The second perspective on effective teaching concerns the acquisition of a repertoire of *models of teaching*, which refers to distinct groups of teaching approaches. It is clear students learn in different ways and what helps one student learn may be different from what helps another. Hence, it is important the teacher possesses a range of teaching models to suit a range of learning orientations. Although it is the learner's activity that results in the learning, it is the teacher's responsibility to provide the conditions that will increase the probability of student learning. Teachers help students to learn by exposing them to different models of teaching (Joyce *et al.*, 1997). Consequently, the more models of teaching a teacher acquires, the greater the probability different kinds of learning will occur.

Teaching models

At the core of the teaching process within any subject area is the arrangement of a *learning environment* within which students can interact and study how to learn (Dewey, 1916). It has been suggested there are models of teaching which describe a particular type of learning environment (Joyce and Weil, 1996). Such descriptions include curricula, courses, units and lessons, or instructional materials (books and workbooks) designed to promote a particular learning context. Most of these models of teaching are designed for specific purposes (i.e. the teaching of concepts, ways of thinking or how to study values).

Some models focus on delivery by the teacher while others develop as learners respond to a task. However, all models of teaching emphasise how to help students learn to construct knowledge (i.e. learning how to learn). Joyce and Weil (1996) suggest that, in nearly all cases, the mastery of a model of teaching by students is the key to learning effectiveness (i.e. the students have to learn how to engage in the learning process emphasised by that model).

The most recent overview of models of teaching has been provided by Hopkins and Harris (2000). This book builds upon the seminal work in this area conducted by Joyce and Weil (1996). They suggest there are four families of models of teaching based upon the types of learning they promote and on their orientation towards people and how they learn. In both books the authors detail all the models and provide a thorough interpretation of each in classroom practice. Clearly, this chapter cannot replicate the depth of analysis offered in the work of Joyce *et al.* (1997). What is presented here is an introduction to this expansive and important research field.

The four families of models of teaching proposed by Joyce and Weil (1996) are as follows:

1) Behavioural systems family.
2) Information processing family.
3) Social family.
4) Personal family.

The models of teaching within each of these four families are those that have been identified as leading to specific learning outcomes. Furthermore, they are adaptable in so far as they can be adjusted to the learning styles of students and to the requirements of different subject areas. These models are relevant and useful to all subject areas and span both the primary and secondary sectors. Most importantly, there is a wealth of research evidence that demonstrates they work in enhancing students' ability to learn (Joyce and Weil, 1996). In summary, the four models are as follows:

Behavioural systems family

This set of models may also be known as behaviour modification, behaviour therapy and cybernetics. Essentially, this family of models is premised upon the stance that all human beings learn through feedback and adjustment. The most famous studies in this area became known as stimulus and response, with psychologists like Skinner (1938) organising task and feedback structures to make it easy for human beings to self-correct and to learn.

The information processing family

Information processing models emphasise ways of students organising data, sensing concepts and generating solutions to problems. Some models in this family provide the learner with information and concepts; some emphasise concept formation and hypothesis testing by the learner; and other models generate creative thinking. The information processing models help students learn how to construct knowledge as they focus directly upon intellectual capacity. These models help students to operate on information obtained either from direct experience or from mediated sources so that they develop conceptual control over the areas they are studying.

Social family models

This family of models is premised upon the importance of students working together within a social context. The social models of teaching are constructed to take advantage of co-operative relationships in the classroom and to produce integrative and productive ways of interacting with each other that support vigorous learning activity. The social family of models helps students learn how to sharpen cognition through interactions with others, how to work productively with individuals and how to work as a member of a team. In terms of cognitive and academic growth, the models help students to use the perspectives of other persons, both individually and within a group. Through this interaction students are encouraged to clarify and expand their own thinking and conceptualisation of ideas.

Personal family models

The personal models of teaching begin from the perspective of the self-hood of the individual. They attempt to shape education so that individuals can come to understand each other and themselves better, to take responsibility for individual development and can be more sensitive and creative in the search for high-quality lives. The cluster of personal models of teaching pays great attention to the individual perspective and seeks to encourage productive independence so that students can become increasingly self-aware and responsible for their own destinies.

Despite research evidence demonstrating how these models impact positively upon students' learning (e.g. Joyce and Weil, 1996; Joyce *et al.*, 1997), many teachers remain unaware such alternative models of teaching exist. Part of the problem resides in the inaccessibility of some of the research evidence but also in the fact that, within most schools, little time is devoted to developing new approaches to teaching. In England and Wales, teaching expertise is currently centred upon curriculum content for each subject domain. Much teacher time is devoted to 'delivering' the curriculum and relatively little is allocated to considering alternative ways of teaching.

In order to extend and develop the teaching repertoires of colleagues within the subject area, it is initially important the subject leader provides opportunities for teachers to reflect upon their teaching. Research has shown that effective schools and effective subject teams are collegiate and give priority to teachers' professional development (Scheerens, 1992; Harris, 1999b). Consequently, it is important the subject leader creates a climate within the team where discussion of teaching and learning is commonplace and non-threatening. This can be achieved by the following:

- Ensuring some meeting time is devoted to developmental issues.
- Creating opportunities for mutual sharing of good practice within the team.
- Providing support for classroom observation and peer review.
- Sustaining a dialogue about teaching within the team.
- Focusing upon learning outcomes rather than curriculum coverage.

Artistry

The third and final perspective on effective teaching is of a different order from that associated with teacher behaviour/skills and teaching styles/models. Within this research tradition there is the central recognition that teaching involves creativity and is carried out in a highly personalised way. This dimension emphasises the personal responsibility for creating the conditions for effective learning undertaken by the teacher. While effective learning *can* take place in the absence of effective teaching, optimum results will occur when there is a good match of the two. The ability to match these two has been characterised as *artistry*. Artistry characterises a highly personalised and individualistic approach to the study of teaching (Hopkins *et al.*, 1994).

The idea of artistry in teaching was summarised by Rubin (1985: v):

> There is a striking quality to fine classrooms. Students are caught up in learning; excitement abounds; and playfulness and seriousness blend easily because the purposes are clear, the goals sensible and an unmistakable feeling of well-being prevails. Artist teachers achieve these qualities by knowing both their subject matter and their students; by guiding the learning with deft control – a control that itself is born out of perception, intuition and creative impulse.

Artistry incorporates the recognition that teaching is a highly creative and personal activity. Unlike the previous research on teacher behaviour and models, the research evidence here does not lend itself to specifications or lists of features. Yet this perspective on teaching is one which has received much attention (Armstrong, 1980; Rowland, 1984; Gray, 1990; Louden, 1991). The importance of a good and vital inter-relationship with students is at the core of artistry.

Many studies of effective schooling have demonstrated that the teacher–student relationship is at the heart of the learning process. It is a consistent theme which appears in the research and writings concerning effective classrooms. At the core of such relationships is 'unconditional positive regard', which is defined by Brandes and Ginnis (1990: 23) as follows:

> The most enabling quality that one person can display to another is unconditional positive regard, a phrase which describes the clear, non possessive, non manipulative attitude which seeks the growth and the empowerment of the other: neither submissive or subordinate, nor superior but aligned with the students in following their endeavours and achieving the goals of the School.

As might be expected, within different subject areas the extent to which such 'authentic relationships' are in evidence varies considerably (Hopkins *et al.*, 1997b). Where there is a lack of positive regard the potential for learning is greatly diminished. Showing acceptance of students and having specific strategies for communicating positive regard to them are important determinants of classroom relationships. Gipps (1992) identified some important factors that mark out effective primary teaching. Amongst these was the importance of a good positive atmosphere in the classroom with plenty of encouragement and praise. Effective subject areas place an emphasis upon reward rather than sanction and provide opportunities for autonomous student learning. They also provide regular feedback to students and are knowledgeable about the learning process (Harris, 1999b). For improvement to take place within a subject area requires teachers to understand not only what constitutes effective teaching but also how students learn most effectively.

Effective learning

The research on effective learning is extensive, complex and somewhat bewildering, but subject leaders need to understand the key principles and concepts contained in the literature to assist them towards a better understanding of the learning process (e.g. Wood, 1988). Effective learning involves some modification of what the learner already knows or believes. What students are doing as they learn can be understood only in terms of the way their previous experience has set them up to construe the new situation. Learning, therefore, can be guided and assisted successfully only in the light of this understanding. If what is taught does not engage with the learner's current understanding in this way, it will be ignored or the learning will be ineffective (Claxton, 1988).

To learn effectively students need to be effective gatherers, organisers and expressers of knowledge (Kyriacou, 1986). The main channels for gathering knowledge in school are listening, reading, asking questions and discussing. One thing that distinguishes successful from unsuccessful learners is the ability to recognise and articulate what it is they do not know, or do not understand. The skill of being articulate about intellectual knowledge provides an important strategy for amplifying that knowledge. It actually helps the students to learn as well as providing them with the ability to express what they know during exam time or during discussions and tests. In the case of teachers, this also applies to their professional learning. Many teachers are excellent practitioners but are unable to describe this practice with any precision. This tacit knowledge is implicit in the practice of all teachers but when teachers are encouraged to articulate and explain their practice, this has a powerful effect on their professional learning (Day, 1999).

At its simplest, effective learning is the translation of complex information, concepts and knowledge by the teacher. Sometimes, however, the barriers to effective learning may lie in the subject matter itself rather than in general qualities of the teaching or learning activities in which learners are engaged. Consequently, subject leaders need to take the lead in making their subject area accessible to students and showing colleagues how to make the subject area accessible. The subject complexities of science or history may require careful translation for students in order that learning can take place. The subject's 'taken for granted' phrases or terminology might require careful translation if learners are to get to grips with complex phenomena or concepts. The subject leader has to take the lead to ensure this happens. This is an important aspect teachers need to address if students are successfully to access the subject domain.

Another important part of effective learning is the extent to which learners feel they are expected to learn and how this expectation of learning is reinforced (Gipps, 1992). Subject leaders have an important role to play in ensuring the department has high expectations of all students. The importance of teacher expectations upon student learning has been well documented and emphasises the importance of teachers' judgements about ability affecting subsequent student performance. Where teachers hold high expectations of students' ability then students are more likely to achieve. Thus, for subject leaders, a central task must be to ensure all teachers hold high expectations of students, irrespective of socioeconomic context.

Motivation, whether intrinsic or extrinsic, is a vital factor in effective learning as it is closely related to self-concept and to personal needs. Praise, recognition and approval from the teacher can help satisfy needs for acceptance and are also basic to feelings of self-esteem. Intrinsic motivation occurs in situations in which the motivation for learning comes entirely from the task to be performed. The student learns because of the interest in the topic or activity, or in order to find an answer to a puzzling question or a solution to a pressing problem. This form of motivation arises in situations in which there is a conceptual conflict caused by uncertainty, novelty, conflict or ambiguity.

Extrinsic motivation comes from the portrayal of the subject as being important, interesting and rewarding. The subject leader can play a part in ensuring the subject matter is presented to students with enthusiasm and encouragement. Their level of curiosity and interest is an important factor influencing subsequent learning and affiliation to the subject. Curiosity and interest will increase attention and boredom will be reduced, helping alleviate behaviour problems in the classroom. Teachers using curiosity in this way will find students will be more eager to learn and that their teaching will be more effective as a result of using curiosity and interest in such an overt way.

Learning theory stresses the importance of individual differences amongst learners and underlines the need for learners to believe in themselves as learners (Wood, 1988). The stronger students' feelings of self-efficacy, the higher the level of achievement. Consequently, subject leaders need to encourage colleagues to reward, praise and respect students as a means to improving students' self-esteem and improving their achievement.

Effective learning does not occur by accident. It is usually the product of an effective classroom situation created by a skilful teacher. For, as Joyce and Showers (1991: 10) note:

> Effective learners draw information, ideas, and wisdom from their teachers and use learning resources effectively. Thus a major role in teaching is to create powerful learners. The same principle applies to schools. Outstanding schools teach their students ways of learning. Thus, teaching becomes more effective as the students progress through those schools because, year by year, the students have been taught to be stronger learners.

How teaching is conducted has a large impact upon students' abilities to educate themselves. Research has shown that effective teachers are not simply charismatic and persuasive presenters but they engage their students in cognitive and social tasks that teach the students how to use them productively (Mortimore, 1993: 299). Effective teachers teach their students *how to learn* and thus teaching becomes more productive as students are helped to become more effective learners. As teachers extend their repertoire of approaches, so students extend their repertoire of learning approaches and so improvements in learning result. Improved teaching is a means to improved learning, but how does the subject leader promote and secure improved teaching?

Improving teaching

Within any subject team, teachers' expertise and practical competence will vary. In addition, different subject areas use quite diverse teaching approaches and instructional strategies. Many of these are subject specific and are premised upon a particular pedagogical content knowledge relating to the specific subject area (Shulman, 1997). Other approaches, like whole-class teaching, are relatively generic although their manifestation within different classrooms inevitably varies. For many teachers the methods and approaches used in the classroom are repeated year on year primarily because they are effective. Consequently, there is some reluctance and often a resistance to try out new teaching approaches or to experiment with new teaching models.

The most effective practitioners have a range of teaching skills, styles, models and approaches which comprise a teaching repertoire (Hopkins *et al.*, 1997a). The challenge to subject leaders is to encourage all teachers, even the most effective, to develop and extend their range of teaching approaches. Opportunities to engage teachers in discussion about teaching methodology occur quite naturally as part of the work within the subject area. For example, if the subject leader is approached for advice concerning resources or teaching materials, this provides an opportunity for the subject leader to engage in a dialogue about teaching.

Yet, for optimum professional development to occur, intervention has to be proactive and of a more formal nature (Day, 1999). Strategies for reviewing and sharing teaching practices are of paramount importance in facilitating professional development and growth. Consequently, subject leaders need to consider what procedures they can adopt or instigate to facilitate the process of teachers critically examining their own teaching practices. One proven approach is the introduction of classroom observation within the subject area (Hopkins *et al.*, 1997a).

Classroom observation

Observation plays a crucial role, not only in classroom research but also more generally in supporting the professional growth of teachers (Day, 1999). It is a pivotal activity that links together reflection for the individual teacher and collaborative enquiry for pairs or groups of teachers. It also encourages the development of a language for talking about teaching and provides a means for working on developmental priorities for the staff as a whole (Southworth, 1998). Eraut (1994) has argued that as adult learners we need to be aware of our own and others' perceptions of our practice in order to develop fully as professionals. He suggests the quality of skilled professional behaviour can be improved through the following:

- Gaining feedback from independent observers.
- Recording and reviewing classroom behaviours.
- Developing awareness of the impact of actions.
- Observing others in action.
- Expanding the repertoire of routines.

Drummond *et al.* (1992: 42) describe observation as an essential and invaluable part of any educator's skills: 'Observation means more than watching and listening; it is a process by which educators can understand and give meaning to what they see and hear, drawing on their own knowledge and experience.' Cooper (1989) noted that not only do we learn more about children and their learning by observing but we also learn more about the learning process and our involvement in it. Consequently, classroom or peer observation has to be at the heart of extending or developing teaching repertoires. It offers a prime source of professional feedback, necessary for improvement and the opportunity to engender and develop a language about teaching simply through talking to others about what happens in classrooms.

In setting up a classroom observation process there are a number of questions the subject leader needs to consider. Firstly, how will colleagues respond to the introduction of classroom/peer observation? There is an inevitable tension between accountability and development that exists within the observation process. The use of classroom observation within the appraisal process has had the unfortunate consequence of equating observation with notions of accountability. Subject leaders will need to dispel such interpretations if they are to succeed in using observation in a developmental way. Hence, it is important any observation process must be transparent from the outset and introduced as a means of professional development, rather than professional evaluation.

Secondly, subject leaders need to consider the type of observational process colleagues are encouraged to undertake. Hopkins (1993) usefully distinguishes between different methods of classroom observation: open, focused and structured. In an open observation, the observer simply notes what appears to him or her to be important or relevant. In an observation of this type ideas, issues or concerns are noted by the observer in an unstructured way. The limitation of this type of observation is the variability of the evidence base and the diversity of foci noted by the observer.

An alternative approach to this unstructured approach is a more focused approach where the foci for observation are predetermined and categories exist for recording information. This acts as a filter for the observation process and offers a clearer basis for feedback following the observation. Examples of using observation of this type could be to focus upon questioning techniques, or the interaction of teachers and students. The result of collecting information of this type can be used for discussion with a view to improving teaching.

A more structured observation process will usually employ systems to record activities in some kind of quantitative form. Typically, coding sheets are used to record behaviours in the classroom. Behaviours are recorded by a tallying or category system, as shown in Figures 6.2 and 6.3 respectively. Teachers may wish to develop their own classroom observation pro-forma or recording instrument but may also consider using existing observation instruments that have been tried and tested (e.g. Beresford, 1998). Instruments can be grouped into two categories: those that are used to record behaviour or other aspects immediately in the classroom as in Figures 6.2 and 6.3; and those in which the recording is postponed until later.

A third consideration when introducing classroom observation must be the focus of the observation. If the purpose of the observation is to enhance and develop the teaching repertoires of members of the subject team, then the observation must focus upon those teaching skills, approaches and models that are central to the teaching repertoire. It is essential, therefore, that a clear focus for the observation is both identified and agreed with colleagues. Subject leaders will need to encourage colleagues to focus upon some aspect of their teaching that they want to develop further. Hence, observation becomes developmental rather than judgemental and has a real chance of changing teaching behaviour.

Setting up a peer observation system within the subject area requires the subject leader to be clear with colleagues about the reasons for setting up the process. Where observation fails it is often as a result of a lack of understanding about the purposes behind the process. Subject leaders need to reassure team members that the reasons for the observation are as follows:

- sharing
- development
- support
- enquiry.

Date: **Lesson:**
Teaching strategies   **Incidence**

Accuracy stressed	C	
Accurate recall	As	
Action planning	As	
Brainstorming	D	
Case-study	As	
Choice of activities	C	
Classwork	As	
Clear goals expressed	C	
Comprehension	C	
Data collection	As	
Demonstrations	As	
Discussion	D	
Group interaction	D	
Group work organised	Ac	
Gut feelings asked for	Ac	
Hand outs	As	
Investigations	D	
Lecture	As	
Mistakes allowed	Ac	
Note taking	C	
Open-ended questions asked	D	
Paired work	D	
Planning of work by pupils	C	
Practising skills	C	
Problem-solving	C	
Reflection on experience	D	
Relevance of work explained	C	
Reporting back methods varied	Ac	
Role-play	D	
Scientific experiments	C	
Simulations used	Ac	
Specialisms tapped	As	
Testing	C	
Thoroughness stressed	C	
Variety of approaches	Ac	
Video	As	
Working alone	C, As	
Worksheets	C	

Ac		D	
C		As	

Fig. 6.2 Observation schedule of teaching strategies, based on Kolb's four learning styles
© IQEA – *Collecting Information for School Improvement*

School: Teacher behaviour	Lesson 1 details:				Date: Lesson 2 details:			
1. Accepts feelings								
2. Praises, encourages								
3. Uses pupil ideas								
SUBTOTALS	1.	2.	3.	G/T	1.	2.	3.	G/T
4. Asks questions								
5. Lectures								
SUBTOTALS	4.	5.		G/T	4.	5.		G/T
6. Gives directions								
7. Critises, justifies authority								
SUBTOTALS	6.	7.		G/T	6.	7.		G/T
8. Pupil talk, response								
9. Pupil talk, initiate								
10. Silence, confusion								
SUBTOTALS	8.	9.	10.	G/T	8.	9.	10.	G/T

Fig. 6.3 Observations of teacher behaviour in classrooms
Source: based upon a schedule in Flanders, N. (1965) *Teacher Influence, Pupil Attitudes, and Achievement.* Washington: US Office of Education

Also, the subject leader needs to ensure there are clear ground rules associated with the observation process. A set of questions establishing the ground rules is as follows:

● Is the focus of the observation clear?
● Are the intentions clear?
● Is there an agreed means of recording?
● Is there an agreed procedure for providing feedback?
● Are confidentiality and trust assured?
● Is there a code of classroom conduct for the observation?

In order to use observation to improve the quality of teaching and learning, it is important both observer and observed agree the focus of the observation. Within a classroom setting it will be impossible to look at all aspects of teaching and learning; hence, a specific focus is necessary. For example, if the focus of the observation was to consider the teaching and learning styles in evidence during the lesson, the questions would assist the observer in recording appropriate and relevant information.

Despite the well established benefits of peer observation, there will be situations in which the opportunity to engage in observation will not be welcomed. Where observation is used as a mechanism for accountability rather than development, resistance to observation will inevitably ensue. The following case study is a brief illustration of this particular issue.

Case study: Extending the teaching repertoire

Jackie is a head of department in a large comprehensive school. As head of English she has a team of seven full-time teachers, five of whom are subject specialists. The school is committed to reviewing current teaching practice. Jackie tried to introduce classroom observation to the team before but it was not viewed positively by members of the department. They viewed it with suspicion because of the way in which observation was used in the past as part of appraisal to judge teachers' effectiveness.

However, with a whole-school focus upon teaching approaches Jackie has been able to re-establish observation as a means of sharing good practice across the department. The emphasis upon development rather than accountability has allowed her to persuade staff to embark upon observation. Using external impetus for internal change, Jackie has developed a classroom observation instrument with her team that focuses specifically upon:

- *teaching skills*
- *teaching approaches*
- *teaching models.*

Using a checklist approach, teachers observe each other and tick the frequency of certain types of classroom practice. This subsequently forms the basis for a discussion about teaching and has created a culture of more openness within the department. It has also assisted the department in adding new models of teaching to their practice by providing specific feedback on proficiency in the classroom. Irrespective of what happens within the school, the department has agreed to continue with the observation process and to work together to develop the teaching repertoires further.

This case study demonstrates the importance of trust within the observation process. Essentially, observation is a form of mutual learning for both observer and observed. By focusing upon agreed elements of the lesson, both teachers have the opportunity to reflect in a structured way upon their practice.

Within teaching, peer observation can be a powerful means of self-development and personal growth. If used appropriately, it can also provide the drive and momentum to expand upon and improve teaching practices.

7

Developing Professional Networks: Working with Parents and Communities to Enhance Students' Learning

Working with local communities in all their manifestations – parents, business, local authority, community groups – and a variety of social and cultural contexts is of key importance to subject leaders. Understanding the social contexts in which their students learn helps subject leaders better tailor the teaching and learning processes to meet student needs and help students achieve the best academic performances possible. At the same time it helps students to become more successfully integrated socially and helps parents and students to recognise that schools are part of their local communities as well as communities in their own rights that reflect their local social contexts.

Introduction

Since the mid-1980s in England and Wales there has been growing emphasis in schools on treating parents as partners in education. The Education Acts of 1988 and 1992 gave parents the opportunity to choose to which schools they send their children on the basis of the information schools are required to provide. Amongst other items, school prospectuses have to provide information on extra-curricula activities and on the quality of students' performance in tests and examinations. OFSTED inspections since 1994 have routinely investigated the extent and diversity of parents involvement with, and views on, their children's schools. The Code of Practice for Special Educational Needs 1994 requires parents to be involved to the statementing of their children, compelling special educational needs co-ordinators (SENCOs) and other subject leaders to be directly concerned with explaining to parents the problems their children are experiencing.

Improvements in teaching and learning, from which may arise extra-curricula activities, are directly the responsibility of subject leaders

(Sammons *et al.*, 1997; Harris, 1998). Busher (1992) found those subject leaders who paid attention to developing extra-curricula activities in their areas and developing public displays of students' work in schools were held in greater esteem by senior staff and colleagues than were other subject areas and leaders. Merchant and Marsh (1998) found a main responsibility of subject leaders in primary schools was publicising their subject areas through school displays of students' work. This and other activities and open evenings to which parents are invited help to keep parents in touch with their children's learning activities and, sometimes, with new developments in pedagogy and the curriculum.

Since 1997 the emphasis in England and Wales has moved from encouraging parents to act like consumers of education to becoming partners with teachers in the processes of curriculum and school development and improvement. The central government white paper *Excellence in Schools* (DfEE, 1997) stressed the importance of parents as co-educators with teachers of their children. For example, the Literacy Task Force (1997: 32), set up by the in-coming Labour government, urged that: 'Parents have a vital role in supporting and encouraging children's learning, perhaps most of all in helping that child to read. Attitudes to literacy in the community as a whole are crucial'.

This view builds on carefully researched evidence (for example, Hannon, 2000) of the impact parents can have on improving their children's learning. It coincides with attempts by central government to strengthen parental influence in schools (Bennet and Downes, 1998) by involving them in core curriculum planning processes that, until the late 1970s in the UK, were the preserve of education professionals. On the other hand, it has also been an important strand in professional educators' thinking for a number of years (e.g. Sallis, 1988; Bastiani, 1995).

Working with parents

The notion of parents as partners with teachers in the education of their children faces subject leaders with an intriguing task of working with a wide range of people to develop the curriculum. Some parents may not understand the curriculum. Some may be reluctant to become involved with their children's schools, perhaps in part because of their own experiences as students in school (Merchant and Marsh, 1998; Osler *et al.*, 2000). The complexity of working more closely with parents can be seen in the following extract from Merchant and Marsh (1998: 65). The subject leader, a primary school literacy co-ordinator, explained:

> We have a series of events and structures that are designed to encourage the involvement of parents in their children's reading development. When

children first enter the school or nursery, we give parents copies of a leaflet designed for them which explains our reading policy and show how they can help their child. We offer all parents the opportunity to take part in a three-session course on 'Helping your child with reading and writing'. The course is offered in most of the community languages spoken by our parents. A yearly open evening is devoted to the English curriculum and provides us with an opportunity to develop particular themes. Parents are encouraged to come to school early with their children and share a book in the reading area with them before they go. They are also welcomed into school to take part in reading activities in the classroom. This is not organised on a workshop basis but is flexible to meet the needs of individual parents. A parent library operates in the Nursery. This is limited because of lack of funds, but parents are allowed to borrow up to two texts a week. The wider community is invited into school during literacy-related events, e.g. Book Week. A weekly English class for Asian women is held in the school and occasionally takes part in classroom activities.

Hannon (2000) explores the importance of developing family literacy in order to create a home environment that will support children's learning in school and beyond.

Developing close contact with parents has other benefits for subject leaders and their colleagues, too. Brown and Rutherford (1998) points out that it can help teachers have a clearer picture of their students as learners outside the school context, as well as helping parents to work more confidently with schools. Busher (1992) found that closer understanding of parents and local communities helped teachers to recognise from where particular values and attitudes held by students came. In turn this points teachers towards more effective strategies for working with students to improve their learning. In one case the discovery that many students had difficulty finding sufficient suitable space to do homework at home led a subject leader to set up a homework club for students.

To promote closer liaison between parents and schools, home–school agreements, under the Standards and Framework Act 1998 in England and Wales, are intended to allow teachers to be more explicit about homework requirements and expected standards of student behaviour in schools (Bastiani, 1996). Subject leaders need to develop policies and practices to implement this for their areas. The positive impact of homework on student performance is less clear in practice than in mythology (Farrow *et al.*, 1999), but is symbolically important for indicating the integration of home and school in supporting students' learning.

Involving local communities

The thrust of policy to include parents and the community more fully in the processes of schooling has a broader perspective as well. The

Standards and Framework Act 1998 has encouraged the setting up of Education Action Zones (EAZs) in deprived urban communities in England and Wales. The focus of these is to bring different aspects of local communities together with the schools that serve them to try to improve the quality of student performance in the schools. This strategy is in part based on the view that learning requires people to be proactive in engaging with all possible means of education throughout their lives if they are to have successful lives and be successful citizens (Ransom, 1998). It is not a new perspective. In some local authorities in England and Wales, such as Leicestershire, this commitment to involving schools closely with their local communities has been enshrined in their education structures for many years. It is intended to avoid people experiencing a sense of uselessness in their lives as changing technologies change national economies and make them unemployed (Sennett, 1995). Continued access to education throughout their lives, it is argued, allows them to cope with the changing demands of the labour market.

An important aspect of this perspective is to reduce the number of students schools exclude. Exclusion from school for whatever reason deprives students of access to the curriculum which, in turn, diminishes their opportunities for finding satisfying jobs and building successful lives, as an LEA officer pointed out (Osler *et al.*, 2000). Nutbrown (1998) casts another light on this, arguing children have a right to be educated under the United Nations Convention on the Rights of the Child, which the UK government ratified in 1991. Article 23 of this convention asserts governments should include all children in education in their local communities. The emphasis, then, is for teachers and subject leaders to create inclusive schools which cater for the needs of all the students who come to them (Clark *et al.*, 1999), difficult though that is.

Implementing such a strategy faces subject leaders and senior staff with a range of multiple problems that are likely to be situationally located. Fink (1999: 134) points out tellingly 'that to suggest that poverty has no relationship to school achievement, as some politicians have done, is disingenuous at best and deceitful at worst'. Strand (1999: 180) points out that various studies since 1985 in the UK have shown that differences in students' educational attainments related to ethnic group, economic disadvantage and sex occur as early as 7 years of age. These studies also show these differences may persist or even increase over time.

Schools in lower socio-economic communities find it more difficult to achieve high levels of academic performance (Hodgkinson, 1991; National Commission on Education, 1995). On the other hand, higher socio-economic catchment areas for schools can mask weaknesses in a school's organisation and pedagogy, creating 'cruising schools' (Stoll and Fink, 1998) that do not fully help students to achieve high performance. There is some evidence, too, that schools serving such communities can face determined opposition from parents and staff if they try to introduce reforms (Kohn and Kottocamp, 1993).

To cope with the complexity of the socio-economic contexts in which schools are located, subject leaders need to find ways of differentiating the curriculum and extra-curricula activities, but not the social contexts, to meet the needs of the students and their parents who come to their schools. The inclusive school is a multi-cultural school, whatever the social composition of the local communities it serves.

Encouraging parents to work with schools

Subject areas can gain considerably from:

- looking at ways to work more closely with parents
- making contacts with local community groups.

An interesting starting point for any subject leader beginning to work with parents is to carry out an audit of the different ways in which parents are involved in the curriculum. Bell and Ritchie (1999) suggest this is a good way for subject leaders to involve their colleagues in thinking about the quality of contact there is between their subject area and parents. Macbeath (1998) encourages subject leaders to involve parents in evaluating the quality of contact subject areas have with them, perhaps using a simple questionnaire. OFSTED inspectors expect schools to monitor the quality of contact they have with parents (OFSTED, 1999).

In a project conducted in Cambridgeshire, Bennet and Downes (1998) suggested schools that are successful in building partnerships with parents had a number of factors in common:

- Open and welcoming.
- Communicate clearly and frequently with parents.
- Encourage parents as educators and learners.
- Give strength to parental voices in the development of the school.
- Respond flexibly to parents' needs and circumstances.

At the core of these policies is a respect for all parents and a recognition parents actually want to be involved in their children's education if they can. The term 'parent' is used here as shorthand for a wide range of carers and parents with whom children may be living. Subject leaders need to work with pastoral leaders in schools, such as heads of year in secondary schools, and SENCOs to find out the family backgrounds of all the students taught in their subject area in order to help their subject colleagues be aware of how these social contexts might affect each student's learning. As Merchant and Marsh (1998: 180) point out, subject leaders should not assume every home will have the same opportunities for supporting their children's learning. So even when providing guidance leaflets on how parents might help their children's learning, subject leaders need to indicate a variety of useful practice.

Below the strategic level of school policy are a range of practices subject leaders can implement with their colleagues. Bennet and Downes (1998: 13) suggest these can be separated into the following types of activity:

- Communicating clearly with all parents orally and on paper;
- Providing practical advice to parents on how to support students' homework;
- Being systematic and thorough in exchanging information with parents about the curriculum and their children's progress;
- Creating structures that enable less confident parents to participate and contribute.

The implication of each of the four preceding bullet points on subject area practice for subject leaders and their colleagues is vast in any school, however small, as the quotation on page 90 illustrates.

Enhancing student learning through involving parents

Teachers work with parents in many ways. For example, in many primary schools parents come to work in classrooms as learning support assistants. It is for subject leaders to act as mentors to these parents, inducting them into how they should work with students, what work they should do and what relationships they should develop with teaching and support staff in the school. Merchant and Marsh (1998: 184) suggest parent helpers could be usefully given information by Literacy subject leaders on the following:

- Strategies to use when hearing children read;
- Relevant questions to ask children about their reading;
- How to fill in reading records;
- How to join in with school approaches to reading;
- Introduction to the range of language games in a school;
- Strategies for reading stories to children;
- How to deal with difficult behaviour.

Where parents choose to act as classroom assistants on a more permanent than *ad hoc* basis, it is for subject leaders to fin l ways to support their work with in-service training. This is discussed in more detail in Chapter 12.

On a more *ad hoc* basis, contacts with parents may give rise to a variety of opportunities for subject leaders and their teams to enhance students' learning. Bell and Ritchie (1999: 99) suggest parents can be used to share their 'Particular expertise, enthusiasms, interests or experiences (coming into schools to talk about visits to foreign countries; reminiscing about past times; demonstrating tools and equipment they use at work; teaching a craft that they do)'. In other cases subject leaders may use contacts with parents to arrange for students to undertake educational visits and fieldwork at sites to which they might not otherwise have had access, such as coal-mines, factories, power stations and farms.

Taking account of local community cultures

As well as contributing directly and indirectly to students' access to the academic curriculum, closer contact with parents and the local community can help subject leaders and their colleagues devise suitable social and work-orientated rules and procedures for students working in their areas. In some subject areas, such as physical education, this can mean enforcing appropriate dress codes that, none the less, take account of the values of religious or ethnic minority groups. In other cases it can mean devising suitable strategies for students to manage their bags and outdoor clothing without disrupting important working spaces in classrooms.

Knowledge of the social customs of students' families and local communities can also help subject leaders and their colleagues when devising policies on homework; on submission times for work assignments; and for carrying out fieldwork at certain times of the year. It may also indicate which groupings of students within lessons for, say, small-group discussion work or physical recreation are more or less likely to be successful. Subject leaders and their colleagues can build on this to develop a work-orientated culture within a subject area, which still allows for different social customs and is inclusive of the parents as well.

Teachers in subject areas can benefit from developing connections with local community groups their students attend. It is for subject leaders to explore these as part of their function of building professional networks. For example, knowledge that some students from particular ethnic minority groups are attending learning support sessions run by their heritage communities can be used as a source for supporting the students' further develop of their skills and understanding in particular subject areas (Osler *et al.*, 2000). In some local communities there are people who are willing to mentor disaffected youth from that community (CRE, 1997). This can provide teachers with support for the development of academic work as well as reduction in social misbehaviour in school. Recent research suggests that, in some urban areas, there are a great many self-help groups with which contacts might be made by enthusiastic teachers, schools and subject areas better to support the learning needs of some of their students.

Governors and the local administrative contexts

Within the administrative framework of schooling in England and Wales, LEAs and school governors play a powerful role. Since 1986, school governors have become increasingly important in the internal workings of schools in England and Wales (Riley and Rowles, 1997). Since the introduction of local management of schools under the Education Reform Act 1988, as Riley and Rowles (1997: 74) point out, governors have become responsible for:

> school budgets, for the appointment of staff, for school action plans following an OFSTED inspection, and for the implementation of the National Curriculum and a range of policy initiatives . . . [They have to] have detailed policies on pay and conditions [of work for staff], and clear guidelines on sex abuse, drug abuse, and child abuse. They must follow complex procedures on admissions and exclusions [of students].

Newsam (1994) suggests the roles of governors revolve around issues of management of a school, support for the students and staff in a school, and accountability to the public and to the local authority for the good order of a school.

It is because of these extensive powers, especially over the implementation of the curriculum and the maintenance of effective discipline in a school, that subject leaders have to work closely with school governors. Riley (1994) suggests school governors are reluctant to visit classrooms when lessons are being taught, although some are happy to act as classroom helpers if they have the time available to do this. On the other hand, subject leaders can invite school governors to monitor the quality of the teaching and learning. It can help subject leaders to evaluate that, too. Bell and Ritchie (1999) point out it is becoming commonplace for governors on school governors' subcommittees for their school's curriculum to be assigned to monitor work in particular subject areas.

To help governors become involved in their subject areas, subject leaders need to brief the attached governor on the curriculum of the area, and on the range of policies implemented by the subject team. Merchant and Marsh (1998: 213) quote one such governor as saying: 'It keeps at least one of the governors in touch with what is happening in the school with regard to the literacy curriculum. I go in about once every half term and have a chat with . . . the English co-ordinator. She tells me what has been happening and I ask her about various aspects of the curriculum.'

As in this school, subject leaders can set up a pattern of visits for their attached governors to lessons and subject team meetings. Attached governors also need to be briefed on the range of resources available in a subject area, and to important shortfalls in those resources. Working closely with an active attached governor can be a useful vehicle by which a subject leader can make a case to senior staff and governing body for additional resources for a particular project. Subject leaders can also ask for the opportunity to address governors formally about work in their subject area, when seeking to advertise the quality of work it is doing. In many schools in England and Wales this opportunity is now likely to be offered on a regular rotational basis between subject areas. It has become another arena in which subject leaders can practise the art and politics of leadership.

Another reason for subject leaders keeping close contact with their school's governors is that one of the major channels for voicing parental concerns is through parent governors on a school's governing body (Wallace and Huckman, 1999). As the headteacher of a school is technically accountable to a school's governing body, any questions of concern to be raised about work in a subject area are likely to be raised in the forum of governors' meetings. Close contact can give subject leaders early warning of any such complaint and time to prepare their defence of their or their colleagues' previous actions or lack of actions. Apart from seeking out an active governor to become attached to their subject area, subject leaders can themselves seek nomination to the governing body as a teachers' representative.

Using local authorities to support learning

If subject leaders need to be aware of the internal political processes of their school's governance better to prosecute the goals and objectives of their subject areas, they also need to be aware of the external administrative contexts for the same reasons. For example, some local authorities have established effective monitoring procedures for student absence and misbehaviour and are able to provide this information to

schools in their area to help teachers manage the students more successfully (Leeds, 1998). In other cases local regulations can have a
considerable impact on how, for example, a subject leader can organise fieldwork or a school trip for students and staff.

It may be particularly important for SENCOs, key-stage co-
ordinators in primary schools and heads of year in secondary
schools to know how to contact services outside education, such
educational psychology services, health services, social services and
welfare services in order to gain support for particular students. On
the other hand, subject leaders in areas as diverse as technology,
literacy and physical education may find it valuable to have access to
fire officers and health and safety inspectors. These can give guidance on various *ad hoc* activities such as school plays and open day
activities, as well as on regular workplace hazards. Wenham (1999)
points out how important it is for appropriate subject areas to be
aware of the relevant legislation on, for example, health and safety at
work. It applies to schools equally with other public places and to
students and staff.

The political environment of different local or regional authorities
also affects the way in which teachers are able to work with students.
Whereas in some areas the local council implements policies of pri-
vatising as many local services as possible, encouraging schools to be
as autonomous as possible, other local councils may encourage their
schools to work together and with other local services as closely as
possible.

Working in local political contexts

Subject areas can gain considerably from understanding:

- relevant national legislation;
- the influence and processes of the media;
- local political systems; and
- links with the local business community.

An important aspect of the local political arena is the local media, be
they press, radio or television. Their ability to portray schools,
teachers and students' activities in a variety of different lights has an
impact on local opinion about schools. There is little research done on
this area apart from Weber and Mitchell (1999), but a great deal of
anecdote. In turn, this affects the views of local councillors and local
authority officials on particular schools and teachers. It also affects the
views of parents and other members of the local civic communities in
which teachers work.

Teachers are not merely the victims of such representation, they are able to influence what representation they are given, if they are able to gain access to the media. For example, if a subject leader can persuade local newspapers or a local television channel to visit a forthcoming display of work or a successful activity they can gain useful publicity for their area and for the school. As Busher (1992) discovered, senior staff in schools looked favourably on those subject areas in their schools that were able to gain good publicity for them. Students, too, are usually very pleased to gain publicity for their success, as are their parents.

The development of contacts with local politicians and council officers can help subject leaders to gain extra resources for their areas, or to gain access for their students to particular opportunities. In more extreme cases, the successful development and use of contacts with local political and media processes can help senior staff and subject leaders alter a deleterious public perspective of a school or a subject area within a school into a positive one (Barker and Busher, 1998).

Contact with the business community

The business community that exists around a school can be a source of major support and innovation to teachers. Representatives of this are likely to be parents or governors in a school, providing subject leaders with some initial access to it. Senior staff in these enterprises may be able to offer advice, guidance and support for curriculum development, as well as help with staff development and management processes. Bell and Ritchie (1999: 99) cite the case of an enterprising design and technology subject leader who resourced a whole curriculum project on environments by appealing to local companies for recycled materials.

For the subject leader who is prepared to look for it in the business community, help can be found in several different categories:

- Curriculum materials and equipment.
- Advice and guidance to students for project work or personal development.
- Curriculum development opportunities for staff.
- Management development opportunities for staff.
- Project data gathering for students.
- On-site work experience for students.
- School-site work experience for students through industry subsidiaries.

Engagement in projects with local business can lead to subjects developing work students find creative and can help them to see the relevance of the prescribed curriculum to their daily lives.

Keeping in touch with the professional community

The professional arena has several aspects to it. It is for subject leaders to guide their colleagues in keeping in touch with these different arenas. These can be summarised as follows:

- National Curriculum directives, guidelines and developments and contacts with the QCA (Quality and Curriculum Authority) which oversees the Key Stage Standard Tests.
- Networks that can be built with other teachers, through local curriculum networks, and with relevant local authority officers.
- Links that can be made with national centres of learning, such as universities, and subject associations, such as the ASE (Association of Science Educators) or the Historical Association. These centres and associations can help teachers keep in touch with changing views and understandings in particular areas of knowledge.
- Sustaining awareness of changing resources that are available in particular areas of knowledge, a process that can helped by regular reading of the teachers' professional press, such as *The Times Educational Supplement*.
- Keeping in touch with national assessment procedures for students. For secondary-level teachers, another aspect will be that of engaging with public examination boards which set the syllabi for public examinations in England and Wales for students in Year 11 and Year 13.

Although it might be possible or even advisable for subject leaders to keep track of all changes, there may be good reasons for delegating some of the foregoing responsibilities to other colleagues. Delegating responsibilities for some of these aspects is helpful not only because of the amount of work that is involved, but also to further the professional development of other colleagues. It also helps to construct a culture of interdependency between colleagues (Ribbins, 1992) if a subject leader delegates some of these functions, contributing to the sense of team or community spirit within a subject area (Busher and Saran, 1995a).

Keeping in touch with changes and developments in the National Curriculum allows teachers in subject areas to fine tune their teaching to meet the latest government requirements of schools. In the view of central government this should mean students in those subject areas which are most closely in touch with government requirements are receiving the best schooling possible. In the same way it is important for teachers in subject areas to be kept in touch with the changing demands of the Standard Assessment Tests (SATs) set by the Qualification and Curriculum Authority (QCA) in order to prepare students for these tests.

In secondary schools in England and Wales this liaison with external national bodies also extends to being in contact with the examination boards. This is to find out what changes in syllabus are likely to effect the examination performance and preparation for examination of students in the GCSE examinations taken at the end of Year 11. In schools and colleges offering post-16 education, contact is also needed with the examination boards offering post-compulsory schooling examinations.

Subject leaders can find important sources for new ideas for pedagogy from national subject associations, such as the Geographical Association. These offer teachers, through publications and seminars, a range of ideas for structuring and shaping the contents of the curriculum at various different levels. They also offer a wide range of suggestions on how teachers can develop alternative approaches to the pedagogy they are using. A similar source of information exchange can be found on the World Wide Web. Subject leaders need at least to be able to make their colleagues aware of the range of information available, even distilling it if necessary in order to encourage their colleagues to keep in touch with changing ideas about the curriculum.

Subject leaders who develop contacts with a nearby university can gain valuable access to ideas, to contacts with other teachers and, sometimes, to resources, too. Whether this contact is in the form of attending short or long accredited or unaccredited courses or of attending subject specialist seminars will be a matter of preference for individual teachers. Not only does such contact lead to the development of subject specialist knowledge, but it can also lead to more sophisticated understandings of subject leadership and school improvement. In some cases, subject leaders as part of a whole-school policy can persuade a university department to run courses shaped specifically to their school's needs. Evidence from Harris *et al.* (2000) suggests such courses lead to the most effective implementation of knowledge learnt by teachers on courses.

Local curriculum networks offer subject areas another important source of help in developing their curriculum. This may take the form of networks run by a group of schools for the benefit of their teachers. Such networks may hold regular meetings or workshops to consider different aspects of the curriculum, different approaches to teaching particular topics or the development of resources for particular aspects of the subject (Busher and Hodgkinson, 1996). In cases where these clusters or families of schools include primary and secondary schools, it may be possible for teachers across school phases to acquire and share resources which any one school could not on its own afford. It may be possible for primary students to have access to specialist facilities that are usually housed in the secondary school. It may also be possible for subject specialist teachers in one school to act as advisers to those teachers in other schools who, although teaching in a subject area, are not specialists in it themselves.

In some cases these curriculum networks or networks for school improvement may be run by local authorities, offering opportunities for training as well as for growing contacts with teachers in other schools who might be facing similar challenges. In some cases it may be possible through such networks to locate schools or subject areas which have already workable approaches to these challenges. The success of this will depend to some extent on how well the local authority is able to manage a database of school activities and use it as an information exchange which different schools can access.

Subject leaders need to be aware of what training opportunities are available through the local education authority, as well as those which are being organised as part of a school's in-house staff development programme, so they can help their colleagues access relevant courses. Proactive subject leaders can encourage local authorities to set up courses that are relevant to their colleagues' needs. Within the planning of a subject area, subject leaders and their colleagues can use information about local authority short courses, as well as other professional development courses, to structure the processes of staff development most clearly to meet the needs of their subject area. Obviously this planning process will have to be within the context of school policies.

A final aspect of the professional area subject leaders need to manage is that of searching for new resources for their subject areas. Although some of this information can be gleaned from contacts with other schools, with the LEA and with local universities, some of the most useful sources for this are the professional education press and the occasional travelling education fair. The last has the advantage that teachers can often see new resources in operation. If this is not possible, then subject leaders or the member of the subject area team who has this responsibility have to send off for inspection copies of materials. In some cases, such as that of interactive software, publishers are unwilling to make it available because of the risk of illegal copying.

It is for subject leaders to guide their colleagues in keeping in touch with these different aspects of this arena.

Part III

Leading and Managing Staff

8

The Subject Leader as a
Middle Manager

This chapter explores what it means for a subject leader to be a middle manager in a school, and how that crucially involves working with and through people to create an effectively operating subject area. How subject leaders work with people is seen to have a number of interlocking aspects.

Introduction

In schools, organisational hierarchical distinctions are not neatly delineated. Many staff are involved in a complex switching of roles and lines of accountability between different aspects of their work. Macbeath (1998) sums up this complexity by suggesting that practitioners learn more from the heresies of leadership than from the conventional nostrums. He argues good leaders set unattainable goals to serve a particular and strong vision. To do this they need to work with people who are effective managers and who can organise everyday activities efficiently. On the basis of an international research project, he suggested effective leaders are led by listening carefully to those people and situations around them. Consequently he suggests the preferred style of leadership in schools is feminine. This style tends to be more democratic and supportive of people and is more effective at diffusing conflict between people. Hall (1996) discusses this style for head-teachers at greater length.

Within the complex matrix of leadership and accountability in schools, subject leaders are increasingly acknowledged to be key figures. Huberman (1990) has suggested it is the subject area or department that is the powerhouse that makes whole-school development possible. Glover *et al.* (1998) have argued more recently that the distinction between middle and senior management remains blurred and the spheres of leadership are still not clearly delineated or, possibly, definable. They suggest four key dimensions of activity for subject leaders:

- Bridging and brokering the views and values of senior staff to sub-ject area colleagues and representing the views of subject area staff in whole-school policy-making.
- Leading decision-making collaboratively with colleagues for a sub-ject area.
- Monitoring and improving staff and student performance.
- Being aware of the demands in the external environment for chang-ing practice.

However, they also acknowledged many subject leaders spend a considerable amount of time on relatively low-grade administrative tasks.

Busher and Harris (1999) extended this argument, suggesting there are five main organisational parameters which interact with each other and with which subject leaders have to work. These might be said to construct the cultural framework of a subject area a subject leader has to understand and mould in appropriate ways:

- The organisational structure of a subject area within a school, the impact of which on subject leaders is discussed in the first part of this book. Hannay and Ross (1999) note the importance of this parameter as a potential inhibitor of change.
- The social cohesion, vision and identity of the subject team within a school (Hopkins *et al.*, 1994)
- The status of the subject area in school and the 'realm of knowledge' (Siskin, 1994) it purveys.
- Understanding and liasing with the contexts of the subject area for professional knowledge, national policy guidance and community support for learning.
- The ways in which power is used in the school and subject area – a realm of micropolitics (Ball, 1987; Busher, 1992; 2000).

They argue that no subject leader can implement any of these func-tions without access to and use of power, a hidden but all-pervasive ingredient to successful leadership. A variety of sources of power are likely to be used by subject leaders in working with colleagues, stu-dents and parents (Busher, 1992) and may be used transformationally to work with people, or transactionally to negotiate with or coerce people (Blase and Anderson, 1995). Amongst other sources are in-cluded the allocation of money and time. Blase and Blase (1994) and Bennett (1995), amongst others, discuss the importance of power and authority as a tool of management. The uses of power are discussed in more detail in Chapter 9. Leaders cannot get things done with or through others without having access to:

- moral suasion;
- resources;
- coercion (e.g. authority of position);
- expertise in curriculum and organisational practice which they display in their own work; and
- personal enthusiasm and commitment.

A more technicist or mechanical view of subject leadership is expressed by the Teacher Training Agency. For subject leaders to be effective, it suggests, they need to have:

> - The ability to lead and manage people to work towards common goals;
> - The ability to solve problems and make decisions;
> - The ability to communicate clearly and understand the views of others;
> - The ability to manage themselves effectively and professionally.
>
> (TTA, 1998: 6)

It also suggests subject leaders need to have a selection of personal attributes, which raises some uncomfortable questions about the degree to which preparation for subject leadership is merely a matter of training and education. Hodgkinson (1991), too, suggests that as leadership is essentially a moral enterprise, it requires people to develop certain personal attributes. He suggests leaders have to achieve wisdom in four areas that affect their actions. Knowing:

- the task;
- the situation;
- the followership; and
- oneself.

The last two areas are explored more closely in Chapter 9.

The exercise of leadership and the effective working of subject areas

Working in organisations is often said to have five dimensions (Sergiovanni, 1992). For an organisation, such as a school, or subunit of it such as a subject area, to work effectively leaders need to create coherent policies and practices in each of these dimensions. In England and Wales, weaknesses in any of these dimensions are likely to draw criticisms from school inspectors working under OFSTED guidelines (OFSTED, 1999). These are as follows:

- The technical or curriculum aspect of schooling, its 'production' or task function.
- The operational aspect of how an institution or subject area is organised.
- The human aspect of working with people, staff, students, parents and governors.
- The cultural aspect of creating and maintaining the values, beliefs and vision of an institution or subject area.
- The contexts of decision-making of using power and resources to achieve organisational goals.

Table 8.1 gives some indication of how these dimensions relate to the work of subject leaders.

Managing the task: managing the curriculum

If teaching and learning are at the centre of school activity (Hopkins *et al.*, 1994; Bell and Ritchie, 1999), a key aspect of subject leaders' work is giving advice and guidance to their colleagues in their subject area on effective practice. To do this they not only need to be able to teach effectively themselves, but also to have and articulate an expert understanding of the curriculum, its assessment and its pedagogy. In England and Wales, the formal academic curriculum is prescribed by the National Curriculum, introduced in 1988. Assessment tests are carried out by the Qualification and Curriculum Authority (QCA) at three key stages in a student's career. The school-leaving examinations are administered by different public examination boards.

Subject leaders also need to understand how the subject syllabus relates to other aspects of the National Curriculum, including those cross-curriculum aspects such as ICT (information communication technology) and citizenship. They also need to understand the pastoral curriculum in order to help students become effective learners and effective citizens – a recent new emphasis in UK central government education policy. Deeper understanding of students' attitudes and motives both individually and socially and a knowledge of how people work in groups will help teachers develop imaginative and effective approaches to supporting their learning.

Subject leaders need to help their colleagues become expert in a variety of teaching strategies (pedagogy) and in monitoring and assessing students' work in ways that take account of students' aptitudes as well as of their absolute levels of performance. This is discussed in more detail in Chapter 6.

Table 8.1   Five aspects of organisations, five functions of leadership

Five dimensions	Some of the functions of subject leaders and middle managers
Technical (the curriculum)	• Shaping study programmes to meet National Curriculum programmes of study • Considering the quality and quantity of curriculum materials needed to sustain these programmes • Creating a preparatory programme for Standard Assessment Tests (SATs) and public examinations • Setting clear standards and processes for marking students' work • Provision of special educational needs (SEN) curriculum support • Establishing clear processes for giving feedback and support to students on the quality of their work
Operational development and resource management	• Planning, organising, monitoring and evaluating the work of a subject area • Setting performing indicators and targets • Creating and sustaining deadlines for projects • Linking curriculum development plans to those of the whole school • Allocating resources on a moral basis – budgeting
People/human relationships	• Knowing self: personal values, professional interests and beliefs, technical expertise • Knowing colleagues: personal values, professional interests and beliefs, technical expertise • Respecting other people and self; different needs and aspirations • Understanding different student needs (e.g. ethnicity, gender, poverty) • Critical friend and mentor: helps colleagues reflect carefully on their practice both as a team and as individuals • Appraiser and professional reviewer of colleagues' practice • Creating and applying consistent standards of behaviour
Symbolic and cultural (vision, beliefs, symbols and ceremonies)	• Living proclaimed values and persuading colleagues to do the same • Projecting a vision (e.g. the range of teaching methods possible) • Helping create myths about what a successful lesson looks like • Sharing stories of what works in people's classrooms • Creating ceremonies, symbols and rituals that celebrate key values
Contexts of decision-making: authority, power, environment	• The moral use of power and permission • Gaining access to sources of power through senior staff; LEA • Comparing organisational values and personal (staff) beliefs • Understanding the demands of the environment (e.g. LEA, DfEE, Qualification and Curriculum Authority) • Relationships with school governors

Managing the operations: creating effective departments

Leaders of schools at all levels need to understand the characteristics of effective education organisations. These may be used as touchstones to guide the direction of their steps to school improvement.

Work by Sammons *et al.* (1997) suggests that characteristics which indicate the effectiveness of schools as a whole also indicate the effectiveness of subject areas within schools. This view is supported by Harris *et al.* (1995) who also suggested (Harris, 1998) that the negation of these qualities led to ineffective departments in secondary schools. Sammons *et al.* (1994) suggested the key characteristics of effective schools are that they have:

- A leader who is firm and purposeful and has effective professional knowledge;
- A shared vision and goals among the staff and students;
- An orderly learning environment;
- A strong focus on teaching, learning and high achievement;
- An emphasis on purposeful teaching;
- High expectations of everybody in the school;
- Positive reinforcement of behaviour;
- Effective monitoring of students' performances;
- A clear recognition of students' rights and responsibilities;
- Strong home–school partnerships;
- An emphasis on developing a learning organisation.

Harris *et al.* (1995: 285) suggested that, within effective subject areas, there also needs to be:

- Good resource management;
- Careful and clear structuring of lessons;
- A matching of syllabus and pedagogy to the needs of students.

By contrast, Harris (1998: 272) suggested that ineffective subject areas have the following characteristics:

- Inappropriate leadership and management styles;
- Lack of vision;
- Poor communications within the subject area;
- Poor organisation;
- Inadequate systems for monitoring and evaluation;
- A non-collegial culture;
- Nobody acting as a leading professional within the subject area;
- An absence of professional development;
- Insufficient focus upon teaching and learning.

Subject leaders have a responsibility for ensuring the characteristics of their subject areas correspond more closely to those of the effective subject area than those of the ineffective one. They could, for example, work with their colleagues to consider how closely the characteristics of their subject area match those of effective schools and subject areas and put strategies in place to achieve these characteristics where they do not already exist.

Managing with people

For many subject leaders managing other people is the most difficult task they face. In secondary schools most subject leaders have direct line management of other staff while, in primary schools, such line management responsibilities are rare. This presents subject leaders with the sensitive and sometimes difficult task of motivating and sometimes challenging colleagues. Success in doing so largely depends upon the professional relationships subject leaders have with colleagues. In this respect the effective subject leader needs to be aware of the feelings associated with decisions taken or tasks delegated. The process of delegation is not without anxiety and stress, particularly when the subject leader is taking a risk by delegating to others. Consequently, knowing their own and their colleagues' personal strengths and weaknesses is an important first step in effective subject leadership, as discussed more fully in Chapter 9.

The emphasis here is on the importance of transformational approaches to leadership (Blase and Anderson, 1995) that focus on building trust and shared values (collegiality) between staff in a school. At subject level this establishes a collaborative culture by asserting that staff should be able to influence and share ownership of a school and subject area's core values. Hargreaves (1994) called this perspective genuine collegiality. It requires leaders to know and work alongside their colleagues as individuals, understanding the following:

- How they perceive themselves as professionals – 'most teachers consider students' needs as paramount, even when these may be different from their own as employees' (Hall, 1997: 152).
- The culture of their particular subject areas or key stage areas as it is affected by particular aspects of subject knowledge (Siskin, 1994).
- The focus of staff development in learning organisations.

Hargreaves (1994) draws a distinction between the extent to which a collegial culture in a school is contrived (controlled by senior staff), genuine (controlled by all staff) or balkanised (staff are limited to decision-making in specific areas of a school). The first tends to encourage cynicism amongst staff (Busher and Saran, 1992). Genuine or balkanised collegial cultures facilitate people's sense of ownership of school decision-making (at least within defined areas) and practices, as Blase and Anderson (1995) suggested it would. It also facilitates co-operation between all staff in a school, creating the kind of environment Wallace *et al.* (1997) have referred to as a learning organisation.

In schools where there is only limited formal involvement of subject leaders in whole-school decisions, staff tend to perceive themselves as only being informed about what is happening rather than genuinely participating in the decision-making (Brown *et al.*, 1999). This managerialist approach, they claimed, discourages staff from working together, especially across subject boundaries. Siskin (1997) thought such strongly structured divisions in a school discouraged reform and change because they encouraged a fragmented view of a school rather than notions of a school-wide community.

The position of subject leaders in a school means they have a complicated set of interpersonal relationships to deal with within the school. On the one hand they are directly accountable to the senior management team and managed by them. On the other hand, they have subject area members accountable to them and have responsibility for managing them as a team. It is this Janus-faced aspect of their role that highlights their bridging and brokering functions. In secondary schools not all the teachers of a subject area work full time on a specific subject. In departments with few staff, such as history, there may be only one full-time subject teacher, the subject leader, along with several part-time staff who also teach other subjects. Arguably, the more fragmented the staffing of a subject area, the more difficult it is for a subject leader to create a vision of teaching and learning to which every teacher of that subject, however little of it they do, will subscribe enthusiastically. This has been discussed in more detail in Chapter 4. On the other hand, in primary schools, subject leaders co-ordinate and inspire the work of people who teach a wide variety of subjects to a fixed group of students.

It is important, therefore, that subject leaders set clear parameters within which to work with others. For example, they need to ensure all intrusions on their time have an agreed time limit, purpose and agenda. Subject leaders have to develop effective negotiating skills to assist them in offsetting competing demands upon their time. For example, rejecting ideas from subject area members can often cause resentment and, consequently, needs to be handled sensitively by a subject leader.

Despite the acknowledged difficulties of managing other people, the quality, commitment and motivation of teachers have a direct impact upon performance within the subject area (Harris *et al.*, 1995; Sammons *et al.*, 1997). To develop commitment in others subject leaders need to:

- involve staff in developing a clear sense of purpose and identifying their own targets;
- encourage staff to take ownership for their work;
- value staff and maximise their potential within the subject area;
- articulate a clear sense of purpose or vision (Glover *et al.*, 1998: 285) so that subject area staff know what they are doing and why;
- translate a sense of purpose into clear and realistic objectives for the subject area and individuals; and
- remove barriers to, and provide opportunities for, the achievement of those objectives.

Working in teams

There are many features common to all management teams across all phases of education. Subject leaders in schools tend to work in two types of team: a structured team and a specific-purposes team (Blandford, 1997). Poster (1976) refers to these as formal and *ad hoc* teams. The structured team forms part of the school hierarchy (e.g. in secondary schools departmental teams are part of the middle managerial layer of the school organisation). In primary schools in England and Wales, the structured team may be either a subject area or a key stage area. In contrast, the specific team is one that has been established outside the usual organisational structure for a particular purpose (e.g. to consider whole-school issues). It may have a life span no longer than that of its task.

Focusing on work groups as teams tends to emphasise their formal structures and formal processes, rather than considering how they evolve as groups of people. For example, the size of a team affects how it operates. In some smaller teams one person may have to perform many functions. In some very small departments, one person may have to undertake all the functions. In larger teams or subject areas, there may be opportunities for delegation of responsibility by the team leader or of specialisation by members of the department. It is the mixture of people with a variety of skills and abilities who are in a team that is important to the successful operation of a team (Belbin, 1996). Subject leaders need to reflect carefully on how they can use the strengths of the teachers and other staff in their teams.

Newly appointed subject leaders may find the teams they inherit do not behave as teams or engage in any teamwork. Simply because the staff in a subject area form part of a school's organisational structure does not mean they function as a team. Hence the initial task of any subject leader must be to ensure the department works and functions as an effective team. This may involve reconstituting and redefining the collective identity of a group of people so they begin to perform as a team. According to Handy (1976), this involves the subject leader in taking the group through four specific phases of team development:

1) *Forming* The purpose of the team, its composition and organisation is discussed. Individuals establish their identities within the team and their positions within the group.
2) *Storming* Handling conflicts and challenges by individual members as clearer functions and roles are identified.
3) *Norming* Establish norms and practices, including decisions on how work will be carried out.
4) *Performing* The group starts to work coherently and interdependently to achieve its goals.

Formal processes of working with people through meetings and job descriptions give a clear framework to the operation of a subject area or a school, as Wallace and Hall (1994) suggest. However, only a small proportion of a subject leader's work is likely to take place in this way.

Much of a subject leader's work is likely to take place with colleagues at an informal and individual level, or in informal meetings (Busher, 1992). The last often happen by chance, such as during coffee breaks or before or after lessons, though a skilful leader will know how and where they can be engineered and with which people. Busher and Blease (2000) point out the importance of informal processes of decision-making and job allocation in subject areas to complement formal processes of working. They conducted a study about how laboratory technicians who were female worked with teachers who were predominantly male.

The debate about the relative merits of formal and informal consultation processes goes beyond a technical issue about how bureacratic effective organisational processes need to be. It also raises issues about the impact of gender and ethnicity on people's preferred and actual work styles, and questions the extent to which the notion of a subject area as a team of workers governed by formal contractual processes is misleading. Sergiovanni (1994a) suggests such work groups might be better understood as communities.

Subject areas as communities

Work groups amongst school staff can be characterised in many different ways: as teams; as communities; or as coalitions or alliances. In characterising them in these different ways researchers and practitioners can gain different insights into how the groups function and, as a result, can gain different insights into how they can be led and managed.

Talking about people working in teams or working in communities raises different expectations about how those groups will operate, whether in a school or in another organisation. Sergiovanni (1994b) suggests people working in schools have far more of the characteristics of communities than they do of contractually based organisational teams. The latter emphasises contractual relationships, the former relationships of choice and shared values. Subject leaders need to help their colleagues develop a sense of community since this creates a greater sense of cohesion and the subject area team.

Sergiovanni (1994b: 10) points out that:

> In communities we create our social lives with others who have similar intentions to ours . . . Communities rely more on norms, purposes, values, professional socialisation, collegiality and natural interdependence [to exert control over their members] . . . The ties of community in schools can become substitutes for formal systems of supervision, evaluation and staff development . . . [and] for management and organisational schemes that seek to co-ordinate what teachers do.

Such a view applies to the work of support staff in schools as much as to the work of teachers (Busher and Saran, 1995a; Busher and Blease, 2000).

Such an emphasis encourages staff and students to consider carefully their interdependence, perceiving rules and regulations as a necessary framework to enable them to pursue their own goals as well as to allow other people to pursue theirs. Ribbins (1997) gives an example of this approach by teachers in a primary school where they actively involved students in helping to define the appropriate rules and values for their school. The impact of this was said by the headteacher to have greatly reduced the amount of misbehaviour by students and raised their enthusiasm for work. The latter was attributed to their greater sense of engagement in creating the processes of schooling. Subject leaders can bring about this state by engaging students in consultations about effective learning practices and norms of socially acceptable behaviour.

Involving parents in this community of the subject area has benefits to student learning as well (Merchant and Marsh, 1998). Osler *et al.* (2000) suggests those schools which involve parents as part of their community in supporting the work of students have lower rates of exclusion and inappropriate behaviour by students. This challenging set of evidence encourages subject leaders to acknowledge the importance of using transformational approaches to leadership based on trust rather than depending on transactional and managerial approaches. The latter assume that, unless people are closely supervised, they will not do any work at all – McGregor's Theory X of the 1960s.

Viewing the subject area or key stage area as a community of staff and students does not negate the importance of encouraging and helping staff and students to monitor student academic progress, review staff pedagogy and evaluate subject area effectiveness. However, it does encourage subject leaders to view their colleagues and students positively as wanting to achieve high-quality performance if only they are given appropriate leadership and support. In this scenario subject leaders need to focus on how help can be given to staff and students, rather than on how people should be punished for making mistakes. In terms of subject area and school culture, it encourages subject leaders to create those of improving schools (Stoll and Fink, 1996) or of effective schools (Sammons *et al.*, 1997) or effective departments (Harris *et al.*, 1995).

Managing meetings: a particular sort of teamwork

One of the ways in which teams or communities work together in schools and other bureaucratic organisations is through a series of formal meetings. There are, of course, also informal meetings – sometimes referred to as 'consultations'. The latter often take place over a cup of coffee in staffrooms or in corridors. They can be of great importance to a subject leader in sounding out in advance of formal meetings how staff might respond to certain ideas. They can be a means of gaining knowledge and information out of the glare of formal meetings (Busher, 1992).

For meetings to be successful, Everard and Morris (1996) point out they need to have a purpose. There are many occasions when formal meetings might not be needed for decision-making. For example, in any subject area there is likely to be a range of routine matters on which staff have already agreed policy. All that is required is for subject leaders to implement those policies, taking whatever decisions are needed. On the other hand, over issues of policy or matters of curriculum development or of resource allocation, formal meetings are likely to be necessary. This is because in these cases subject leaders need to agree principles on which procedures can be implemented.

Formal meetings have their own particular dynamics. One of the questions a subject leader has to decide is which people need to attend what meeting. If staff are expected to attend meetings about students or procedures with which they are not involved, they are likely to perceive the meeting as a waste of time, harming the quality of discussion in the meeting and the quality of relationships between staff.

In preparing for any meeting with colleagues, subject leaders need to prepare themselves in all five aspects of the organisation shown in

Table 8.1. For example, they will need to be clear about the technical aspects of their curriculum knowledge that apply to the agenda of a meeting. Every meeting will need to have an agenda prepared, whether that is formal and written, or informal and held either by the subject leader or his or her colleagues.

To give guidance to colleagues on how to begin to find a resolution to particular situations, subject leaders need to consider the operational processes available in particular situations to implement action, including what might be some of the possible outcomes or solutions to problems to be discussed. An important perspective here is the micropolitical processes of a school and the tensions and pressures encapsulated within them. This means subject leaders and their colleagues need to be aware of how power is used in and around their schools through and with people. As well as allowing them to implement decisions more effectively, it will allow them to recognise what solutions are probably achievable in their particular schools.

In any meeting there is likely to be a variety of people with different attitudes to the meeting. Some people might be enthusiastic, others may have only a limited view of what is involved in teaching a subject. Some may be slow to offer their views on particular matters, while others always have lots to say on every topic (West-Burnham, 1992). The different strengths and weaknesses of these people, which might be characterised by Belbin's typology of team members (as is discussed in Chapter 3), will have to be managed by the leader of the meeting. This raises questions about the leadership styles that might be used in meetings and how meetings can be successfully facilitated. Everard and Morris (1996) suggest a range of styles from the autocratic through the consultative to the collegial can be appropriate for meetings on different types of topics.

Most importantly, subject leaders need to be aware of their own and their colleagues' personal and professional views and interests in the matters under discussion. This understanding of people can help them chair a meeting or co-ordinate a discussion through the following:

- Allowing space for colleagues to contribute to discussion.
- Bringing colleagues into the discussion appropriately or sometimes excluding them.
- Taking the lead in shaping the ideas in the discussion when appropriate.
- Paraphrasing and summing up the discussion as a meeting progresses.
- Drawing together the threads of a discussion at its conclusion.

- Helping colleagues devise realistic steps for action.

Day *et al.* (1985: 125) suggests, practically, that subject leaders should ensure the following:

- Meetings start on time, and their duration is clear;
- The purpose and content of the meeting is made clear;
- The feelings and understandings of staff members are regularly checked;
- Late comers should be brought up to date;
- Members' contributions are respected and valued;
- Members are listened to, encouraged, supported;
- Differences and conflicts are talked out thoroughly;
- Questions and concerns are clarified;
- Participation is acknowledged and not taken for granted.

In addition it is often important that some notes of each meeting are taken and circulated after the meeting, partly to check with participants that they are an accurate record of the meeting. A second purpose is to remind people of what decisions they have taken during a meeting and what they agreed to undertake after it. Subject leaders will need to follow up the meeting by discussing progress on various points with their colleagues.

Sustaining development: monitoring performance

Knowing what are the characteristics of an effective department is not sufficient for a subject leader to create a successful subject area. It is also important that subject leaders help staff colleagues to plan development, allocate resources appropriately and monitor performance and progress. This view is also found in the literature on managing change (e.g. Fullan, 1991) and in the literature on development planning (e.g. Hopkins and Hargreaves, 1991) which is discussed more fully in Chapter 11.

Monitoring performance is about making visible what has been or is being achieved. While this includes statistical evidence such as keeping records of the work students have undertaken and the quality of performance students have achieved, it also includes oral and othographic evidence. This might include making visible the effort students have put in to doing their work or improving their behaviour perhaps through the range of wall displays subject leaders encourage teachers use. Sammons *et al.* (1997) suggest student motivation and the expectations teachers hold and display about students are important in creating effective subject areas. Glover *et al.* (1998) suggest processes of monitoring and evaluation not only focus on statistical data but also on literate evidence. They argue the latter can be sufficiently formalised to be used as evidence of improvement.

An important element in monitoring the performance of a subject area is that of setting appropriate targets for students of different abilities. Staff and students need to be helped to perform to these levels in the relevant key stage Standard Assessment Tests (SATs) or first-level public examinations, such as GCSE. Useful guidance on how to monitor and evaluate the performance of a subject area can be gained from the OFSTED guidance to schools. Subject leaders need to be aware of this and be able to help colleagues evaluate theirs and their students' performances against the criteria given.

9

Cultures of Leadership and Professional Autonomy: Managing Self, Developing Others

This chapter explores how subject leaders have a key part in establishing particular educational and social values for their subject areas. These affect critically how people work with each other in a particular subject area, whether they are staff or students. They have to work carefully with teachers who have autonomous perspectives on teaching but, none the less, need helping to reflect on their practice in order to improve it. To do this successfully subject leaders need to facilitate this potentially threatening process by undertaking the role of mentor.

Introduction

At the core of being a subject leader is being clear about one's own self as a creative and dynamic force within a team trying to meet the needs of its students. Hodgkinson (1991) suggests that being a leader is a moral art, a view echoed by Sergiovanni (1992). As Table 9.1 suggests, this involves leaders at all levels in a school developing their personal philosophies, their interpersonal skills and their management of themselves as a first step.

Greenfield and Ribbins (1993) argue that, until leaders have a coherent understanding of self, it is difficult for them to develop themselves as leaders. These identities are constructed in part because of their personal biographies – who they were, where they grew up, what were their formative influences, as Ouston (1997) argues. In other words, their personal environment has a major impact on subject leaders' views on managing subject areas and working with people. In this context gender and ethnic group have to be considered major parameters influencing people's choices (Hall, 1996; Coleman, 1999).

There are, however, many ways of being a leader. Duignan and Macpherson (1992) considered it involved working in three different

Table 9.1   Practical guidance on being a moral leader

Personal
- Learn from feelings and rebuffs
- Don't save stillettos – bury hatchets
- Be authentic
- Be courteous and well mannered
- Draw a line between private and public life

Interpersonal techniques
- As for a proposed solution from problem raisers
- Delegate
- Machiavelli has a rightful place
- Compartmentalise your work
- Do your homework thoroughly
- Understand proper procedures thoroughly
- Rarely is anything simple or complete

Communication
- Observe channels
- Create channels
- Empathise with colleagues
- Read
- Write, fax, email, telephone

Timing
- Delay or retard impulsive action or reaction
- Transact 'business' at the proper place and time
- Be punctual and meet deadlines
- There is always enough time, it is just a matter of deciding priorities

Work
- Nothing is accomplished without work
- Have both commmitment and detachment

Source: After Hodgkinson (1991).

realms: that of ideas for developing values and strategic thinking; that of people for developing appropriate cultures and asserting power (political activity); and that of things, managing what is achievable and evaluating what has been achieved. Such activity is bounded – that is, it takes place within particular contexts or situations.

Leadership and power

Leadership is asserted through the use of power. Power can take a wide variety of forms: coercion, reward, expertise, charisma, traditional norms and rational-legal processes (Weber, 1947 in Bendix, 1962; French and Raven, 1968; Bacharach and Lawler, 1980). In subject areas these different forms of power are to be found in the everyday routines of work. Students and staff are coerced by the rules and regulations of school life, but they are also rewarded for their efforts by praise, financial reward or opportunities to gain something they want. Processes of positive discipline for students are mirrored by staff gaining the opportunity to take field trips they particularly enjoy. Subject leaders may use access to limited resources as a means of controlling the development of the curriculum in particular ways, for example. Subject leaders are likely to manifest expertise in their particular subject area, and can use such knowledge to win arguments about how they prefer a subject area to be organised or how students should be assessed. Other colleagues in subject areas may, too, possess expertise in some aspects of the curriculum. This may be through personal or professional interest and become the basis for delegated responsibilities. If subject leaders delegate authority they, too, will be able to exercise leadership in some aspects of a subject area.

That subject leaders are appointed to their post gives them rational-legal power or authority. This is what Watson (1969) calls authority of office. However, unless they set out actively to use their power to implement actions they may merely exercise what Gibb (1947) calls 'headship' rather than leadership. They may not, of course, always be successful in achieving the developments they want in the subject area or in their classrooms. This is because the other staff and students can also exercise power (Hoyle, 1981) to counterbalance or resist that of the subject leader. At such points leaders are often pressed into seeking the support of more powerful people, such as the senior management team.

Blase and Anderson (1995) suggested power can be asserted in one of three ways: over people, with people or through people. While the first of these might be considered to include aspects of coercive leadership, the other two indicate the importance of leaders exercising their leadership by working in collaboration with other people. Blase and Anderson (1995) suggest it is the last form of leadership and power that contributes most strongly to bringing about organisational improvement through raising teachers' morale. However, as they were writing in a North American context which has particular socio-political norms, it may be that part of the explanation for their most successful model of school leadership is that it supports social values homogeneous with those of the host society. Brundrett (1998) suggest that collegiality as a preferred style of effective working in schools seems to be related to broader socio-political norms in particular societies.

Styles of leadership which seek to work with and through other people, building agreed norms and values and shared approaches to action, are often described as transformational leadership. It is described as an essential approach for building teams or communities of people in organisations who will work together effectively (Blase and Anderson, 1995).

Leaders at all levels in organisations, including subject leaders, often have to negotiate with their colleagues in order to achieve change or maintain equilibrium. This is likely to involve them bargaining with their colleagues. This form of leadership is called transactional leadership. In order to get something implemented subject leaders allow their colleagues to gain something they want in return for helping implement some action the subject leader wants. Subject leaders have many bargaining counters available to them. For example, subject area colleagues may want extra resources (to carry out teaching), the opportunity not to teach an aspect of work they do not like, or the subject leader to take a part of one of their lessons so they can prepare some teaching materials.

Whatever sources of power subject leaders have to support and enact their role, how they conceive themselves as leaders and what style of leadership they use, is likely to have a major impact on the culture of the subject area. It crucially affects how they and their colleagues work together as a team or community. Brown and Rutherford (1998) suggests these styles can be collected into a descriptive typology of subject leadership, although any one leader may use elements of several of these depending on the situation or action required. The styles are as follows:

- *Servant leader* Leadership through a web of interpersonal relationships.
- *Organisational architect* Creating organic forms of organisational working.
- *Moral educator* Creating a shared collection of deeply held values and beliefs.
- *Social architect* Constructing social networks for staff and students to support learning.
- *Leading professional* Highly knowledgeable and up to date, and an expert practitioner.

A much older catalogue of leadership styles creates a continuum from that of autocrat to that of abdicator (Tannenbaum and Schmidt, 1973). As Busher and Saran (1995a) point out, whatever style a leader adopts as his or her preferred or normal style of leadership, it will shape the culture of the organisation or subject area. Ribbins (1992) explains how different cultures heavily influence the ways in which different staff act. For example, staff working for an autocratic subject leader are likely to be very dependent in their actions, waiting to be told what to do rather than risk innovations which might draw criticism. Table 9.2 illustrates this point, showing how leadership styles, through helping

Table 9.2   Staff/teachers' styles of work as outcomes of leaders' styles

Visionary	Company baron	Traditionalist	Team coach		**Leader styles** (Kakabadse and Parker, 1984)
Prophets	Sheiks	Bureaucrats	Shepherds	Craftworkers	(Mahil and Busher, 1998)
					plus ↓
Charisma	Normative	Rational/legal	Interpersonal		**Source of social authority** (after Weber, 1947 in Bendix, 1962: 32)
					leads to ↓
Tells	Tells	Sells/consults	Consults/ delegates	Abdicates	**Leader relationships** (after Tannenbaum and Schmidt, 1973)
					creates ↓
	Corporate	Managerialism	Collegiality		**Organisation culture** (Hargreaves, 1991)
	Club	Role focused	Task focused	Existentialist	(Handy, 1976)
Autocracy		Consultation/ views sought	Participates in/ influences decisions	Autonomy	(Busher and Saran, 1992)
					leads to ↓
Dependent		Quasi – interdependent	Interdependent	Independent	**Teacher styles of working** (Ribbins, 1992)

Source: Hugh Busher, University of Leicester, School of Education, 1998.

to construct particular subject area cultures, are likely to influence the way in which subject area staff and students prefer to work.

Cultures of schools and departments: social constructions of reality

At the core of effective departments are the cultures constructed by staff under the guidance of subject leaders, key stage co-ordinators or heads of department. The main building blocks of these cultures seem to be the attitudes of people of different status in a school to particular curriculum subjects; the attitudes of subject leaders and senior staff to their colleagues and to processes of social cohesion or control; and teachers' perspectives on pedagogy. However, the culture is also affected by the way in which formal organisational structures are created and the ways in which power and authority are used. The culture of the school and the history of the subject area will undoubtedly affect the working relationships between staff and the habits that already exist. Siskin

(1994) points out that the core knowledge of a subject area also affects the culture subject leaders and staff in a subject area create.

A variety of different terms are used to describe organisational culture: ethos, climate and atmosphere, among others. Whilst not exactly synonymous they usually refer to a rather amorphous quality which is difficult to define but which, none the less, many experienced teachers would claim to recognise when they meet it on entering a school. Crudely, culture is sometimes defined as 'the way we do things around here'. A great deal has been written about the cultures of schools (Hopkins *et al.*, 1994; Dalin and Rust, 1996) and the relationship between school culture and teacher development.

Schein (1992: 125) defines culture as:

- A pattern of basic assumptions and values;
- Invented, discovered or developed by a given group;
- As it learns to cope with its problems of external adaptation and internal integration;
- That has worked well enough to be considered valid;
- Is to be taught to new members;
- Is perceived by group members as the correct way to perceive, think and feel in relation to those problems.

Not only is culture created by a group of staff but it also reflects the history of that group and how it has developed through coping with a series of situations. It creates for its members a lens through which every aspect of school life is likely to be perceived. It incorporates core values for the group members and gives them a sense of identity. Sharing a group's culture leads to membership of the group who created it. Rejecting the culture of a group means, for a member of staff, placing him or herself outside that group.

Within a school, different groups of teachers may operate sub-cultures that diverge from what a headteacher may claim is the overall culture or ethos of a school. Siskin (1994) offers some explanation for this. She points out the impact of the cultures of different subject specialisms on teachers' professional identities. Subject leaders need to work with their colleagues to develop the views, values and beliefs which form a subject area's culture. They need to consider carefully how far they want to use symbols, badges and language to indicate their unique identify within the confines of a school's culture.

In primary schools, on the other hand, especially in very small schools, this process of differentiation is unlikely to happen, with a school's culture focusing around core values of teaching students (Nias, 1999). On the other hand there may be different sub-cultures between Early Years teachers, say, and the Key Stage 2 team in primary schools in England and Wales.

New staff in a school have to be taught the appropriate cultures of a school and the sub-cultures of its subject areas to help them belong. This is an important function for subject leaders who are inducting new members of staff. On the other hand new members joining a group themselves influence the values held within the culture.

Leaders, be they headteachers or subject leaders, need to analyse carefully what is the existing culture of the staff with whom they work as well as creating their own vision for a subject area. This is because all members of staff have their own views of their preferred working cultures, as is discussed below. This is not only in terms of what values they want to implement through changes in practice, but also of the quality of relationships they want to see established between colleagues, and between colleagues and students, parents and school governors. Subject leaders also need to be aware that their own styles of leadership, with their implicit values of how people should interact with each other, heavily influence the culture that emerges among their subject area colleagues.

There have been various attempts to create typologies of different organisational cultures, one of the best known, perhaps, being that of Handy (1976) in his book *The Gods of Management*. In this he described four different types of organisational culture. These ranged from an autocratic culture, dominated by one person or oligarchy, through a bureaucratic culture to an autonomous culture where people pursued

Table 9.3   The expression of a school or subject area's values

Verbal expression	Behavioural expression	Visual expression
Statements of aims and objectives	Rituals	Facilities
Descriptions of the curriculum	Ceremonies	The display of artefacts and memorabilia
Descriptions of organisational structure	Operational procedures	Use of badges, mottoes and uniforms
Metaphors of how people work	Rules, sanctions and rewards	
Stories of success or failure		
The language people use about other people and events		

Source: After Beare *et al.* (1989).

their own work only loosely held together by agreed processes and norms. Table 9.2 on page 124 indicates other possible typologies of organisational cultures.

Less successful have been the attempts to define and make visible in practical terms the key attributes of different types of culture, although Prosser and Warburton (1999) discuss interestingly how an organisation's cultural features can be mapped. On the other hand, Beare *et al.* (1989) offer a comprehensive view of how the different factors and values which make up the culture of a school or subject area can be mapped (see Table 9.3).

Collaborative cultures and professional partnerships

Blase and Blase (1994) suggest that effective leaders (they are talking about headteachers, but their views apply to subject leaders in a school as well) need to facilitate effective communication; encourage openness and trust between people; and develop and model understanding of other people's practices. An important aspect of this is that successful leaders have to practise their 'process' skills (i.e. they have to practise and model effective practice in getting on with other people in a variety of different ways and circumstances). One consequence of this is they are likely to be seen to be handling and diffusing conflict effectively, helping colleagues to feel involved in activities without compromising agreed core values. Blase and Blase (1994), looking at some headteachers in the USA, suggested that leaders acting like this had a fundamental trust in their colleagues which was not necessarily found in other types of leaders. Busher and Saran (1995a) also found the same in their survey of research on leadership of school staff in the UK. Hopkins *et al.* (1997a: 10) list six conditions they say create effective environments for learning and collaboration:

- Authentic relationships – the quality of openness and congruence of relationships in the classroom;
- Boundaries and expectations – the pattern of expectations set by the teacher and school of student performance and behaviour within the classroom;
- Planning for teaching – the access of teachers to a range of pertinent teaching materials and the ability to plan and differentiate these materials for a range of students;
- Teaching repertoire – the range of teaching styles and models available for use by a teacher, dependent on student, context, curriculum, and desired outcome;

- Pedagogic partnerships – the ability of teachers to form professional relationships within and outside the classroom that focus on the study and improvement of practice;
- Reflection on teaching – the capacity of the individual teacher to reflect on his or her own practice, and to put to the test of practice, specifications of teaching from other sources.

The development of this type of collaborative culture is dependent on leaders cultivating particular styles of leadership that facilitate this. However, changing educational contexts in England and Wales in the late 1990s which, as Brundrett (1998) points out, make increasingly bureaucratic demands on staff, may make it very difficult for such collegial ways of working to be sustained. Further, central government policy in the UK emphasises that high standards of teacher and student performance might be better served by tightly hierarchical approaches to leadership and management that specify clear standards of practice for teachers and students to follow.

Even within tightly constrained organisational frameworks leaders make a difference. If leaders, be they headteachers or subject leaders, implement collaborative working despite whatever organisational constraints there are, staff are more likely to want to engage in the activities being undertaken. None the less, subject leaders need to recognise different people prefer to be led in different ways. Subject leaders need to discover how to incorporate colleagues into the subject area team while allowing them space to retain their own professional identities – a difficult balancing act. The quality of the relationship within the subject area will determine the quality of teaching and learning within that area. On the other hand, consultation does not mean every decision can only be taken through a committee meeting!

Where teachers develop a collaborative community under the guidance of a subject leader or headteacher, this is often described as a learning school or a learning organisation. Wallace *et al.* (1997: 125) describe some of its key cultural attributes as follows:

- the willingness of staff to reflect and discuss what is being done in teaching and learning;
- the development of a collective focus by staff on student learning;
- the development of shared norms and values;
- an openness to innovation and reasonable risk-taking;
- staff empowerment.

These are brought about in part by:

- people having time to meet and discuss;
- the development of trust and respect amongst colleagues;

- supportive leadership; and
- a deepening professional knowledge by staff of pedagogy, curriculum (subject area) and organisational process.

The subject leader must, therefore, aim to lead and encourage staff in a subject area to:

- participate in agreeing the aims of the subject area;
- share their skills and knowledge;
- realise potential opportunities and synergies from co-operation; and
- reduce stress and anxiety.

It is interesting to note how closely these cultural attributes overlap with the characteristics of effective schools and departments discussed in Chapter 8. They are sometimes described as collegial cultures, although the extent to which real collegiality can ever be achieved in organisations where there are imbalances of power between leaders and led is open to dispute (e.g. Hargreaves, 1994).

The feeling of being part of a professional group within the school is an important factor in enabling teachers to function effectively and to continue to improve their teaching. Hargreaves (1995: 15) has characterised such an environment as a community of learners: 'Collaborative cultures turn individual learning into shared learning. Attending to structures so that they help people connect and designing tasks so they increase the capacity and opportunities for learning, spreads such learning across the entire organisation.'

The process of performance management for staff proposed by the UK central government (DfEE, 1998) could provide the structure to which Hargreaves refers. Whether those structures are used to assert subject leaders' control or indicate teacher empowerment will have a vital impact on the cultures leaders and colleagues construct in subject areas and schools, and the enthusiasm with which teachers and students carry out their work.

Schools vary greatly in their ways of working and in their cultural norms. Collaboration increases teachers' opportunities to learn from each other between classrooms, between subject areas and between schools (Darling-Hammond, 1990). The insulated and often segregated subject departments of secondary schools make it difficult for teachers to learn from each other. Consequently, subject leaders need to build a climate of collaboration within their area that fosters communication, sharing and opportunities for staff to work together. Collaboration is important because it creates a collective professional confidence that allows teachers to interact more confidently and assertively and so allows them to address the quality of student learning by addressing the quality of teaching.

Brundrett (1998), however, raises a note of caution about collegial or collaborative cultures, wondering to what extent they are cloaks for transformational leaders to reassert their power. Findings by Busher and Saran (1992) suggested that where teachers become aware that consultation and quasi-collaborative approaches to decision-making were being used in this cynical way they rapidly became cynical themselves. In these cases collaborative approaches do not lead to the benefits outlined above. Hargreaves (1994) also decried the impact of 'false collegiality', as he called it, on staff morale and enthusiasm for school improvement.

Managing individuals

Subject leaders have to work with teachers and support staff as individuals as well as as part of a subject area team. How people respond to the ways in which they are managed revolve around how people construct their life stories, and how these are related to their careers and their ambitions (e.g. Goodson and Hargreaves, 1996). Some of the development of professional identities is, of course, related to the conditions of service and work people experience and to the ways in which alternative life opportunities are presented to them.

Teachers and other staff, as well as students, develop their professional identities through their interactions in a variety of contexts. Crudely, these interactions can be divided into those in people's personal environment, those in people's organisational or school environment, and those which occur through time as part of a person's growth and/or career development. Subject leaders need to get to know their colleagues as individual people as well as as teachers.

Teachers' personal frameworks are strongly influenced by socio-economic frameworks, as well as by how people perceive teachers and how teachers perceive themselves (Weber and Mitchell, 1999). At one level this includes questions about people's interests outside their school work, such as whether they have care of dependent relatives, or what social activities or voluntary organisations they are engaged with, and the importance they give to these activities compared with their school work. These concerns are likely to affect the way in which teachers respond to demands subject leaders make on their time (Busher, 1992). The value staff give to such activities is a legitimate part of their own construction of personal and educational values. Where these differ from those of the subject leader, and this leads to

tension with subject area policy, subject leader and staff have to negotiate a compromise.

Teachers' views of what it means to be a teacher will affect their
vocational values – what they think they should be doing as teachers
(Crowther, 1993). In turn, this will affect their views of professional
development, of how schools and subject areas should be run, of the
role of a subject leader and the relationship of this role to other
teachers and to senior staff. Teachers' education in particular subject
areas affects their views on how particular subjects should be taught
(Siskin, 1994) and how teachers of particular subjects should behave.
In the mid-1980s in England and Wales, many PE teachers found it
very uncomfortable to stop taking after-school and weekend sports
sessions for their students during the teachers' industrial action of
that period, because these sessions were an accepted part of PE
teachers' culture (Busher, 1992). These vocational values are shaped
through a process of dialogue not only in people's personal and
social lives, but also in their professional ones. Subject leaders need
to engage in such conversations to shape the professional views
underpinning the cultures and practices of teaching and learning in a
subject area.

In primary schools teachers are likely to hold different views
of being a teacher from those held by teachers in secondary
schools. Not least, primary school teachers are likely to be concerned
first with the needs of the students they teach daily for a wide variety
of subjects rather than with the nuances of each individual subject
(Nias, 1999). As a result of central UK government guidance in the
late 1990s on the importance of literacy and numeracy, which is
probably reinforced by school-level policies, they are likely to focus
much of their energies on teaching in these core areas, perhaps at the
expense of enthusiasm for other subject areas they have to teach.

Subject leaders not only need to become familiar with the wide
variety of views and values held by their colleagues but also to take
these into account when managing their subject area. At one level this
means using teachers' (and students') interests as the basis for
negotiating changes and developments. These interests can be divided
into two main areas, professional and personal, as has already been
discussed, and into four categories. Busher (1992: 384) suggests the
latter can be described as follows:

- Institutional – how a school is organised; which classrooms and resources are available; the esteem in which a subject area is held; how
  students are disciplined; preferred relationships with senior staff and
  other colleagues;

- Technical/Curriculum – preferred pedagogy; subject topics; resources available; how students are grouped for learning;
- Work-oriented – career; self-esteem; extra-curricular activities; job satisfaction; educational values;
- Social – personal interests inside and outside a school.

These views are likely to be linked to views on what it means to be a teacher. Teaching can be viewed in four ways: labour, craft, profession or art as, for example, Ozga (1988) argues. Overlaying this are perspectives held by teachers as to whether their work is narrowly restricted to what they do with students in their own classrooms or whether it has a broader perspective. Hoyle (1980) refers to this dichotomy as people holding a restricted or extended focus for their work. The latter perspective is likely to encourage teachers to engage creatively in every aspect of school work. It is the latter perspective subject leaders need to encourage if they are to create collaborative cultures.

The narrower perspective might be akin to that described by various competence-based or technicist approaches to teaching. An example of this is the Catalina Foothills district of Arizona, which describes teaching in the following terms:

- Effective lesson planning;
- Effective classroom management;
- Effective teaching practices – teaching to the objective, monitoring student progress;
- Positive interpersonal relations – with parents, colleagues and students;
- Professional responsibility.

(Fraze and Hetzel, 1990: 135)

Green (1994) quotes a longer list of 12 competencies which the Education Assessment Centre at Oxford Brookes University used to evaluate teacher performance. Esp (1993) discusses competence-based training and education for teachers in some detail.

While the development of such competence-based understandings of what is meant by effective teaching can be useful, it can also lead to a limited and mechanistic understanding of what is involved in teaching. As well as overlooking the artistry and professional judgement involved in effective teaching (Hopkins and Harris, 2000), it also ignores the central importance of subject leaders establishing with colleagues the core values that are to underpin their work. This guides the manner in which core competences, whether those listed above or those suggested by OFSTED as criteria for effective teaching (OFSTED, 1999), are to be implemented. Usefully, competence perspectives can provide a focus through which subject leaders can give guidance to new staff and help existing staff to evaluate their own practices through processes of professional development.

A final aspect of individual teachers' perspectives on their activities which subject leaders need to take into account is the view people hold of their career. This is likely to influence strongly the enthusiasm teachers have for processes of professional development or for collaborating excitedly with new approaches to pedagogy or education management. For example, teachers in the early stages of their career may be excited and eager to adapt to new approaches to teaching, seeing it as a means of improving students' learning and developing their professional expertise. On the other hand, teachers within a few years of retirement, particularly if they are already successful at their job, may be unwilling to undergo extensive training to learn new pedagogical practices. The availability of resources may be a factor in both these dichotomous and stereotypic scenarios.

At any given stage in their lives and careers, then, teachers will be at a particular phase in their personal and professional development. As such, the meaning of teachers' development is located in their personal and professional lives and in the policy and school settings in which they work. The nature of teaching demands that teachers engage in continuing professional development but particular needs and the ways in which these are met will vary according to circumstance, personal and professional histories and current dispositions.

Mentoring: promoting professional reflection and development

Lomax (1990) suggests staff development can be viewed through four paradigms:

1) A research perspective, which might also be described as an extended professional approach since it requires teachers to consider their practice in its national, institutional and personal professional perspectives. This approach is considered in more detail in Chapter 10.
2) A political perspective which defines how staff development meets national and local policy agenda regardless of the relevance of particular developments to teachers' improved support for learners.
3) A managerialist perspective which emphasises the importance of a school's corporate goals and needs with little regard for teachers' individual professional needs.

4) A restricted approach which focuses only on working in classrooms.

The first and last encourage staff to think critically about their work in order to improve their practice, assuming that through this process they retain legitimate if partial professional ownership of it. To reflect successfully on one's own practice, however, often requires the help of other people to act as a lens through which practitioners can analyse personal action rigorously (Schon, 1987). Such 'other persons' are sometimes called 'critical friends'. Within organisations these 'other persons' are often more senior colleagues. Alongside this has to be set the findings about effective departments or subject areas. Earley and Fletcher-Campbell (1989: 105) noted in their research on middle management that the planning of staff development was seen as one of the hallmarks of a successful department. Other studies (e.g. Harris *et al.*, 1995; Sammons *et al.*, 1997) similarly point towards staff development as being central to subject area performance.

Consequently, a key function of subject leaders is to provide help and encouragement to their colleagues to think critically about practice in order to develop teachers' professional skills and knowledge to meet the needs of the students – see, for example, McIntyre and Haggar (1996) or Moyles *et al.* (1998). Hopkins *et al.* (1997a) called it *pedagogic partnerships*. By that term they meant groups of teachers working together inside and outside the classroom to bring about improvement in teaching and learning. Other facets of this role involve subject leaders arguing with senior staff in their schools for adequate resources for staff development and training in their subject area, and considering how best to allocate in-service training resources provided by outside agencies to develop teaching further within the subject area.

Subject leaders have a key role to play in these 'pedagogic partnerships' as mentors to their colleagues. Mentors need to sustain a collaborative culture to carry out this role effectively, leaving ownership of the practice and of the changes in practice with their teacher colleagues. However, they also have to encourage colleagues to evaluate practice carefully against agreed norms of effective pedagogy for particular students. In this context OFSTED criteria for effective teaching (OFSTED, 1999) can provide useful benchmarks for thinking about teaching practice and how that can be effectively adapted to local situations. Moyles *et al.* (1998: 43) found mentors in their study had six key functions:

- Professional supporter – who encourages and reassures their colleague in their actions;

- Professional trainer – who coaches colleagues and helps them to clarify what situations need;
- Professional educator – to encourage colleagues to reflect critically on an evidence base of their actions;
- Professional assessor – to offer an evaluation of performance according to agreed criteria;
- Professional sponsor – able to help colleagues negotiate the organisational structures;
- Personal friend and counsellor.

To work closely with their subject area colleagues in this way, subject leaders need to develop effective procedures and personal skills and knowledge. Hopkins *et al.* (1997b) suggest some useful procedures. Moyles *et al.* (1998) found effective mentors in primary schools possessed good interpersonal skills and good communication skills as well as sound knowledge of professional practice. They also noted effective mentors had to be able to model that knowledge effectively in practice. They (*ibid.*: 45) list the skills needed as follows:

- flexible in their style of working with staff;
- use a wide range of interpersonal skills effectively;
- effective communication;
- sound professional practice;
- sound professional knowledge involving a wide range of pedagogic and analytical skills;
- negotiative and enabling skills;
- fostering self-esteem;
- patience.

Mentoring is a key strategy for subject leaders wishing to bring about change in the curriculum and pedagogy of their subject areas. Foci for this may arise out of ongoing subject area planning meetings when staff recognise the need to introduce change. On the other hand it may be necessary for a subject leader to broach the matter of change with a colleague or colleagues who are resistant to or unaware of the need for it. These latter situations are ones of potential conflict and need to be handled with some care. Even helping colleagues to evaluate an aspect of practice they have chosen for review can pose fragile interpersonal situations.

Almost inevitably, effective mentoring involves the mentor observing the practice of the other teacher. This is an uncomfortable experience for many teachers, especially the first time they experience it. The fact they are observed and their practice monitored on a daily if informal basis by dozens of students and any visiting classroom assistants and stray visitors to a school makes no difference, it would seem, to this sense of anxiety. To allay this sense of anxiety it is important observer and teacher agree in advance what is to be observed; how those observations are to be made – according to a preagreed schedule, perhaps; and how the debriefing session is to be conducted. This is discussed in more detail in Chapter 10.

10

Professional Development and Action Research

This chapter considers the way in which teachers' continuous professional development contributes to and enhances performance within the subject area. The modes of professional development associated with improved teaching and learning are those focused upon and located within the classroom. When teachers work collaboratively, the possibility and potential for improved classroom practice are greatly increased.

The success of a particular subject in school is affected by the kind of professional relationships subject leaders develop with their team members. Also, it is affected by the relationships team members have with each other. The process of action research is one means of generating and sustaining a collaborative culture within the subject area that is premised upon improving teaching. Consequently, it is a process all subject leaders should endorse and support.

Introduction

Subject leaders now have an increased responsibility for the quality of teaching within the subject area and for developing others within their team (Field *et al.*, 2000). In one of the first studies of middle management, a commitment to professional development was seen as one of the hallmarks of a successful department (Early and Fletcher-Campbell, 1989). Contemporary writers on this theme (Bell and Ritchie, 1999; Harris, 1999b) similarly point towards continuing professional development as being central to improving departmental performance.

In their role as developers of others, subject leaders need to be aware of the tensions that exist between professional development and school development. While the positive link between teacher development and school development has been firmly established, in practice there may be competing demands on limited resources (Day,

1996). Subject leaders, therefore, have to make the case on behalf of their teams for adequate and appropriate resources for staff development. It is the responsibility of subject leaders to ensure there is sufficient support and training to enable teachers to be most effective in the classroom.

Continuing professional development

In supportive school environments there are usually structures already in place to effect change and improvement (Hopkins *et al.*, 1996; Lieberman, 1996). In all schools, in-service training programmes exist to encourage development and change (Day, 1999). However, the impact of such training remains variable because of the lack of connection between what Joyce (1992) terms 'the workshop' and 'the workplace'. In Joyce's (*ibid.*) view, the workshop is the training ground for developing new skills and knowledge (e.g. an INSET course or a professional qualification). Alternatively, the workplace is the classroom, department or school where new skills and knowledge are utilised.

Skill acquisition and the ability to transfer 'workshop' knowledge to a range of situations necessitate 'on-the-job support'. The failure of traditional in-service training within schools to affect practice has been widely documented (Hopkins, 1986; Bolam, 1990; Day, 1999). This implies changes to the way in which staff development is organised in schools. In particular, this means establishing opportunities for immediate and sustained practice, collaboration and peer coaching within the subject area (West, 1995). It is difficult to transfer teaching skills from INSET sessions to classroom settings without alterations to the workplace conditions within the classroom, department and school. However, few schools have adapted the workplace to meet such staff development needs. In most schools the workshop and workplace remain separate and in-service training has little impact upon day-to-day classroom practice.

For staff development to change classroom practice requires a commitment among teachers to review their performance as a prelude to development. Joyce and Showers (1980b) have identified a number of key training components which, when used in combination, have much greater power than when they are used alone. The major components of effective staff development are as follows:

- Presentation of theory or description of skill or strategy.
- Modelling or demonstration of skills or models of teaching.
- Practice in simulated classroom settings.

- Structured and open feedback (peer observation).
- Coaching for application.

Based on this analysis, mutual observation and professional partnerships are key to improving the quality of teaching and learning. The establishment of critical friendships within the subject area will increase professional learning and decrease feelings of isolation. By linking with one or more colleagues there is the possibility of mutual sharing of good practice. Provided they are skilled and trusted, professional partnerships can:

- Stimulate reflection in, on and about teaching;
- Generate new ideas and ways of working;
- Break down subject barriers and remove feelings of isolation;
- Create a more collaborative culture where mutual support is the norm.

(Hopkins *et al.*, 1997a: 7)

Subject leaders can promote professional partnerships among colleagues by providing the opportunity and time for teachers to work together. They can also encourage a climate within the subject area where classroom-based enquiry is the norm and where teacher reflection upon practice is encouraged. The nature and type of the opportunities provided will depend upon the priorities set by the subject leaders and individual staff development needs.

At any given stage in their lives and careers, teachers will be at a particular phase in their personal and professional development (Bolam, 1986). As such, the meaning of teacher development is located in their personal and professional lives and in the policy and school settings in which they work (Goodson, 1992). The nature of teaching demands that teachers engage in continuing professional development but particular needs and the ways in which they may be met will vary according to circumstance, personal and professional histories and current dispositions (Hargreaves, 1994). Sometimes professional learning may be informal, opportunistic and unplanned. At other times, professional learning occurs as a result of the structured guidance, input and support of the subject leaders.

Whether informal or formal, continuous professional development is central to maintaining and enhancing the quality of teaching (Levine and Trachtman, 1997). Within this endeavour subject leaders have an important part to play. They will be best placed to know the profile and expertise of the teachers within the subject area and will be able to judge their developmental needs and requirements. The challenge facing subject leaders is to assist colleagues in identifying individual needs and requirements through dialogue and personal review. This necessitates building professional trust and recognising the tensions that exist at a micropolitical level (Blase and Anderson, 1995; Busher and Saran, 1995a). Needs may be identified by listening to, or watching, other colleagues in action. Also, through talking with colleagues about classroom-related issues, developmental priorities may become apparent. Subject leaders need to explore as many ways as possible of identifying professional needs and of providing the necessary support for others.

It is clear any new learning will require considerable internalisation and reprocessing if it is to influence practice. As Steadman *et al.* (1995: 49) note:

> Change in the classroom which involves more than extending the repertoire by acquiring new skills will mean changing attitudes, beliefs and personal theories and reconstructing a personal approach to teaching. IN-SET therefore needs to provide new experiences, support the anxieties which accompany not just the threat but the genuine difficulties of change and give people time to reflect, work things out and think things through.

As noted earlier, every teacher has a set of developmental needs that relates to his or her age, experience, expertise and teaching context. A major consideration, therefore, in planning and encouraging staff development will be *how* it will contribute to individual and subject area development. Effective professional development has to be focused upon classroom change and developing new teaching behaviours.

Joyce and Showers (1991) further endorse this view by suggesting that effective training is that which provides for a combination of presentation, modelling, practice, feedback and coaching. In Figure 10.1 the relationship between training method and the degree of impact is outlined. This matrix suggests the problem of transfer of knowledge can be solved by practice, feedback and coaching. Simply hearing a presentation is likely only to raise awareness but have little chance of changing or affecting teaching practice.

The lessons emerging from this for subject leaders are clear:

- Team members must have sufficient opportunity to develop skills they can eventually practise in classroom settings.
- Follow-up work within the subject area, such as coaching and classroom observation, will be necessary if changes in teaching behaviour are to occur.

In short, teacher development is most likely to occur where there are opportunities for team members to work together and to learn from each other. Working with colleagues not only dispels feelings of professional isolation but also assists in enhancing practice. Teachers are more able to implement new ideas within the context of supportive collaborative relationships or partnerships (Hargeaves, 1994).

Training method/ Component \ Level of impact	A. General awareness of new skills	B. Organised knowledge of underlying concepts and theory	C. Learning of new skills	D. Application on the job
1. Presentation description (e.g. lecture) of new skills	●			
2. Modelling the new skills (e.g. live or video demonstrations	●	●		
3. Practise in simulated settings	●	●	●	
4. Feedback on performance in simulated or real settings	●	●	●	●
5. Coaching/ assistance on the job	●	●	●	●

Fig. 10.1 Training matrix
Source: Joyce and Showers (1988).

Collaboration among teachers strengthens resolve, permits vulnerabilities and carries people through the frustrations that accompany change in its early stages. It also eliminates the possibility of duplication and allows greater co-ordination and consistency of teaching approaches (Little, 1993).

By working collaboratively teachers are able to consider the different ways in which the subject matter can be taught (Nias, 1989). Collaboration pools the collected knowledge, expertise and capacities of teachers within the subject area. Collaboration improves the quality of student learning by improving the quality of teaching. It encourages risk-taking, greater diversity in teaching methods and an improved sense of efficacy among teachers. The principle of teacher collaboration is at the core of constructing a positive working community and is consistently listed in the effective schools' literature as correlating positively with student outcomes (Mortimore *et al.*, 1994).

Collaboration in dialogue and action can provide sources of feedback and comparison that prompt teachers to reflect on their own practice (Schon, 1983). Those teachers who recognise that enquiry and reflection are important processes in the classroom find it easier to sustain improvement effort around teaching and learning practices (Hopkins *et al.*, 1997a). The reflective teacher is one who turns attention to the immediate reality of classroom practice. Reflection is centrally concerned with improving practice rather than collecting knowledge (Day, 1993). As each school, subject area and classroom are unique, reflective teachers develop their practice through engaging in enquiry and critical analysis of their teaching and the teaching of others (Calderhead, 1993).

For teacher development and school development alike, committing to certain kinds of collaboration is centrally important (Dalin and Rust, 1996). It is a means to securing greater teacher effectiveness and school effectiveness (Harris, 1999b). However, collaboration without reflection and enquiry is little more than working collegially (Hargreaves, 1995). For collaboration to influence professional growth and development, it has to be premised upon mutual enquiry and sharing (Grundy, 1994). In order for teachers to be reflective about their practice there has to be 'a feedback loop', a means by which they can consider their work in a critical way. One powerful way in which teachers are encouraged to reflect upon and improve their practice is through a process of action research or action enquiry (Elliott, 1991).

Action research

There is a growing literature that demonstrates the importance of evidence-based research as the basis for improving teaching (Louden, 1991; Atkin, 1994; Day, 1999). The analysis and application of research findings by teachers as part of their routine professional activity have been shown to have a positive effect upon the quality of teaching and learning (Hopkins and Harris, 1997; Harris and Hopkins, 1999). Processes of collaborative enquiry and development can be a powerful way of helping teachers and schools to respond to and to cope with often competing mandated requirements. The importance of the development of the skills of enquiry has been recognised by Hopkins (1993), who suggests improvements in teaching and learning are dependent on the qualities and skills of the teacher.

The arguments for teachers adopting the role of researcher have been made most persuasively by Stenhouse (1975; 1979; 1981) and, subsequently, by Rudduck (1985), Whitehead (1986) and Whitehead and Lomax (1997). The argument for research as a basis for teaching rests upon two main principles: first, that teacher research is linked to the strengthening of teacher judgement and consequently to the self-directed improvement of practice; and secondly, that the most important focus for research is the curriculum in that it is the medium through which knowledge is communicated in schools (Rudduck and Hopkins, 1995). As Stenhouse (1981: 16) noted: 'it is not enough that teachers' work should be studied: they need to study it for themselves. What we need is a different view of research which begins with our own work and which is founded in curiosity and a desire to understand; which is stable, not fleeting, systematic in the sense of being sustained by a strategy.' Furthermore, Stenhouse (1979) argued for a change in what counts as research and the need to look for opportunities for teachers to engage in their own research and to communicate this to other practitioners.

Stenhouse (1979) proposed that action research should contribute not only to practice but also to a 'theory of education' and teaching which is accessible to other teachers. In this respect action research is a teacher-based form of curriculum development that is premised upon teacher trust and collegiality. The main aim of action research is to encourage reflection both in and on action. Consequently, it is both a powerful and potentially liberating form of research that can contribute centrally to school and departmental development (Elliott, 1991).

Gathering and using evidence about practices at subject area level have been shown to improve outcomes for teachers and for students (Blandford, 1997). Engaging in action research, however, does not mean subject leaders have to encourage colleagues to engage in high-level research that demands both expertise and time. Instead, they need to encourage team members to invest in their own development as well as the development of the subject area. To be most effective, action research needs to be focused upon the immediate issues within the subject area and to address questions of particular relevance to teachers.

Action research holds considerable potential for the teacher-as-researcher wanting simultaneously to implement and evaluate a curriculum innovation. Furthermore, it draws upon the widest range of data collection methods and encompasses techniques from different methodological positions. Stenhouse (1981: 34) described action research as 'systematic enquiry made public' and elaborated this definition further to outline action research as: 'Systematic and sustained enquiry, planned and self critical, which is subjected to public criticism and to empirical tests where these are appropriate.' While there are many competing views upon the process of action research, for subject leaders and their team members, it constitutes research by individuals upon their own professional practice.

The process of action research

The term 'action research' originated with Kurt Lewin who de-scribed it as a form of research involving experimental interventions in institutions and communities (Lewin, 1948). The Lewinian ap-proach to action research differs from contemporary interpretations in the respect that it is externally initiated to assist a client system normative in orientation and prescriptive in practice (Hopkins, 1994). Yet Lewin's research cycle of planning, data collection, evalua-tion and further planning has become an integral part of many school improvement projects that locate action research centrally (Hopkins *et al.*, 1994).

According to the proponents of action research it 'uses strategic action as a probe for further improvement and understanding' (Brown *et al.*, 1982: 7). Action research is involved with practical issues of the kind that arise naturally as part of professional activity. This practical orientation is one of the reasons why action research remains a popu-lar form of research for teachers and has the potential to contribute to school and departmental improvement.

Since there is the desire to improve one's own practice within action research, it implies there must be a perceived problem or some dissat-isfaction with an aspect of teaching. The stages of an action research enquiry, based upon the identification of a problem, are then as follows:

1) Identify the problem
2) Plan to overcome the problem
3) Put into practice the solution
4) Evaluate the effect of your action
5) Reflect upon your actions.

(McNiff, 1988: 23)

However, Kemmis and McTaggart (1981: 34) note that: 'You do not have to begin with a "problem". All you need is a general idea that something might be improved. Your general idea may stem from a promising new idea or the recognition that existing practice falls short of aspiration.' Their approach to action research asks a different set of questions:

- What is happening now?
- In what sense is this problematic?

● What can I do about it?

This will inevitably involve taking action of some sort and reflecting upon that action in a systematic way. Action research is disciplined enquiry; it is not *ad hoc* or random investigation. Whitehead (1986) suggests action research is based upon systematic procedures that subsequently generate knowledge. He suggests a schema for action research is provided in the following stages:

- I experience problems;
- I imagine solutions;
- I act in the direction of the preferred solution;
- I evaluate the outcome of my action;
- I modify my problems, ideas, action in light of my evaluation.

Action research is a means to an end but not an end in itself – the process is ongoing and self-evaluative. For those teachers involved in action research the purpose of undertaking an enquiry is not to *prove* but to *improve*. In educational research the action research cycle can be used to assist the teacher in improving his or her practice. Kemmis and McTaggart (1981: 27) note that: 'Action research is a systematically evolving, lived process of changing both the researcher and the situations in which he or she acts; neither the natural sciences nor the historical sciences have this double aim.' Good action research projects are highly rigorous and entail a well conceived methodology. Brown *et al.* (1982) suggest the cycles of action research themselves provide a means of internal cross-checking and evaluation. The forms of self-study and self-analysis that occur as part of an action research cycle ensure the collecting and analysing of data are thorough and carefully undertaken.

By its very definition and practical nature, action research is participatory in design as it involves the active participation of the researcher. It involves some type of social or educational intervention and therefore it by its very nature demands involvement from practitioners. The collaborative nature of enquiry promoted by action research involves practitioners in the process of mutual investigation. Elliott (1979) noted the importance of participative enquiry in securing research activity that made a difference to teachers' practice.

Clearly, if the processes of research and action are integrated, then action research must involve the 'practitioner' very closely. However, it is not simply enough for the research to be undertaken as a routine part of the job but to be built in as a form of investigation designed to provide feedback on practice in order to improve practice. In this respect, action research is directly linked to the process of change. It provides a way forward for the professional to reflect upon and improve practice.

Issues connected with the use of action research

When subject leaders are introducing both the concept and process of action research to team members there are a number of issues to consider. The first issue of importance in relation to action research is *ownership*. The participatory nature of action research brings with it the issue of who owns it. With other approaches to research this tends to be more straightforward because the researcher is outside the process. With action research, the researcher is very much 'inside' the process and often in conjunction with others. Consequently, if focused upon a subject-related issue or problem, it is important that, at the outset, expectations of the research process are agreed among team members.

Another important issue in action research is one of *ethics* because the research focuses upon the activity of the teacher. This inevitably raises issues of confidentiality. Those teachers who engage in action research need a strong code of ethics to protect them from possible breaches of confidentiality. The following set of ethical guidelines has been produced to assist action researchers in ensuring confidentiality about their work:

- The development of the work must be transparent and visible.
- Permission must be obtained before making observations or examining documents produced by, or for, others.
- Descriptions of others' work must be negotiated prior to publication.
- Confidentiality must be assured and anonymity where requested.

Another related issue concerns the *validity* of action research enquiry as a research process. As with any other research method, action enquiry requires validation to demonstrate the intrinsic truth of the research undertaken. In addition, it requires validation in order to establish the credibility of the research findings generated. This is particularly important in the case of action research because it is often the means of a person's individual review and enquiry.

To ensure validity requires more than simply designing a detailed methodology or rigorously applying that research methodology. The private encounter between teacher and practice requires that, at some point, the research findings must be made public. Peer validation, therefore, is an important dimension of action enquiry and necessarily involves researchers presenting their claims or findings to others (Whitehead, 1986). The setting up of validation groups is part of the action research process and allows the individual researcher's claim to knowledge to be challenged and questioned. Through this process individual claims are validated and the research process is strengthened.

One way of securing validity within both action research and other forms of research is the use of different types of triangulation. Elliott and Adelman (1976: 17) describe one approach to triangulation as 'Gathering accounts of a teaching situation from three quite different points of view: namely those of teacher, students and a participant observer'. Who in this triangle gathers the accounts, how they are elicited and who compares them depends largely on the context. By comparing the three different accounts and standpoints there is the opportunity to test ideas and to compare perspectives. Such an approach is particularly relevant to subject-level and classroom research.

Action research in practice

The fundamental aim of action research is to improve practice rather than to develop theory. The improvement of practice consists of realising the implicit values that lie within the practice itself. For teachers, values such as empowerment of learners and respect for students' views may be at the centre of their action research activities. Improving practice is about realising such values and necessarily involves a continuing process of reflection on the part of teachers. However, the kind of reflection encouraged by the action research process is quite distinctive from an ends-driven type of reasoning. The reflection is about choosing a course of action or a particular set of circumstances based upon a set of values or principles.

Action research improves practice by developing teachers' capacity to make judgements about their own practice. It constitutes the development of a very practical form of knowledge and allows teachers to consider the complexity and difficulties inherent in their own teaching situation. As a form of insider research it is not without associated problems or difficulties. There are a number of dilemmas teachers will face when undertaking action research. These have been described in depth by Elliot (1991) and are worth summarising here because they outline some of the potential difficulties subject leaders might encounter when encouraging team members to embark on enquiry of this kind.

The first problem concerns the issue of sharing data with other teachers. Problematic areas of practice can be exposed and teachers may be reluctant to share such data with others. While sharing data promotes a reflective conversation, it may create some tension if the

teacher feels it demonstrates weakness and a gap in teaching expertise. To offset such difficulties it is important the subject leader emphasises that critical friendships will be based upon confidentiality and
that the action research process is primarily about development rather
than accountability. For action research to work most effectively there
must be a culture of respect and trust between teachers.

A second problem concerns a tendency among teachers to opt for a
data collection method that distances them from the enquiry. Simons
(1978) observed that teachers prefer to use questionnaires in order to
distance themselves from the potentially disturbing effects interviewing and observation can have on personal relationships within
the school. She suggests teachers will tend to select data collection
methods that separate the role of teacher and researcher. In this way
they remain detached from the enquiry and safe from looking at their
own practice too closely or too critically.

One way of trying to resolve this problem is through subject leaders
modelling forms of action research that incorporate observation by
colleagues and student feedback. By taking the lead and demonstrating the process of action enquiry that is about improving practice, it is
more likely teachers will adopt a similar approach. Within effective
subject areas, the subject leader has been shown to be the 'lead professional' with a responsibility for demonstrating good practice and for
leading by example (Harris *et al.*, 1995).

A third problem concerns teachers' reluctance to seek student feedback on teaching and classroom practice. Eliciting student views will
inevitably result in some challenge or critique and, hence, there is a
reticence to seek such views. James and Ebbutt (1980: 7) illustrate this
point by describing how a teacher had sought feedback from students
which was subsequently relayed to her colleagues: 'On another occa-
sion her practice of interviewing students to obtain feedback on her
own lessons in one area of the curriculum had apparently encouraged
students to volunteer criticism to other teachers who were unprepared
for such a response, whether negative or otherwise.'

The dilemma here for the 'teacher-as-researcher' arises from a
conflict between the critical openness of students and their right to
share this criticality more widely. There are a number of ways in
which the subject leader can protect teachers from being caught up
in such a conflict. The first way is to encourage colleagues to share
their research agendas so that teachers can contextualise any negative or critical comments made by students about other teachers. The
second way is to encourage teachers to explain the process of enquiry to students and offer them ownership and responsibility in the
process. Research has shown that, when students are involved in the

process of enquiry and have some ownership in the process, they are more likely to respond in a mature and sensitive way (Rudduck *et al*, 1997).

The activities associated with action research are largely dictated by the stages in the action research cycle. Taking Elliott's (1991) guide to action research, the stages are as follows:

- Identifying and clarifying the general idea.
- Data gathering.
- Developing next action steps.
- Implementing action.
- Evaluation.

These steps are similar to those contained in the action research planner by Kemmis and McTaggart (1981). They represent the fundamental stages in the action enquiry process and offer a practical guide for teachers embarking upon action enquiry.

Through the process of action enquiry it is possible for subject leaders to orchestrate departmental improvement. To be successful, subject leaders need to introduce the process as a response to a shared problem. By embarking on a process of enquiry, teachers within the subject area will have a common focus for discussion and the opportunity to work together. Both these components are centrally important in school and subject area improvement.

The following case study is provided to illustrate each of these steps.

Action research: case study

As a head of a large science department in an inner-city comprehensive school, Robert Smith, was faced with the task of improving the department's GCSE grades. Over the past few years the average scores had fallen from 35% A–C to 27% A–C. This marked decline was a cause for concern at the senior management level and pressure had been placed upon the head of department to improve the performance of the subject area. To address the problem it was agreed within the department to engage in some action research, first, to locate the source of the problem and, secondly to decide upon strategies for improvement.

Identifying and clarifying the general idea

The department met to discuss the issue of performance across the department and to clarify the research question. From the discussion it was proposed that a lack of consistency in teaching across the department could be the cause of the problem. As a large department where teaching took place in different parts of the school with little time for teachers to meet and talk, it was felt that communication within the department, particularly about teaching, had deteriorated. Consequently, the issue of consistency in teaching was agreed as the main focus of the enquiry.

Data gathering

The department agreed to conduct some data gathering on this issue in the form of interviews with students and classroom observation. Groups of Year 9 and 10 students were interviewed about the teaching of various science topics. This was undertaken in order to ascertain whether they experienced a common approach by different teachers. In addition, peer observation was set up with the prime purpose of teachers watching colleagues teach the same topic area. From the data analysis it was clear individual practices differed quite considerably and that topics were being taught in quite different ways. The net result of this lack of consistency meant students' understanding of topics varied considerably.

Constructing a general plan

Using this feedback the teachers met as a department to agree upon some strategies to improve the situation. These strategies included revising schemes of work, agreeing the most effective way to teach a topic and continuing with peer observation to check a higher degree of consistency was in operation.

Implementing action

The next stage in the enquiry process was to implement the action steps identified. This involved adopting the revised schemes of work and teaching topics in the way agreed within the department.

Evaluation

Through follow-up interviews with the students and the peer observation feedback, there was sufficient evidence that greater consistency was occurring across the department. The data also highlighted differences in the homework set by different teachers and the way in which this led to differences in student understanding of the topic.

Consequently, the issue of homework became the next focus of enquiry for the department.

Commentary

Having established a process of enquiry within the department, the head of department was able to sustain a culture of continuous improvement. The outcomes from this development were an increase in staff morale, a shared focus upon teaching and learning, greater consistency in teaching and improved GCSE results (40% A–C).

Part IV

Efficient and Effective Deployment of Staff and Resources

11

Planning Development and Resource Utilisation to Improve Students' Learning

This chapter discusses how development planning can be carried out effectively and linked to appropriate resource allocations. This chapter only considers the allocation of physical and financial resources as the allocation of staffing is considered elsewhere. It raises questions about how issues of equity and priority can be addressed when trying to meet the needs of different students.

Introduction

There is considerable debate about how far subject leaders should be involved in strategic planning for a whole school or just in strategic planning for their own subject area which will then have to be incorporated into a whole-school plan. Fidler (1997) suggests that senior staff in a school can either create a 'grand design' and ask subject areas to create development plans to fit in with this, or can ask subject areas to create their own strategic plans and then meld these into a whole-school plan. Brown *et al.* (1999) found that in schools where subject leaders were deliberately involved in strategic planning by head-teachers, subject area plans correlated closely with a school's plan. However, of equal importance for the development of an integrated approach to development planning throughout a school, was the belief by subject leaders and staff that the headteacher and senior staff were genuinely concerned to promote a collegial culture in the school.

An alternative approach which expects subject leaders to be engaged only in development planning for their subject areas within the framework of a strategic plan for the school prepared by senior staff assumes a strongly hierarchic view of organisations. In this, middle-ranking staff are delegated discrete areas only to manage operationally or developmentally. This view under-rates the interactivity of staff of all levels in schools, especially in smaller schools, and conflicts with notions of collegial cultures, the implementation of which effective learning organisations seem to sustain (Wallace *et al.*, 1997).

Strategic planning is, as Fidler (1997) admits, a rather vague concept which, none the less, focuses on the overall co-ordination of the processes of a school in the contexts of its current and future socio-political environment. It is future orientated in a way in which development planning is said not to be. Strategy might include considering the whole scope of a school's activities, including the contribution of subject areas to these. Strategy might include considering a school's long-term direction in terms of parent involvement, for example, or the changing demography of its natural catchment area. For example, since the mid-1990s in England and Wales some state schools have had the opportunity to consider whether to become Technology Colleges and focus their curriculum to some extent on particular subject specialisms.

All schools and subject areas need to plan for development in a coherent and rational way, even though future changes in the environment even during the lifetime of one plan may invalidate key aspects of it. These changes might be externally driven – a new government directive, a change in the social profile of the student intake – or internally driven by changes in staffing or equipment or accommodation availability. At least a plan provides a carefully structured approach to development which, if carefully monitored, can be modified through a process of annual or biennial review to meet changes in a school or subject area's environment.

Development plans are constructed to carry forward the vision of the school or subject area, maintaining good practice and improving other practice. They are constructed in the light of the changing environment school or subject leaders have surveyed and analysed. To make these plans achievable, leaders, possibly with their colleagues, then need to identify targets to be fulfilled within certain time frames to move towards the desired improvements, and tasks which staff need to undertake to make the targets achievable.

Hopkins and MacGilchrist (1998) suggest such plans need to be drawn up in one of three different ways, depending on how well a school or subject area is performing at the time when it audits its activities. Type One focuses on strategies to assist low-performing schools in England and Wales to become adequately effective in terms of the OFSTED criteria (OFSTED, 1999). It requires staff to use external help to support their development. These are the struggling or sinking schools to which Stoll and Fink (1998) refer. Type Two strategies help a school or subject area to progress from adequacy by refining its development priorities, focusing on specific teaching and learning issues and improving its management arrangements to support these.

These are the cruising schools to which Stoll and Fink (1998) refer. Teachers using both these strategies are likely to benefit considerably from help from external sources. Type Three strategies help schools or subject areas that are already very effective according to recognised performance criteria to sustain this level of performance.

Development planning cycles were first recommended to schools in England and Wales in 1989 (Hargreaves *et al.*, 1989) as a means of improving the way in which schools could respond effectively to the changing needs of their students and to develop their working practices. Subject area development plans have to take place within the framework of agreed school plans and subject area aims, since these guide the purposes the development plans are intended to implement. Such plans consider a range of different aspects of school or subject area work:

- The curriculum (syllabus, teaching, and learning process and performance).
- Human relations processes and values.
- Staff development.
- Decision-making and resource allocation.
- Links with external contexts.

These aspects form a collection of linked programmes of development for a school or subject area. Each aspect might require its own plan for action within the framework of a subject area's overall development plan. After creating a development plan, the next step is for a subject leader and colleagues to decide which aspects of the plan are given what priority for implementation, and to create a timetable to allow that implementation. This involves them considering what actions are to be taken and what targets achieved. Figure 11.1 shows a stylised planning cycle (Hargreaves *et al.*, 1989).

A more recent description of a school planning cycle (DfEE, 1997: 8) highlights the importance of schools and subject areas reviewing the progress of their performance. Future developments have to take account of the evaluations of previous development plans if rational planning processes are to be sustained. The DfEE (1997) planning cycle also emphasises the importance of using benchmarks during the audit phase (see Figure 11.2) to check one school or subject area's performance against those of other similar entities. However, as Hopkins and MacGilchrist (1998) point out, such data needs to be treated with caution. Even small differences in the intakes of student groups in different schools – such as students' social background, or dates of birth within a year group, or gender or ethnic balance – and of other 'input indicators' (OFSTED, 1995b), can have a noticeable

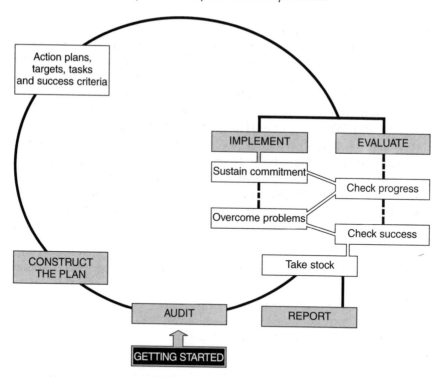

Fig. 11.1 A stylised planning cycle
Source: Hargreaves *et al.* (1989: 14).

influence on schools' cultures and on the practices that are possible
within them, even if schools are deemed to be 'similar' by some criteria.

Auditing: setting the baseline from which to develop

Planning processes initially involve senior staff and subject leaders
auditing the current situation of a school or subject area and evaluating how well they are performing in it. In a marketing framework this
involves staff carrying out a SWOT analysis, looking at current internal strengths and weaknesses and the external opportunities for and
threats to improvement and development (Murgatroyd and Morgan,
1992; West-Burnham, 1992).

The reason for beginning a planning cycle with an audit is to ensure
the plans for development are based on a reasonably accurate assessment of the current situation of a school or subject area. Trying to
construct other routes to development might lead to important aspects
of a subject area's work being overlooked, although Fidler (1997) suggests approaches of 'creative muddle' can be successful with well
established teams.

Context 1   Basic information about the school. 'Input indicators': student teacher ratio; contact ratio; annual budget/recurrent funding; expenditure per student per group; unit costs per student per group. 'Background indicators': staff profiles (qualifications, jobs); student profiles (include gender, ethnicity, ESL, school meals, social class).

Context 2   Relationships of subject area to school; fit of departmental development plan to whole school; application of school codes of conduct within subject area; relationships with school governors; involvement of staff with whole school; meet national regulations (e.g. health and safety).

Task   Curriculum/syllabus; teaching; student learning/work; assessment/recording; teaching differentiation; achievement on SATs/GCSE/internal tests; provision for SEN; extracurricular activities.

Operations   Resource allocation to students and topics; unit costs/expenditure per class/topic – compared with key values; use of accommodation; decision-making/minutes of meetings; style of meetings – involvement of staff.

People   Relationships with staff/students/parents; staff development and appraisal schemes; job descriptions and actual functions; student grouping/equal opportunities; social acivities.

Culture   Symbols and values: work displays; codes of conduct – work, behaviour, dress; administrative board displays.

Fig. 11.2   Audit – what is going on

Figure 11.2 summarises what aspects of a subject area might be audited. This draws heavily on guidance from OFSTED (1995b; 1999). OFSTED (1999) argue that until an institutional framework is known, it is not possible to judge the quality of a school or subject area's performance. For this reason it is very important for subject leaders and their colleagues to undertake the audit of both Contexts 1 and 2 in Figure 11.2 as well as auditing the other aspects of their work.

If subject leaders undertake this audit with the help of their colleagues it is likely to sustain or develop a collegial culture so staff will work enthusiastically to achieve the plan that will eventually evolve from it. Hopkins (1987) suggests subject leaders can involve their colleagues in:

● carrying out sections of the audit (for example, for different year groups);
● giving information to other colleagues about aspects of it;
● analysing the data for aspects of it; and
● co-ordinating the process of aspects of it.

It is likely the subject leader will be the overall co-ordinator of the process for a subject area.

Involving staff has several purposes. First, it helps staff to feel they have a part to play in monitoring and evaluating their own work practices. It lessens the chance of them perceiving the auditing and planning process as a control strategy belonging to the subject leader. Secondly, it emphasises that current practice in a subject area is the responsibility of the staff in that area and therefore changing practice where needed is also their responsibility. This argument can be extended to include students as well. Thirdly it helps to promote staff development (Busher, 1988) by engaging staff in a variety of activities beyond the core one of teaching. In so doing it helps to make all staff in a subject area aware of their interdependency in creating an effective subject area. This helps to sustain and develop collegial approaches to working, helping to create an effective subject area.

Planning for development

Effective planning is based on five interlocking processes:

1) Working with staff.
2) Establishing baselines: measuring current performance.
3) Having a clear vision of where to go.
4) Creating sensible maps, timetables and ladders to achieve the preferred goals.
5) Creating a means of monitoring progress on the road to achieving the goals (target-setting).

The planning process has to build on the current quality of a subject area's performance. Crudely, this can be measured in terms of students' performance outcomes on a variety of internal and national tests. However, such raw score data, often expressed in terms of the numbers of passes of a particular test obtained by students, may not accurately reflect the quality of teaching and learning. Gray and Wilcox (1994) point out that value-added data can give a more accurate view. These data compare the level of student performance when they entered a school with subsequent levels of performance. For example, students making large improvements in performance from a low baseline (measured against, say, the expected levels of performance of students of a particular age on Standard Assessment Tests (SATs) in England and Wales) may be discounted by external observers if those students still attain only relatively poor performances compared with students in other local schools. While relatively low raw-score student examination results might suggest a relatively ineffective school, the large improvement shown by value-added measures is likely to indicate the reverse. However, value-added or student gain scores are difficult to calculate accurately, especially over short periods of time.

Other aspects of a subject area's work that are not easily amenable to quantification, such as the quality of relationships between staff or between staff and students, also need to be evaluated as part of this baseline measure of performance.

All these aspects of current performance need to be evaluated against the vision for a subject area held by a subject leader and his or her colleagues and by the senior staff of a school. The appropriateness of this vision also has to be burnished in the light of current external demands and pressures on a school and subject area, before it can form the spirit and direction for the development plan which is to guide improvement of practice.

To create sensible maps and timetables for implementing a development plan, having established the current situation of a subject area and its preferred vision, subject leaders need to incorporate the following elements into their subject area plans:

- Goals/objectives/targets (e.g. what they want to achieve).
- Steps to be taken (e.g. how they plan to fulfil their goal).
- Milestone timings for objectives and goals.
- Individual staff tasks and responsibilities in achieving goals.
- Resources/support needed.
- Areas of further information needed to support/implement development.
- A monitoring process to gauge progress and to recognise completion.

Targets are a powerful means of identifying what needs to be implemented to bring about change. *Setting Targets to Raise Standards* (DfEE, 1996) discusses in some detail how quantifiable targets can be set. For example, a subject area might set out to raise the proportion of students achieving a particular level on the Key Stage SATs, or the proportion of students achieving five or more A–C passes at GCSE. Each target is then broken down into a series of tasks on which staff can work. Subject leaders and their colleagues can then decide who is going to undertake which tasks in order to achieve the targets the area has set itself. In some cases such targets may have been set for a subject area by the senior staff of a school either in response to an inspection report or as part of the school's development plan.

The targets themselves should be as follows:

- *Specific* – detailed and focused rather than general and vague.

- *Measurable* – but qualitative targets need to have agreed measures of success.
- *Achievable* – realistically achievable (if necessary, split into smaller steps).
- *Relevant* – to the subject area and member of staff.
- *Time bound* – with milestones to measure ongoing improvement.

There is some debate as to whether targets should only be statistical and quantifiable. There are many aspects of a subject area's work that are not easily measurable by quantitative outcomes. For example, improving the quality of student display work may be an important target for raising the enthusiasm of students for work in a subject area. Other qualitative targets might include the following:

- Quality of student thinking.
- Teachers' presentational skills.
- Interpersonal relationships between staff in a subject area (or between staff and students).

Such targets may need to look for non-quantifiable outcomes, perhaps based on the connoisseurship of expert witnesses, or the expressed and compared views of participants in situations. The analysis of such data can indicate strong trends that are at least as valid as simple descriptive statistics on which no tests of inference have been made.

To discover the worth of a development plan, subject leaders need to monitor its progress and outcomes. This should be built in when the targets are being devised. It will need to take account of what might be considered a satisfactory performance on each target and the likely views of the school inspectors during the next full inspection on that. Guidance on this is easily available from the OFSTED (1999) inspection handbooks. In these not only does OFSTED set out on what aspects of subject areas schools' inspectors will require information, but it also indicates what quality of performance in every area of a school the school inspectors are likely to judge to be satisfactory. Performance below this level risks schools in England and Wales being perceived as having areas of serious weakness or worse.

In England and Wales after a school has been inspected, subject leaders and their colleagues need to incorporate into their subject area development plans relevant aspects of the school's action plan. This has to be put forward in response to inspectors' criticisms.

Managing resources ethically and effectively to promote development

Development planning is not a value-neutral activity since it prioritises some activities over others. This can raise some serious ethical dilemmas. For example, raising the performance of students in a secondary school to increase the number of A–C grades at GCSE which students in that school gain may be possible only by investing a disproportionate amount of resources in a small group of students. These are likely to be those in Years 10 and 11 and predicted to gain Grade D. The opportunity cost of such investment is to lessen the quality of learning opportunities for other students both in those year groups, who are non-D Grade, and throughout the school by taking away or not giving resources to these other students. High-cost courses or small groups of students which incur high costs, possibly because of high staff:student ratios, can cause subject areas major problems if they are trying to pursue a policy of equitable budgeting for all their students.

Managing the resources of a subject area faces subject leaders with a series of difficult value choices. Although only a means to an end, resource allocation involves subject leaders and their colleagues in prioritising the competing claims of different groups of students for support (Simkins, 1997). It engages subject leaders and their colleagues in what Thomas and Martin (1996) call a 'dialogue of accountability' between themselves and senior staff to meet the needs of the students they have identified. It is an aspect of subject area management that is now carefully scrutinised through school inspection (OFSTED, 1995b; 1999) in England and Wales.

These value conflicts can be outlined as follows:

- Balancing efficiency and effectiveness.
- Balancing professional and managerial approaches to resource allocation.
- Balancing performance maintenance and performance development.
- Considering equitable resource allocation.
- Balancing resource creation, student benefits and staff time.

Effective schools and subject areas achieve their purposes using whatever resources are needed. The risk is it may not be possible to afford the resources needed. OFSTED (1995a: 121) defines the efficient school as that which 'makes good use of all its available resources to achieve the best possible educational outcomes for all its students – and in doing so provides excellent value for money'. The same definition might be applied to a subject area. When finance is tight, the temptation is to emphasise efficiency over effectiveness. Yet it is the latter which leads to a subject area fulfilling its purposes.

This conflict faces subject leaders with invidious choices about opportunity costs. This is a notion in which the consequences of investing in one type of resource are weighed not only against its financial costs but against the other opportunities or purchases forgone by investing in such a way. It can make apparently sensible decisions seem much less reasonable. For example, a heavy investment in new books or videos may give some students some attractive new resources. Undoubtedly many parents of those students will be pleased to see this. Yet it may mean the majority of students and most of the teachers in that subject area have access to many fewer duplicated resources and the flexibility to learning these can bring.

Maintaining or developing resources for student learning

Another area of tension for subject leaders is between what Simkins (1997) calls the professional and the managerial approaches to using resources. Whereas the first is likely to focus on how resources can best be deployed to support the learning needs of students, the latter concerns itself particularly with the efficient use of resources. To some extent subject leaders can address this tension by emphasising on what they prefer to spend money (e.g. particular curriculum objectives), and then considering the mix of resources they wish to use to achieve this (books, staff, time, space/rooms, equipment, consumables such as paper and chemicals). The alternative approach tends to focus on the artefacts on which subject leaders prefer to spend money than on the policies they wish to implement. These artefacts might be:

- new books
- replacement books
- materials (general)
- equipment
- stationery
- photocopying
- computer hardware
- computer software
- other consumables.

Subject leaders and their colleagues also have to maintain a balance between maintaining performance and extending or developing performance (Hopkins *et al.*, 1996). Resources are not usually sufficient to attain both at the same time for every group of students taught by staff in a subject area. To routinise and make easier subject area decision-making, many subject leaders may be tempted to place an emphasis upon maintaining the status quo, maintaining standards and maintaining performance. However, to improve work in subject areas, investment needs to be made in the development of new work as well.

The problem is compounded for subject staff because, within the area of maintenance there are two different thrusts. One is for the replacement of materials – buying additional copies of those books and consumables that have worn out or been lost or used. This alone can generate a considerable drain on resources. A second thrust is renewal – buying different books and materials to sustain existing processes in the curriculum. While this can lead to a broadening of the resource base of a subject area, perhaps permitting the incremental or organic development of new pedagogic practices, it can eventually lead to there being insufficient quantities of some resources to be of use with any student group.

To balance adequately the demands for new resources against replacement or renewal, subject leaders need to be scrupulous in keeping records of equipment, books and consumables. As well as indicating the total level of stock of resources, this needs to indicate the level of wear and tear on them, helping a subject leader to identify what proportion of stock is likely to need replacing each year. While this record-keeping has to be reviewed regularly by the subject leader, it is important that members of the subject team feel they, too, own the problem of adequate and equitable resource allocation between the different student groups. Parts of the record-keeping process can be delegated by a subject leader to various members of the team, so long as the records are reviewed regularly, perhaps at a team meeting.

Equitable resource allocation

Some groups of students in subject areas need to be resource rich in order to work effectively. In secondary schools in England and Wales students in Years 12 and 13 have notoriously soaked up more resources than they are entitled to for their size of teaching group. In any school, small groups of students absorbing a lot of teacher time and using expensive resources are not likely to be cost-effective, but may be necessary to ensure adequate student progress. Special education groups are an example of this.

To address this problem of equitable allocation of resources subject leaders and their colleagues have to engage in what Thomas and Martin (1996) call 'long-term thinking'. In this way staff have to think strategically within subject areas about how they balance long-term development and disproportionate investment in one group of students in one year, against a similar process for other groups of students in subsequent years. Such targeted 'over-investment' in one year has to be balanced by relative 'under-investment' in other teaching groups in the same financial year. But such development needs also have to be set against and combined with maintenance expenditure.

As resources such as materials, equipment, time, money and staff are in finite supply, they need to be distributed optimally to meet the values of the subject area and its preferred styles of pedagogy. This faces subject leaders with the dilemma of constructing an optimal resource mix for each group of students within an overall equitable allocation of resources among all their students. For example, subject leaders need to decide which teachers to allocate to which groups of students in a secondary school to meet student learning needs and staff preferences. They have to decide when particular groups of students can be taught certain aspects of their subject, especially if their subject area uses expensive equipment or facilities which have to be shared by the whole school, like PE, music or technology facilities. They may have to develop a complex matrix to show how limited resources of materials, staff and equipment are shared out and balanced out amongst student groups. How, for example, might they balance out increased reprographic and stationery costs against decreases in book costs without worsening the resourcing of the curriculum?

Creating resources efficiently

Two major questions for subject leaders wanting to create new teaching and learning resources are the benefits that students will gain from them and the costs of staff time and energy in producing them. Resources available to subject areas can be crudely characterised as those within the control of the teaching team and those they can access through negotiations with other colleagues in other subject areas. For example, borrowing equipment from another subject area may save a subject leader considerable expenditure, but the equipment may only be available at certain times during the week. The lending subject area may expect repayment in kind as well. Subject leaders may also have access to resources other than their own (e.g. special needs support staff, information communication technology (ICT), reprographic facilities and a library) in the school or in the local community. The skilled use of these extra resources can significantly enhance the quality of learning provision across a subject area.

Where particular resources are not available, and senior staff in a school do not think it justifiable to provide them, subject leaders might explore proactive ways in which they can acquire these additional resources (Mountfield, 1993; Marsden, 1997). By this Louis and Miles (1990) are not only thinking of physical resources but also how staff time might be used creatively to set up task groups, collect materials or carry out staff development. However, all such activities, including the creation and duplication of high-quality worksheets, have considerable cost implications for staff. It can take time away from their work with students, facing subject leaders with other difficult decisions.

Managing the budget

The role of the subject leader as financial controller and gatekeeper is crucially important in ensuring high-quality teaching and learning within the subject area. The way in which the budget is monitored and managed will have a major impact upon the resource flow to and through the subject area. If this is well managed then the resources required to fulfil the job effectively will be available. If poorly managed then the subject area will soon find itself in a difficult position and, over time, may lose valuable resources as a result of financial mismanagement.

Subject leaders have to represent the resource demands of their subject areas to their school's senior staff and governors at the school's annual budget negotiations (Hamblin, 1990). They also have to help their colleagues work within the budget frameworks set by senior staff. This is a good example of the Janus-faced nature of a subject leader's role that Glover *et al.* (1998) refer to as 'bridging and brokering'. In order to exert most leverage in the budget negotiations, subject leaders need to have a clear understanding of budget negotiation and construction processes (Levacic, 1995), be well prepared with their own case for requesting resources and have a clear understanding of the micropolitical process of negotiation (Busher, 1992).

In England and Wales since 1988, financial allocations to state schools are largely based on the age-weighted student formula (AWPU). This is the amount of money each student of a different age brings into the school's budget which is allocated by its local authority. In many schools senior staff vary this allocation from subject area to subject area depending on the cost of equipment and consumer perishables different areas need. It often results in science subject areas having higher weightings in school budgets than, for example, the teaching of literacy. Using the AWPU, subject leaders can work out the income generated by a particular group of students when considering what costs might be reasonably spent on it. This gives them a mechanical formula for distributing resources to student groups, but does not resolve questions about what might constitute an equitable distribution of resources across all student groups.

Within subject areas, as in schools, there are many ways to manage a budget. Knight (1993: 96) suggests there are four, offering insights into how subject leaders might allocate money to student groups:

- Incrementalism – last year's allocation plus a little extra (for inflation, perhaps) for each group of students;
- Benevolent despotism – decided on the whim of the leader, perhaps after discussion with colleagues;
- Open market – where subject leaders or teachers within a subject area bid for what they want;
- Formula allocation – finance allocated on the basis of the costs of operations.

Whilst the first of these systems has the disadvantage of tending to preserve the status quo, it does avoid the worst risks of annual micropolitical battles between teachers representing different student group interests. The third of these systems, on the other hand, invites such conflict. It is based on what is sometimes called 'zero-sum' budgeting. This means every allocation of money to student groups or projects has to be explained in every aspect of its expenditure before money is granted by a budget holder. Although possibly creating a fair negotiating arena, it creates a very cumbersome negotiating process, and therefore is probably practically unworkable.

An alternative approach which seeks to place agreed values at the centre of the budget is called programme budgeting (Blandford, 1997). This involves creating a budget directly related to the priorities in the subject area development plan. To implement this, subject leaders need to agree with their colleagues how such priorities are related to each student group and how the needs of each student group are met equitably, at least through time, say over a three-year span. The cost of funding each priority is built up from the costs of each type of resource required – e.g. equipment and supplies, teaching support staff (Fidler *et al.*, 1991). This is a way of ensuring the appropriate resource mix is available to support the subject area development plan within the budget allocated to it by senior staff in a school.

12

Working with Support and Supply Staff to Improve School Performance

This chapter considers the range of support staff with whom subject leaders have to work in schools, indicating in passing what the findings of various research projects suggest as more effective strategies for managing support staff to promote school improvement and more exciting learning opportunities for students. The author would like to thank Loughborough University, of which he was a member at the time of the studies referred to here, for the research grant that supported an excellent research assistant, Lesley Boyd, and provided much of the material which forms the basis of this chapter.

Introduction

Support staff are essential to the effective running of a school. Without them the gates would not be opened, the heating would not work, and school accounts and students' records would be completed only with considerable stress on teaching staff. In some subject areas such as science in secondary schools, practical science lessons would virtually cease altogether. In primary schools, OFSTED (1995a: 12) found that 'extensive use of classroom assistants in primary schools was beneficial,' particularly to children in Early Years education, to children with special educational needs and to students using English as a second language, a view sustained by Moyles with Suschitsky (1997). For subject leaders these staff are not only a vital resource to support teachers in improving the learning opportunities of students, they are also cost-effective. A study commissioned by the STRB (School Teachers' Review Body) from the London University Institute of Education confirmed this (STRB, 1996: vii).

Staff in this category of support staff are the secretaries and caretakers, technicians and cleaners, classroom assistants, midday supervisors and caterers. It is not at all clear that such staff form a homogeneous group in a school, performing many different functions, some of which are proximate in their activity to teaching and learning and others of which are remote from it. On the other hand, HMI (DES, 1992) perceived support staff as a homogeneous group, using the term 'non-teaching staff' for it. Riches (1984: 31) defined non-teaching staff in schools as including 'all those who in some sense support the educational purposes of schools'.

Nor is it clear what is an appropriate umbrella term for these staff. The term 'support staff' is used widely (Riches, 1981; Lyons and Stenning, 1986; Bullock and Thomas, 1994; OFSTED, 1995a). However, Mortimore *et al.* (1994) preferred a term of their own coinage 'associate staff', which has since been partially adopted by the STRB (STRB, 1996). This chapter focuses on what such staff do: supporting the teaching and learning processes of a school, and how subject leaders can work with them. So the term 'support staff' is preferred.

Since the introduction of local management of schools in England and Wales in 1988, there has been a considerable increase in the number of support staff in schools (STRB, 1996). Farrell *et al.* (1999) note the increase in the numbers of classroom assistants is expected to continue, partly to support the numbers of students with special learning needs who are being increasingly included in mainstream schooling in England and Wales. How this group of staff view their work as part of a school community (Sergiovanni, 1994a) and, in turn, are viewed by teaching staff or parents, raises questions for senior staff and subject leaders about how to manage them effectively. One of the key questions is the extent to which such staff can be incorporated into subject area or pastoral area teams and decision-making. Another is the range of skills and knowledge such staff have or can be trained to have to support the work of teachers and students more effectively.

Support staff and their conditions of service

Some categories of support staff can be more easily integrated into the work of subject areas than others. This is partly because some support staff are more to the periphery of a school's mission than others (Torrington and Weightman, 1989). A school's core mission is defined here primarily in terms of academic teaching and learning (Millett, 1996). Under this definition, premises officers and clerical staff could be said to be further towards the periphery of a school's purpose and might require different strategies of management by subject leaders than classroom assistants and laboratory technicians. The latter could be said to work closer to the core sites (the classrooms) of a school's activities. The STRB lend credence to this distinction by talking about 'classroom assistants and other associate staff' (STRB, 1996: para. 25).

None the less, premises officers and clerical staff play a vital part in the maintenance of the operations of a school and its subject areas.

The terms of employment of many of these categories of support staff can make their integration into subject area teams difficult. They also pose problems for subject leaders trying to schedule patterns of work that include some members of the support staff. In a study by Busher and Saran (1995c), the majority of support staff were on part-time contracts of which some were for full-time work but during term time only (FTTO contracts). Torrington and Weightman (1989) defined full time as working for at least 35 hours a week, but some staff in this study regarded themselves as full-time workers although they worked for fewer hours. There are also important differences contractually between those staff who are part of a school's establishment, such as many of the learning support assistants and secretaries, and those who are bought in on a service provision basis – education welfare officers, school meals services and cleaners (Riches, 1988). For example, in England and Wales schools are supposed to organise internal staff development activities only for staff who are employed full time at the school.

Table 12.1 attempts to indicate all the different types of employment relationships between a school and its support staff to create a framework to guide thinking about the management of support staff in schools.

Many of the support staff of a school are women, but their managers are often men. For subject leaders and their colleagues this raises some problematic issues about the impact of gender and staff commitments outside work on work-based relationships. Riches (1981) considered gender a major issue in the management of support staff. In a study by Busher and Saran (1995b), the support staff in their eight schools were mainly women, with a few men in manual, technical or administrative roles. All the women had chosen their jobs initially because they fitted in with family commitments and, in some cases, gave them the opportunity to pursue skills and interests they had developed earlier in their lives. Of the men, all but one had come into their jobs because of redundancy in their former work.

Despite the excitement and enthusiasm with which many support staff claimed to work, Busher and Saran (1995b) found that most support staff in their study were poorly paid for the work they had to do. For example, apart from the director of finance in a grant maintained school (who earned over £26,000 a year, commensurate with a professional wage), the salaries of the more senior support staff ranged from £12,000 to £16,000 per year, less than the annual average wage in England and Wales. The other support staff would have

Table 12.1 Categories of support staff by proximity to school central process

	Learning support	Technical support	Clerical/administration	Premises and site	Welfare/catering
Location/type of work base	Classroom based	Preparation room based: classroom proximate	School offices (central): classroom distant	Peripheral office: classroom environment	Access to office space: classroom environment
Likely type of employment:			Senior secretary; bursar; registrar	Site premises supervisor	
Full time, term only (FTTO)	Nursery nurse; special needs assistant;	Technician; laboratory; ICT; workshop librarian	Clerical assistant	Caretaker	
Part time	Classroom assistant; language support; special needs	Library assistant	Receptionist; reprographics assistant	Site maintenance	Senior cook; school nurse; midday supervisors
Voluntary helper	Classroom ancillary				
Contract				Cleaners, grounds staff	Caterers
Site visitors: LEA based	E.g., education care officer				Education welfare officer
	Education psychologist		Attached part-time bursar		
Other	E.g. OFSTED inspector			Contractor (e.g. plumber)	

Source: Adapted from Busher and Saran (1995b: 173).

earned between £8,000 and £11,000 a year if fully employed, but many were not. Worst paid of all were the midday supervisors. They claimed to earn about £5 an hour and worked between 6 and 8 hours a week. Yet in one school ten of them supervised over 1,000 pupils during lunchtime with little visible support from teachers and no training for their work.

The impact of support staff on subject areas

For subject leaders and teachers support staff conditions of service raise problems when time is needed to discuss student progress, perhaps with a learning support assistant (LSA), or to prepare additional materials for a science lesson. It also means support staff are likely to have very tight time schedules for completing their tasks. So, for example, at the end of a school day cleaners are likely to want to gain immediate access to classrooms, whether or not teachers need to complete some work. Another example of this is that subject leaders need to ensure that requests from colleagues for duplicating materials are handed in to the reprographics assistant, if a school has such a post, some time before the lessons for which the materials are being prepared, as that member of support staff is likely to work for a limited number of hours only each week.

Support staff come with a wide variety of skills and knowledge. Effective subject leaders recognise the contribution such staff can make and the delegated responsibilities they might be able to take. Some support staff are well qualified for their jobs. Busher and Saran (1995b) found many clerical staff had relevant RSA (Royal Society of Arts) qualifications. One of the classroom assistants in their study was a qualified teacher, although she had not practised for many years, and another had run a hairdressing business. Many of the premises officers had engineering backgrounds, one being a trained fitter. In a different study by Busher and Blease (2000), most laboratory technicians were well qualified for their posts, having at least A-level qualifications or the equivalent, but underpaid for what they might have earned in industry with their qualifications. It raises questions of what further training subject leaders can provide for staff and how that can be arranged.

The availability and quality of support staff in schools makes a considerable difference to the quality of learning and teaching that takes place. The availability of some support staff such as laboratory technicians is almost essential if some types of lessons are to be taught (Busher and Blease, 2000). Moyles with Suschitsky (1997) noted that the availability of classroom assistants to teachers in Key Stage 1 classrooms in England and Wales makes a considerable difference to the work pupils are able to carry out effectively.

Working with support staff

Support staff can be grouped into four categories: classroom based, classroom proximate, classroom distant and classroom environment, as Table 12.1 suggests. Subject leaders need to work with each of these groups in different ways. Many members of the support staff work directly in classrooms supporting the curriculum (learning support assistants (LSAs), special needs assistants) or in close proximity to them (technicians of all sorts). The latter category may at times also fulfil the functions of LSAs. Other categories of support staff who might be considered proximate to the learning process without having much contact with students are, where schools have them, librarians and library assistants.

Other categories of support staff provide important administrative support to subject areas, for example in monitoring the attendance of students or maintaining a clean environment. With these staff, subject leaders teachers may have only irregular contact for matters of work. On the other hand in primary schools, teachers and midday supervisors are likely to have regular daily contact and will need to develop joint approaches and ways of working for supervising students. Failure to do so is likely to disrupt the beginnings or ends of lessons either side of lunchtime (Busby, 1991).

It is for subject leaders to decide with their colleagues the most effective ways of working with support staff to support the learning of students. In primary schools, the relevant middle manager may be a Key Stage Co-ordinator who manages such relationships in collaboration with his or her colleagues. In Busby's (1991) study in a small school this function was carried out by a deputy headteacher. In primary schools and the smaller unitary departments or diffuse departments of secondary schools, this co-ordination may be done by individual teachers. None the less, the process of co-ordinating staff to sustain the curriculum is a middle management or subject leader function, whoever is implementing it.

Successful styles of management

It is important for subject leaders to make support staff feel valued members of staff (Busher and Saran, 1995c; Moyles with Suschitsky, 1997; Busher and Blease, 2000) who belong to the staff team, rather than merely being servants of it. This sense of interdependence between staff is one of the known features of effectively working teams (e.g. Stoll and Fink, 1996). In part this sense of empowerment is achieved through the ways in which teaching staff treat support staff. In part it is achieved through the styles of leadership used by subject leaders. Both Busher and Blease (2000) and Moyles with Suschitsky (1997) noted the importance of informal processes of management supplementing formal aspects, such as job specifications.

Although formal job descriptions are necessary to define the role of support staff, many support staff in the study by Busher and Saran (1995c) said they were keen to be involved in whatever work needed undertaking because of their sense of commitment to helping students and supporting the school. In primary schools, support staff are routinely included in school and classroom social events. Within some subject areas in secondary schools, this sense of belonging to a community is enhanced by support staff being:

- Consulted regularly, if informally, about departmental decision-making;
- Delegated important aspects of decision-making within a department;

- Included in social events on an equal footing with academic staff;
- Praised and thanked by teachers for the work they do.

(Busher and Blease, 2000: 105)

To build a collegial culture, subject leaders like senior staff in schools in the study by Busher and Saran (1995c) encouraged all staff to regard each other as of equal worth. One means of doing this is to develop a subject area or school policy that all staff are invited to use the staffroom as well as to attend social functions. Despite such policies in some schools, Busher and Saran (1995c) noted that some support staff admitted to feeling unwelcome (science technician) or to choosing not to use the staffroom (assistant bursar). One premises officer said that when he had started to go in '[he] got a few strange looks but that was no trouble . . . at the end of the day I'm a human being'. In due course, he thought 'something like eighty-five per cent of the teachers now treat me as equal'. A senior administrative officer in another school noted: 'When I first started [17 years ago] it was definitely them and us. You knew they [teachers] didn't want you in there.' She added that the status of catering and caretaking staff had improved in recent years as well.

The style of leadership preferred by many support staff from teachers, subject leaders and senior staff seems to be a collegial one. In this, subject leaders demonstrate their support for and trust in the support staff – a quality Blase and Blase (1994) thought essential for school leaders to generate to build effective teams. Busher and Blease (2000) found an important aspect of this culture was ensuring support staff have adequate training for the job they are expected to do, and that the need for training is kept constantly under review. Another important aspect is delegating responsibility to staff to work autonomously on aspects of a subject area's work. However, as Moyles with Suschitsky (1997) point out, that process of delegation has to take place within the quality of knowledge support staff already have, as well as that they can gain from training.

Working with classroom-based staff

Subject leader and teacher responsibility for classroom-based support staff is problematic, not least because there is often so little time for teachers and classroom assistants to engage jointly in lesson and curriculum planning, even where teachers acknowledge the need for this (Moyles with Suschitsky, 1997). Further, for some categories of these staff, such as special needs assistants, the person directly responsible for supervising how and what work they do with identified students is the school's co-ordinator for special needs (SENCO) rather than the subject area's leader. This raises questions about how subject leaders and the SENCO liase successfully to give integrated and effective guidance to the LSA for each subject area and, so, give the most effective help for the students' learning needs.

Classroom assistants appear to see their role as enabling teachers to cope better with student needs (Busher and Saran, 1995c). Many think it is important to build effective relations with students as they have extensive contact with them, albeit for brief periods only. On the other hand some LSAs in Busher and Saran's study (1995c) thought some teachers 'are a little wary of you at first', but that as they realised the value of in-class support to students and to themselves, it was possible to develop good working relationships. A senior teacher thought older teachers seemed more understanding of support staff than younger ones, who tended to regard the classroom as 'their kingdom'. Subject leaders need to help teachers to incorporate LSAs into their lesson planning, classroom management and teaching and learning strategies.

Support by LSAs to students with learning difficulties allows teachers to look after the rest of the students, particularly necessary in larger classes, and gives the weaker students essential intensive individual tuition. It is for subject leaders to develop policies of how support staff are to work in classrooms alongside teachers in order to make this effective learning support for students. Where subject leaders or teachers and classroom assistants can plan the work of students together, they need to include discussion of the following:

- Intended outcomes of classroom assistants' interventions with students.
- Records which need to be kept of the outcomes of interventions.
- Ways in which classroom assistants should intervene (e.g. encouraging independence in students).
- The quality of relationships classroom assistants should build with students.
- Resources classroom assistants need to carry out their work.

OFSTED in England and Wales suggest other criteria that could also be addressed (OFSTED, 1995b). Teachers and LSAs also need to find time to evaluate the impact of the classroom assistant's work on students' learning and on the management of the lessons.

Another aspect of classroom action that subject leaders, teachers and classroom assistants need to agree are the 'rules of engagement' with students (i.e. what behaviours should be praised or sanctioned). As well as avoiding tensions of values between teachers and classroom assistants, this avoids students becoming confused about which behaviours are permissible in the classroom and which are not, and so becoming more difficult for teachers and classroom assistants to manage. An important aspect of this will be for subject leaders to encourage classroom assistants to become careful listeners and prompters of children's expressed needs and worries (Moyles with Suschitsky, 1997).

None the less, there are tensions in the employment of LSAs. A shortage of time at the end of a lesson before moving on to the next event or LSAs being employed on part-time contracts often make it difficult for teachers and subject leaders to find time to plan lessons jointly with LSAs. This not only effectively disempowers LSAs from the curriculum decision-making process but limits the quality of the contribution they make to lessons (Moyles with Suschitsky, 1997). The head of an English department in the study by Busher and Saran (1995c) thought lack of clarity of role definition between teachers and assistants led to some friction. Further, many LSAs work in more than one teacher's or subject area's classrooms and have to balance the demands being made in one area against those demands being made in another. This poses further difficulties for subject leaders, involving them in negotiating with other subject leaders as well as the LSA about how work should be carried out in their classrooms.

Working with classroom-proximate staff

Subject leaders also have a major responsibility for managing classroom-proximate staff, such as technicians. These staff are usually based in laboratory preparatory rooms or in stock cupboards near workshops where they carry out much of their work. However, some of their work is likely to be carried out in the nearby classrooms where teachers work with students. For this reason subject leaders need to agree with support staff on what basis and in what ways and at what times they may work in classrooms. In some schools some such support staff work directly with students. Busher and Blease (2000) found laboratory technicians keen to undertake this role.

The importance of these support staff to teaching and learning is clear. Some science teachers in a study by Busher and Blease (2000) claimed it was impossible to run practical science lessons without laboratory technicians, though in one school teachers were doing just this because there was no physics technician. Laboratory technicians recognised their importance. As one explained 'if we make a mistake it can ruin a lesson' (Busher and Saran, 1995c).

To work effectively with such support staff, subject leaders need to make sure technicians and teachers maintain close liaison with each other about what materials to prepare for each practical lesson. In federal and confederate departments in secondary schools (see Chapter 3), such support staff are likely to have to engage with a number of teachers. Science departments or faculties of eight teaching staff are not uncommon in secondary schools in England and Wales. As with classroom-based support staff, subject leaders need to set out careful guidelines about how work can be given to support staff if those people are to avoid feeling overwhelmed by the competing demands different teachers might make upon them. Creating such a framework has the added advantage of allowing support staff the permissive freedom of planning their own work in such a way it most effectively supports the work of the teachers in classrooms (Busher and Blease, 2000).

Subject leaders can also delegate important responsibilities to well qualified support staff. Science technicians in one school were made responsible for ordering stock and keeping the science department's account books because they knew best what equipment and consumables the department needed at any one time (Busher and Blease, 2000). In two schools in the same study, laboratory technicians also played an advisory role, offering guidance to teachers on the carrying out of experiments and to students on the use of equipment. Other areas of responsibility which were allocated to senior technicians included organisation of curriculum materials and equipment in stock cupboards, and oversight of health and safety procedures.

To promote a sense of interdependence between support staff and teachers, even if the hierarchies of schooling are implicitly present and acknowledged, subject leaders need to find ways of involving support staff in subject area decision-making. This can be carried out through informal consultative processes, or through involving support staff formally in subject area staff meetings, or through some process of representation. For example, the last could be implemented by one member of technical staff attending subject area staff meetings to put forward the views of his or her technical colleagues and to listen on behalf of them. Subject leaders also need to find ways of reviewing support staff performance and considering what further training is needed or wanted and how that can be implemented. Involving support staff in the social activities of the subject area team is also an important means of helping such staff to have a sense of belonging to the subject area team (Busher and Blease, 2000).

Working with classroom-distant and classroom environment staff

Subject leaders have an important liaison function on behalf of their teaching colleagues with classroom-distant staff, such as clerical staff and reprographics staff. For example, subject leaders need to agree with teaching and support staff colleagues how they are going to duplicate various paper-based resources needed for lessons. In addition to agreeing a time schedule for creating these materials, they need to agree how they are going to be duplicated and by whom. This is likely to involve subject leaders in some adroit micro-politics in negotiating which teachers can have how much access to photocopying resources (Busher, 1992).

Part of that negotiation, however, has to be with a school's central administration, agreeing how much time and to what quality of work the school's reprographics assistant needs to produce such materials – if the school has such an assistant. A failure to agree these matters in advance of the production of materials can lead to conflict between members of a school's central administration and the management of a subject area. Lack of understanding of the work of administrative support staff can cause problems. For example, in the study by Busher and Saran (1995c), a reprographics technician had to cope with teachers who wanted instant delivery of their work, even though it had been handed in late!

Administrative and clerical staff fulfil a variety of functions from reproducing materials for teachers, to typing letters (mainly for senior staff), collating data on students for LEA returns, and overseeing and balancing a school's accounts (Busher and Saran, 1995c). Subject leaders need to work carefully with these staff, respecting them for the skills and knowledge they have and the important posts they hold. School bursars, whose work is discussed in some detail by Mortimore *et al.* (1994), oversee the budgets of the subject leaders, for example. The central location of the place of work of clerical and administrative staff, often in a school's reception area, means they meet a wide variety of people including many of the senior staff. Central, here, is both in physical terms and in terms of being at the hub of communications. A headteacher's personal assistant described herself as a go-between for the headteacher and other staff (Busher and Saran, 1995c).

Classroom environment staff, such as site supervisors and cleaning staff, are also important to subject leaders although they may have only irregular negotiations or contact with them. Negotiations may be about the quality of cleaning in certain areas or at certain times. It might be about the level of heating at certain times of the year. It might be about carrying out mundane but important maintenance, such as the replacing of light bulbs or door handles, or the renovation of blackboard or whiteboard surfaces. Trivial as such matters might seem, as one premises officer pointed out, the quality of the environment makes a lot of difference to the attitude of students towards working in particular subject areas or classrooms (Busher and Saran, 1995c). As he remarked, 'If you come to a filthy school everything else goes by the board'. This view was echoed by teachers in two different schools in the same study.

Subject leaders need to plan the use of their rooms to take account of the continuous maintenance work carried out by cleaning and premises staff. Premises officers do not enjoy undertaking emergency work, such as clearing up vomit or replacing light bulbs urgently, because it disrupts the routine of the work they have planned (Busher and Saran, 1995c). As one finance officer explained 'caretakers get a bit peeved at being at everybody's beck and call, but caretakers have always been like that'. The buildings manager in one school explained how he wished teachers 'would work with us in the same way we work with them' (Busher and Saran, 1995c). He explained how willing he and his assistant were to help teachers with room arrangements, for example, for examinations or parents' evenings, but thought teachers were 'not practical people' who had little idea of how long jobs took. 'I've stopped trying to explain,' he grumbled.

When subject leaders need to open rooms and buildings after normal school hours that needs to be agreed in advance with premises officers. Premises officers are usually responsible for the security of school buildings at all times, sometimes working late into the evening when there are late meetings.

Subject leaders need to agree policies and practices both with their teaching colleagues and with midday supervisors – another group who supervise the environment of schools – for the use of rooms during lunch and break times in England and Wales. This is especially important for those days which are wet. Apart from the risk of personal injury to students if they are in rooms and unsupervised, there is the potential risk of serious damage to expensive equipment. Teachers and supervisors need to agree a common framework of rules for student behaviour (Busby, 1991) if students are not to be confused about how they should behave and get punished unnecessarily. Many midday supervisors see their role as enabling teachers to cope better with student needs (Busher and Saran, 1995c). They think it is important to build effective relations with students as they have extensive contact with them, albeit for brief periods only. Lunchtime duty by midday supervisors gives teachers a reasonable break from some of their work.

Working with supply teaching staff

An important area of any subject leader's work is coping with emergencies successfully when they occur. One of the most common of these is the absence of staff. When this absence is of support staff there is often little a subject leader can do apart, perhaps, from rearranging the work schedules of the remaining support staff, be they laboratory technicians or LSAs. Inevitably it means some students and some teachers receive less support than was planned and has to raise questions about how the quality of the learning opportunities is affected. However when the absence is of teaching staff, subject leaders need to take urgent action to sustain the teaching and learning programmes of students.

The problem of absent teaching staff comes in three different categories. One is of short-term, temporary absence that has been planned. Another is of short-term absence that has not been planned. A third is of long-term absence. Subject leaders need to have in place with their subject area colleagues policies and practice to cover these three scenarios.

When teaching staff are absent for a short period, especially at short notice, subject leaders are faced with covering their classes, since it is unwise, as well as illegal in England and Wales, to leave students without any adequate supervision. While part of this problem for subject leaders is one of bridging to senior staff to find out what staff resources are available to deputise for the absent teacher, part of it is making arrangements for students' work to continue in as uninterrupted a manner as possible. Senior staff are likely to make either internal arrangements to deputise for the teacher (cover the lessons) or external arrangements. In the latter case they buy in temporary staff to supervise the absent teacher's lessons. In the former, they use teaching staff of the school to take the lessons of their absent colleague. In such cases those staff with any non-contact time available are likely to be asked to deputise. In small schools, it may well be only the headteacher or deputy headteacher who are available.

Whichever means the senior staff of a school use to cover the lessons, subject leaders are faced with the same problem: how to ensure the students in those lessons continue to follow the appropriate schemes of work. For the cover or deputising staff the mirror image of this problem exists: knowing what work to undertake with the students in these lessons and in what manner. In many schools subject leaders are expected to set work for the lessons of absent teachers, but unless the subject leader is aware of exactly what that teacher was going to teach next, this temporary curriculum may, itself, only sustain students progress ineffectively. In many subject areas and schools, then, subject leaders and senior staff ask teachers who know they are going to be absent to set work in advance for the students whose lessons they are going to miss. When teachers return to school they are expected to evaluate the quality of work carried out by students during their absence. Where teachers are absent unexpectedly, perhaps through sickness, subject leaders might ask them if they can at least suggest work their students might undertake, perhaps indicating what part of a syllabus they intended to tackle next. Where subject areas have a policy of staff keeping up-to-date lesson-planning books, it is relatively straightforward for subject leaders to set appropriate work for the students of absent teachers.

For the cover or deputising staff the problem is often one of being faced with an unknown group of students working in a subject area that is unfamiliar to them both in terms of its knowledge structures and in terms of the location of resources and equipment needed for teaching and learning. Subject leaders need to be able to give cover staff guidance on what curriculum work to supervise and where to find the necessary resources and equipment for a lesson, as well as what to do with these artefacts at the end of a lesson. They also need to give guidance to the cover staff on what to do at the end of the lesson with the work the students have undertaken. Subject leaders need to explain to such staff at least how the particular lesson fits into the general scheme of work the students have been following, even if there is not time to discuss in more detail the epistemological frameworks that surround the topic for the lesson and about which the students might ask questions. Galloway and Morrison's (1994) study explores in detail the problems faced by supply staff and how their work can be supported by subject leaders. Part-time teachers' rights on pay, training and holidays are now covered by European legislation (TES, 2000: 11).

While internal cover staff are likely to know the normal rules and procedures for the subject area and school, external bought-in staff may be unfamiliar with these. Further, they may be unfamiliar even with the site layout of the school. It is up to subject leaders to create a process of temporary induction to the subject area for them. This involves at least explaining to external cover staff what are the policies and practices of a subject area on processes of teaching and learning, on student discipline, on health and safety procedures (where relevant) and on procedures for managing resources. Where it is not possible to explain these details face to face, subject leaders can prepare a booklet of guidance for external cover staff.

When staff are absent for longer periods, perhaps for maternity leave or major ill health, subject leaders need to develop a more comprehensive strategy than the temporary tactics already suggested. This could involve re-timetabling the remaining staff of a subject area to minimise the impact of the absence on students. It is likely to involve inducting a new part-time teacher into the workings of the subject area, even if that new teacher is only on a temporary contract.

13

Subject Leadership and School Improvement

The focus of this chapter (and this book) is the relationship between improving subject areas and whole-school improvement. The purpose of this book has been to offer subject leaders a better grasp of the dynamics of subject development and its link to school improvement. This means, among other things, taking seriously differential strategies for development. By selecting different strategies for change and development that match the particular needs of the subject area, the potential for improvement at both the subject level and school level is enhanced.

It is inevitable schools will face continuous change in the years ahead. Consequently, it is clear that the need and demand for supportive leadership and management at all levels within the school organisation will become even stronger. Whatever the rhetoric concerning the 'self-managing' school, the reality is that those responsible for leading and managing others will have further and higher expectations placed upon them. For subject leaders this presents the opportunity to secure high standards within the subject area by improving the quality of teaching and learning. In achieving this, subject leaders will inevitably contribute to whole-school improvement and improved standards of achievement for all pupils.

Introduction

Subject leaders have traditionally placed teaching and learning at the forefront of their improvement efforts. This emphasis is now being endorsed by politicians and policy-makers who are searching for more effective ways of raising standards of teaching, and through this learning and achievement. In recent years there have been many government initiatives aimed at improving the leadership and management of schools. There is now much wider responsibility and accountability at the school level through the local management of schools. As a result, pressure has been exerted from a wide range of sources, including the government and teaching profession, for a more coherent approach to leadership. This has been coupled with a general desire for improved performance across all schools and a fundamental belief in the need for quality leadership for schools of the future.

Research findings from diverse countries and different school contexts have revealed the powerful impact of leadership on processes related to school effectiveness and improvement (e.g. Van Velzen *et al.*, 1985; Stoll and Fink, 1996). Essentially, schools that are effective and have the capacity to improve are led by headteachers who make a significant and measurable contribution to the effectiveness of their staff. Whatever else is disputed about this complex area of activity, the centrality of leadership in the achievement of school effectiveness and school improvement remains unequivocal.

Most recently, research evidence concerning school effectiveness and improvement underlines the importance of devolved leadership at different levels within the organisation (Fullan, 1991). The importance of mobilising development at school level, subject area level and classroom level change has been shown to be essential in successful school improvement programmes (e.g. Hopkins *et al.*, 1994; Hopkins and Harris, 1997). Recent research has shown that a substantial proportion of the variation in effectiveness among schools is due to variation within schools, particularly between different subject areas. This work has emphasised the importance of exploring differential effectiveness, particularly at the level of the subject team (Creemers, 1994).

The work of UK researchers such as Harris *et al.* (1995), Sammons *et al.* (1997) and Harris (1998) suggests subject leaders can make a difference to subject area performance in much the same way as headteachers contribute to overall school performance.

In particular, the leadership role of middle managers has been advocated as important in explaining differential school effectiveness (Sammons *et al.*, 1997). Similarly, there are increasing calls for and acceptance of a leadership role for teachers in achieving goals in the context of their own areas of direct responsibility. Yet, there is research evidence that suggests there is an ever-growing divide between 'leaders' and 'followers' as a result of the changes arising from the self-governance of schools (Wallace and Hall, 1994). The strong managerialist culture apparent in many schools has reinforced the separateness of the senior management team and has claimed leadership as an activity for the few, rather than the many (Gunter, 1997).

Promoting a more dynamic and decentralised approach to leadership is associated with school improvement. Hopkins *et al.* (1994: 155) noted that 'A school that looks to the headteacher as the single source of direction and inspiration is severely constrained' Yet school structures often reinforce this rather limited view, confusing a hierarchy of roles with the real distribution of knowledge and skills. Recent assessments of the leadership role of the headteacher imply that giving others real responsibility and developing others is the best possible way of an organisation moving forward. This means relinquishing the idea of structure as control and viewing structure as the vehicle for empowering others.

Contemporary views of leadership

This current broadening of interest in and understanding of leadership roles parallels the pattern of development of leadership theory generally. There has been an increasing emphasis upon the links between leadership and the culture of the organisation. This has led to a movement away from the notion of leadership as a series of transactions within a given cultural context towards a view of leadership as transformational, having the potential to alter the cultural context in which people work. The literature concerning leadership, effective schools and school improvement offers a bewildering array of theories, models and strategies for aspiring and serving headteachers (see Leithwood *et al.*, 1996). Various theoretical models have been espoused concerning the impact of leaders on school performance and upon school improvement (Southworth, 1995). Most recent leadership studies have focused upon values; the 'moral purposes' and moral craft of leadership (Sergiovanni, 1992); the roles of leaders in creating a 'community of learners' (Barth, 1990; Senge, 1990); and the capacities of leaders to 'make a difference' through their ability to 'transform' (Sergiovanni, 1995) or 'liberate' (Tampoe, 1998). In attempting to bring about change, it has been shown that effective leadership is a key determinant in deciding whether anything positive happens within the organisation (Leithwood *et al.*, 1999; Day *et al.*, 2000).

Within the UK government's overall strategic vision for education, the training, reskilling, managerialisation and certification of heads occupy a central place. Much of the impetus for implementing successive national reforms rests primarily with the leaders of individual institutions. As a consequence, headteachers are increasingly being viewed as 'managing directors', publicly accountable for improving the performance of their school in ways that are measurable: 'We know that effective teaching must be supported by high quality management and leadership at middle and senior levels in the profession

. . . Managers and leaders also need to be accountable for progress, at whatever level they manage' (Millet, 1996: 9).

Ball (1997) argues that the dominant discourse of leadership embodies a mixture of direct control (old managerialism) and so-called people-centred management (new managerialism). Glatter (1997: 3) encapsulates this point:

> We in 'mainstream' educational management have become preoccupied with what might be called the institutional side of leadership and management to the extent of disregarding, or at least under-emphasising policy and contextual factors. In doing so we may be playing into the hands of those who accuse educational management of being too technocratic and mechanistic and of paying insufficient regard to values.

This claim directly contrasts the popular view that the leader's main role is to influence the quality of teaching and learning in the school through purposeful 'transformative leadership' (Leithwood and Jantzi, 1990).

Subject leaders have an important role to play in changing the internal conditions of the school. They are uniquely placed within the school organisation to bring about change where it matters most, i.e. in the classroom. They are key agents to improved teaching and learning because they have a direct influence over the professional practice of others. They are also in a position to create a culture and a set of values about teaching and learning within their subject area. As Hargreaves (1994: 54) points out, 'what the teacher thinks, what the teacher believes, what the teacher assumes . . . have powerful implications for the change process'. Consequently, the culture of teaching within a subject area can either promote, or prevent, school improvement.

The subject leader can greatly influence the culture of teaching within his or her subject or curriculum area (Busher and Harris, 1999). To make such a contribution, however, subject leaders need to be given the recognition and responsibility for school improvement. Yet, the centrality of the subject leader's role within school improvement has yet to be fully realised in practice (Harris, 2000). Status and power-based recognition for subject leaders is often complicated by the multiplicity of tasks required of the role. Similarly, the micropolitics of the school can often prevent subject leaders taking an active part in school development (Busher and Harris, 1999).

While subject leaders working with their teams are very much in the front line, this does not necessarily mean they are involved in strategic matters or organisation decision-making. Levels of involvement are likely to vary according to the nature of the organisation, the management approach of senior staff and the culture of the organisation. Most importantly, perhaps, levels of involvement are a function of the confidence, expertise and skill in management exhibited by the subject leader (Blase and Anderson, 1995). If subject leaders are expected to lead others within the organisation and to affect change at the classroom level then the capacity leaders have to make a difference will depend upon their interpretation of and responses to the constraints, demands and choices they face (Ribbins, 1995).

Centrally important within subject leadership is the co-operation and alignment of others to the leader's values and vision. As Bhindi and Duignan (1997: 10) have proposed in their visionary paradigm for leadership in 2020:

> Organisations are not solely concerned with outcomes, processes and resources. They are also concerned with the human spirit and their values and relationships. Authentic leaders breathe the life force into the workplace and keep the people feeling energised and focused. As stewards and guides they build people and their self-esteem. They derive their credibility from personal integrity and 'walking' their values.

Another important dimension of effective leadership is the influence of context. In managing people and cultural change subject leaders manage external as well as internal environments. Effective leaders need to combine a moral purpose with a willingness to be collaborative and to promote collaboration amongst colleagues, whether through teamwork or extending the boundaries of participation in decision-making.

In order for schools and subject areas to develop, each has to create and sustain the internal conditions for improvement. Research into effective school improvement (Fullan, 1991; Ainscow *et al.*, 1994; Harris, 2000) emphasises the need to make sure that efforts to raise standards of achievement are accompanied by a comparable drive to build the capacity of the school as a whole to manage change. The focus on the classroom enables the school to keep on moving forward. Interventions in teaching and learning are essential but, on their own, will not result in sustainable school improvements in levels of achievement. The crucial point is that, in terms of school development, neither *external* nor *internal* strategies will impact upon the progress of students *unless* the strategy itself impacts *at the same time* on the internal conditions or change capacity of the school or subject area.

During the past five years or so work has been taking place with 40 schools in England, and more recently in Iceland, Puerto Rico and South Africa, on a collaborative school improvement project known as 'Improving the Quality of Education for All' (IQEA). The IQEA work has demonstrated that, without an equal focus on the development capacity, or internal conditions at the school, subject and classroom level, innovative work quickly becomes marginalised. These conditions have to be worked on at the same time as the curriculum or other priorities the school has set itself (Harris and Hopkins, 2000).

Creating the conditions for improvement

The conditions that underpin improvement effort at the subject level reflect the school-level conditions that have been shown to influence change and development (Hopkins *et al.*, 1997a). These relate to the classroom-level conditions which focus primarily upon changes in teaching and learning. The internal conditions that have been shown to foster improvement at subject area level are as follows:

- leadership
- communication
- co-ordination
- evidence-based change and development
- planning.

These conditions are not presented in any order of priority: all are equally important. What subject leaders need to do is to develop all of them if they are to create and sustain the internal capacity successfully to implement and realise their improvement targets. To provide a clearer picture of these conditions and the way they operate at subject area level, the ideas developed within the IQEA project will be drawn upon in conjunction with the research findings concerning subject team effectiveness (Harris and Hopkins, 2000).

Leadership

Research has shown that successful subject areas have a 'climate for change' or 'a climate for improvement', i.e. the subject area is committed to improvement and is prepared to change existing practices. Developing this climate has been found to be a necessary prerequisite of effective subject level change. Without this climate subject areas will continue to modify incrementally, rather than change, existing practices. Such a climate is influenced by the subject leader and can be set by the particular leadership style adopted.

The most effective leadership approach within a subject area is that of the 'leading professional'. This is where the subject leader is considered by other team members as a model to follow. In short, he or she is viewed as an expert practitioner and is viewed by members of the subject area as a source of good practice. The way leadership is conceptualised and perceived within a subject area is a factor which influences improvement in teaching and learning. Subject leaders need to have a clear vision for the development of the subject area and an ability to share this vision with colleagues to ensure developments are taken forward. Where leadership is too authoritarian, or alternatively too *laissez-faire*, development will not occur and improvement will be difficult to achieve (Harris, 1998).

Communication

One of the most striking findings from the various research studies into team effectiveness has been the collegiate vision adopted by subject areas. Effective subject areas are marked by a constant interchange of professional information at both a formal and informal level. Similarly, schools that are improving seem to have ways of working that encourage staff, governors, parents and students to feel involved. These ways of working provide support for the school's improvement efforts.

In order to generate involvement within a subject area, clear communication systems have to be in place. To achieve optimum levels of involvement, information flows have to be transparent. Where communication is unclear, or muddled, there is evidence to show this restricts effective collaboration (Harris, 1998). The subject leader should ensure, therefore, there are opportunities for consultation and staff participation in decision-making. By providing such opportunities, feelings of involvement should increase to create a sense of community and commitment to high standards.

Co-ordination

Across subject areas the ability to organise key elements of teaching and learning in an optimum way is essential. This requires co-ordination to ensure key tasks are undertaken efficiently. As schools are busy places and there are numerous developments occurring at once, the need for co-ordination is of paramount importance. For the subject leader this will necessitate delegating some core tasks and activities to other members of staff. In doing so, subject leaders will need to ensure they work with colleagues to establish systems of communication and forms of monitoring and evaluation that will inform future developments.

Ultimately the success of a subject area depends upon the success teachers have in working with their respective classes. There is a body of evidence that demonstrates teachers work most effectively when they are supported by other teachers and work collegially (Hargreaves, 1994; Lieberman, 1996). Consequently, the role of the subject leader should be to formulate working partnerships between teachers and to foster mutual sharing. Hopkins *et al.* (1996: 177) note that: 'successful schools encourage co-ordination by creating collaborative environments which encourages involvement, professional development, mutual support and assistance in problem solving.' Within subject areas and across subject areas, these forms of collaboration should similarly be encouraged if sustained improvement is to be achieved.

Evidence-based change and development

The importance of enquiry and reflection within the process of school improvement has long been established. In their study of unusually effective schools, Levine and Lezotte (1990) noted that a 'commitment to enquiry' was a consistent feature of such schools. Hopkins *et al.* (1996) have pointed to the fact that school improvement has to be a process that is data driven. In other words, that appropriate information should be used to inform the school improvement process.

There is now a growing literature that demonstrates and endorses the importance of evidence-based research as the basis for improving teaching (Louden, 1991; Atkin, 1994; Day, 1999). The analysis and application of research findings by teachers as part of their routine professional activity have been shown to have positive effects upon the quality of teaching and learning (Hopkins and Harris, 1997; Harris and Hopkins, 1999). Potentially, action research offers teachers tremendous opportunities to engage in professional development through the systematic investigation of self and practice. This need not demand the use of advanced research techniques but can focus upon simple data collection approaches, or utilise existing sources of information. Consequently, subject leaders need to consider how to make the best use of existing data and how to encourage teachers to engage in their own investigation and enquiry.

Planning

Within the school effectiveness studies, planning has been shown to be an important factor in determining effectiveness. The centrality of developmental planning within school level and subject area level change further endorses the importance of planning as a lever for school improvement (Hargreaves *et al.*, 1989; Hopkins and MacGilchrist, 1998). Development planning is a strategy that is becoming increasingly widespread in schools, as teachers and school leaders struggle to take control of the process of change. Besides helping the school organise what it is already doing and what it needs to do in a more purposeful and coherent way, effective planning is about helping teachers manage innovation and change successfully.

There have been a number of studies that have focused on the impact of development planning on schools, teachers and classrooms, and many of these have been summarised in *Development Planning for School Improvement* (Hargreaves and Hopkins, 1994). This research suggests unsurprisingly that although many schools have development plans they do not always lead to school improvement. Harris and Hopkins (1999) suggest that:

- the organisational and cultural arrangements of the school predispose it to certain types of (more or less effective) plan;
- there can be a dialectical relationship between the plan and the organisational and cultural conditions of the school.

In the latter aspect, the approach to planning taken by the subject leader can have a positive and developmental impact on the internal conditions of the subject area.

A central focus upon teaching and learning

At the heart of school and subject-level improvement is a central concern with the quality of teaching and learning. Effective schools and subject areas are those that place an emphasis upon the teaching and learning processes and invest in teacher development time. However, most interventions still are made at the school rather than the classroom level (Hopkins and Harris, 1997). At this level, change is mainly of a managerial and administrative nature and has led to schools defining and redefining roles and responsibilities, introducing monitoring systems and generally concentrating their efforts upon infrastructural change. This approach stresses the administrative arrangements rather than the human factors and neglects the importance of ensuring change is focused upon improvement in teaching and learning (Joyce *et al.*, 1997).

Effective subject areas enhance the quality of student learning through involving students centrally in the learning process and ensuring they feel empowered to learn. Many studies of effective schooling have indicated that the teacher–student relationship is at the heart of the learning process. Indeed, many of the school effectiveness studies show that factors at classroom level which lead to effective teaching and which subsequently impact upon effective learning are crucially important in effective schooling (Creemers, 1994). Of all the school effectiveness characteristics it is those that relate to teaching that have the most empirical support (Scheerens, 1992). Furthermore, Scheerens has noted that many of the classroom factors related to school effectiveness are concerned with the process and practice of effective teaching and have multiple empirical research confirmation. Consequently, subject leaders have a key role to play in ensuring colleagues provide the best possible learning opportunities for all learners within their subject areas.

These six conditions represent the main levers for change and development within a subject area. As noted earlier these conditions are intrinsically linked to school and classroom-level conditions that have evolved as a result of the IQEA project (Hopkins *et al.*, 1997a). These conditions are connected intrinsically to teacher development, as this has been shown to be centrally important in school development. By working upon these sets of conditions simultaneously (i.e. school, subject level and classroom), there is the potential to build capacity within and across the organisation.

It is these enabling conditions that allows school improvement to impact upon student learning and achievement. These conditions will obviously differ from school to school and from school context to context. However, without a focus upon these enabling conditions, the chances of sustained innovation and improvement are substantially lessened. More importantly, the possibility of raising student performance and achievement becomes even more remote.

If school improvement is to be seen holistically as encompassing all levels within the school organisation then the implications of intervention at each level need careful consideration. More importantly, it is the integration of change at the different levels that sustains school improvement. It is change at different levels within the organisation that contributes to cultural change and it is cultural change that supports the teaching and learning process which leads to enhanced outcomes for students (Hopkins *et al.*, 1994).

School improvement has been defined as 'a strategy for educational change that enhances student outcomes as well as strengthening the school's capacity for managing change' (Hopkins *et al.*, 1994: 3). Building capacity, however, necessitates involvement of all partners in the school improvement process. But what are the implications for subject areas, and how can subject leaders secure improved practices within their subject area?

Improving subject areas

The conclusion to this chapter considers how subject areas may be changed and improved. Departmental effectiveness research (Harris *et al.*, 1995; Sammons *et al.*, 1997) suggests a number of practical strategies subject leaders can adopt to improve the performance across their subject area.

Engage in data collection and analysis

The regular collection and use of information about students' educational outcomes within the subject area is an important source of evidence for subject-level change. The analysis of externally generated data plus regular monitoring of student's work can inform the selection of areas for change and development. The research concerning effective subject areas highlights the importance of regular feedback to students about progress made in the subject area. As such, the analysis of student-level data offers a means of self-review within the subject area, plus the opportunity to set developmental targets closely related to teaching and learning.

Rudduck *et al.* (1997) have demonstrated the potency of listening to students' views about teaching and learning within the subject area. While this might appear a rather high-risk strategy, it has been shown to be an important contributor to school improvement. For example, focusing attention on under-achieving groups, or looking for patterns in classroom behaviour, can provide very useful feedback to teachers. Within the IQEA project collecting students' views is an important dimension of the school improvement work and has been shown to have had positive effects upon improving the teaching and learning within subject areas (Beresford, 1998).

Focus upon the quality of teaching

The quality of teaching is a crucial component of subject-level effectiveness. Sammons *et al.* (1997: 207) suggest from their work that a basis for reviewing the quality of teaching would include the following:

- Work focus of lessons (are most of the students on task most of the time?);
- Strong academic emphasis;
- Clarity of goals for student learning;
- Student responsibility (independent learning is encouraged);
- Lessons generally challenge students of all ability levels;

- Teacher enthusiasm;
- Effective classroom control;
- High teacher expectations for student performance and behaviour;
- Promptness starting and finishing lessons;
- Regular monitoring of student progress;
- Consistent marking policy;
- Homework given a high priority;
- Teachers knowledge of the content of the subject and the GCSE syllabus.

Such a checklist would be useful in evaluating teaching performance across the subject area. Possibly, it might contribute to classroom observation within the subject area by incorporating some of the factors within an observation schedule. While there is no prescription for good teaching, the benefits of a fairly structured approach, of teacher enthusiasm, positive student–teacher relationships and good classroom control on students' academic achievements are well established (Harris, 1998).

Within the most effective subject areas it is the case that heads of subject area attached considerable importance both to team building and actual teamwork within their subject areas (Sammons *et al.*, 1997; Harris, 1999b). In addition, effective subject leaders tend to lead by example by demonstrating good practice and effective teaching approaches. Consequently, by encouraging a climate within the subject area of observing, reviewing and talking about teaching there is more possibility of improved teaching and student learning.

Reinforcing values

It is part of a subject leader's role to articulate the subject area's values and to reinforce them at every opportunity. These values need to be embedded within the institution and shared by staff and also by parents and students. Subject areas tend to be loosely coupled systems despite the existence of a conventional chain of line management causality. Consequently, subject areas need to be clear about the interpretation and articulation of educational values within their individual subject area context.

Avoid complacency

Effective subject areas constantly strive to raise expectations of teachers, students and the wider community regarding potential student achievement. This means subject areas need to be explicit, eloquent and prolific in their definition of achievement. They then need to celebrate it, communicate it and develop a reward system which will eliminate the need for most sanctions. Such a process is likely to ignite the enthusiasm of staff and generate motivation amongst students. It is additionally important to give students and the wider community ownership of the subject area's achievements too and to involve them in organising and participating in regular celebrations of the subject area's success.

External support

Even the most effective subject area eventually becomes inward looking and atrophies if it becomes too self-sufficient. Isolation from external stimulus and support can be damaging to any subject area irrespective of its performance level. A subject area which is developing seeks out best practice elsewhere and uses outside support to develop the knowledge base and to initiate networks. External expertise and support can also offer alternative teaching practices and new ways of teaching and learning. Teachers can become skilled in these new processes by working alongside others both within the classroom and in functional teams.

Risk-taking

Effective subject areas need to encourage experimentation and risk-taking. They need to accept messiness and muddle rather than aim for efficiency. They need to subscribe to the view that safe teaching is mundane teaching and aim high and take joy in the successes, while being willing to analyse the reasons for the failures. Indeed, real learning lies in understanding the failures rather than the successes.

Recognise success

All subject areas at whatever stage in their development need to take joy in every demonstration of success. They need to aim to orchestrate optimism and celebration of teacher *and* student achievement. Everyday professional and social interactions of teachers and students need to focus upon the positive rather than the negative, upon success rather than failure to ensure this permeates the whole subject area and every classroom. Cynicism about students, the subject area, the profession needs to be eroded by making it totally unacceptable within the subject area.

This list of strategies for developing subject areas are still in an early stage. Three characteristics are worth highlighting. The first is these strategies are not homogeneous but holistic and eclectic. The second is this combination of strategies has a disparate focus; they are at the same time directed at the structure/organisation of the subject area, the achievement of students, and the intangible 'culture of the subject area'. Thirdly, these strategies represent a combination of external and internal strategies. The particular blend of strategies is modified to fit the 'context specificity' of each individual subject area. Collectively they offer the possibility and potential for the improvement of subject areas and provide a basis for ensuring that subject leaders contribute importantly to school improvement.

References

Adey, K. R. (1988) Methods and criteria for the selection of teaching staff for appointment to posts in secondary schools, with special reference to head of department appointments: a study of practice in one local education authority. *Collected Original Resources in Education*, Vol. 12, no. 3.

Ainscow, M. (1995) Would it work in theory? Arguments for practitioner research and theorising in the special needs field. In Clark, C., Dyson, A. and Millward, A. (eds.) *Towards Inclusive Schools?* London: David Fulton.

Ainscow, M., Hopkins, D., Southworth, G. and West, M. (1994) *Creating the Conditions for School Improvement*. London: David Fulton.

Armstrong, D. (1995) *Power and Partnership in Education*. London: Routledge.

Armstrong, F. (1998) Curriculum management and special and inclusive education. In Clough, P. (ed.) *Managing Inclusive Education: From Policy to Experience*. London: Paul Chapman.

Armstrong, M. (1980) *Closely Observed Children*. vLondon: Writers & Readers.

Armstrong, L. (1993) *Managing to Survive: Vol. 2: Relationships*. Lancaster: Framework Press.

Atkin, M. (1994) Teacher research to change policy: an illustration. In Hollingsworth, S. and Sockett, H. (eds) *Teacher Research and Educational Reform*. Chicago, Il: University of Chicago Press.

Bacharach, S. and Lawler, E. (1980) *Power and Politics in Organisations*. San Francsico, Ca: Jossey-Bass.

Bailey, P. (1973) The functions of heads of departments in comprehensive schools. *Journal of Educational Administration and History*, Vol. 5, no. 1, pp. 52–58.

Ball, S. J. (1987) *The Micro-Politics of the School*. London: Methuen.

Ball, S. (1997) Good school/bad school: paradox and fabrication. *British Journal of Sociology of Education*, Vol. 18, no. 3, pp. 317–36.

Ball, S. J. (1999) Labour, learning and the economy: a policy sociology. *Cambridge Journal of Education*, Vol. 29, no. 2, pp. 195–206.

Ball, S. J. and Bowe, R. (1992), Subject departments and the implementation of National Curriculum policy: an overview of the issues. *Journal of Curriculum Studies*, Vol. 24, no. 2, pp. 97–115.

Barber, M. and Sebba, J. (1999) Reflections on progress towards a world class education system. *Cambridge Journal of Education*, Vol. 29, No. 2, pp. 183–94.

Barker, B. and Busher, H. (1998) External contexts and internal policies: a case-study of school improvement in its socio-political environment. Paper given at the British Educational Research Association Annual Conference, Queen's University, Belfast.

Barth, R. (1990) *School Improvement from Within: Teachers, Parents and Principals can Make a Difference*. San Francisco, Ca: Jossey-Bass.

Bastiani, J. (1995) *Working with Parents: A Whole School Approach*. London: Routledge.

Bastiani, J. (1996) *Home–School Contracts and Agreements – Opportunity or Threat?* London: RSA.

Beare, H., Caldwell, B. and Milikan, R. (1989) *Creating an Excellent School.* London: Routledge.

Becher, T. (1989) The National Curriculum and the implementation gap. In Preedy, M. (ed.) *Approaches to Curriculum Management.* Milton Keynes: Open University Press.

Bell, L. (1992) *Managing Teams in Secondary Schools.* London: Routledge.

Belbin, M. (1996) *Team Roles at Work.* London: Butterworth-Heinemann.

Bell, D. and Ritchie, R. (1999) *Towards Effective Subject Leadership in the Primary School.* Buckingham: Open University Press.

Bendix, R. (1962) *Max Weber: an Intellectual Portrait.* London: Methuen.

Bennet, C. and Downes, P. (1998) Leading parents to fuller involvement. *Management in Education,* Vol. 12, no. 5, pp. 12–14.

Bennett, N. (1976) *Teaching Styles and Student Progress.* London: Open Books.

Bennett, N. (1995) *Managing Professional Teachers: Middle Management in Primary and Secondary Schools.* London: Paul Chapman.

Beresford, J. (1998) *Collecting Information for School Improvement.* London: David Fulton.

Bhindi, N. and Duignan, P. (1997) Leadership for a new century: authenticity, intentionality, spirituality and sensibility. *Educational Management and Administration,* Vol. 25, no. 2, pp. 117–32.

Bibby, P. and Lunt, I. (1996) *Working for Children.* London: David Fulton.

Blandford, S. (1997) *Middle Management in Schools.* London: Pitman Publishing.

Blase, J. and Anderson, G. L. (1995) *The Micropolitics of Educational Leadership: From Control to Empowerment.* London: Cassell.

Blase, J. and Blase, J. (1994) *Empowering Teachers: What Successful Principals Do.* Thousand Oaks, Ca: Corwin.

Bolam, R. (1986) Conceptualising in-service. In Hopkins, D. (ed.) *In-service Training and Educational Development: An International Survey.* Beckenham: Croom Helm.

Bolam, R. (1990) Recent developments in England and Wales. In Joyce, B. (ed.) *Changing School Culture through Staff Development: The 1990 ASCD Yearbook.* Alexandria, Va: ASCD.

Bradley, C. and Roaf, C. (1995) Meeting special educational needs in the secondary school: a team approach. *Support for Learning,* Vol. 10, no. 2, pp. 93–99.

Brandes, D. and Ginnis, P. (1990) *The Student Centred School: Ideas for Practical Visionaries.* Oxford: Blackwell.

Brown, L., Henry, J. and McTaggart, R. (1982) Action research notes on the national seminar. In Elliott, J. and Whitehead, D. (eds.) *Action Research into Action Research. CARN Bulletin No 4.* Cambridge: Cambridge University Press.

Brown, M., Boyle, B. and Boyle, T. (1999) Commonalities between perception and practice in models of school decision-making in secondary schools. *School Leadership and Management,* Vol. 19, no. 3, pp. 319–30.

Brown, M. and Rutherford, D. (1998) Changing roles and raising standards: new challenges for heads of departments. *School Leadership and Management,* Vol. 18, no. 1, pp. 75–88.

Brundrett, M. (1998) What lies behind collegiality, legitimation or control? An analysis of the purported benefits of collegial management in education. *Educational Management and Administration,* Vol. 26, no.3, pp. 305–16.

Bullock, A. and Thomas, H. (1994) *The LMS Impact Project: Final Report*. London: National Association of Headteachers.

Busby, S. (1991) The management of children in the dining room at lunchtime. In Lomax, P. (ed.) *Managing Better Schools and Colleges: The Action Research Way. BERA Dialogue 4*. Clevedon: Multilingual Matters.

Busher, H. (1988) Reducing role overload for a head of department: a rationale for fostering staff development. *School Organisation*, Vol. 8, no. 1, pp. 99–103.

Busher, H. (1992) The politics of working in secondary schools: some teachers' perspectives on their schools as organisations. Unpublished PhD thesis, Leeds: School of Education, University of Leeds.

Busher, H. (2000) Schools, effectiveness and improvement: a political analysis. In Bennett, N. and Harris, A. (eds.) *School Effectiveness and School Improvement: Searching for the Elusive Partnership*. London: Cassell.

Busher, H. and Blease, D. (2000) Growing collegial cultures in subject departments in secondary schools: working with science staff. *School Leadership and Management*, Vol. 20, no. 1, pp. 99–112.

Busher, H. and Harris, A. (1999) Leadership of school subject areas: tensions and dimensions of managing in the middle. *School Leadership and Management*, Vol. 19, No. 3, pp. 305–17.

Busher, H. and Hodgkinson, K. (1996) Co-operation and tension between autonomous schools: a study of interschool networking. *Educational Review*, Vol. 48, no. 1, pp. 55–64.

Busher, H. and Paxton, L. (1997) HEADLAMP – a local experience in partnership. In Tomlinson, H. (ed.) *Managing Continuing Professional Development in Schools*. London: Paul Chapman.

Busher, H. and Saran, R. (1992) *Teachers' Conditions of Employment: A Study in the Politics of School Management. Bedford Way Series*. London: Kogan Page.

Busher, H. and Saran, R. (1995a) Managing staff professionally. in Busher, H. and Saran, R. (eds.) *Managing Teachers as Professionals in Schools*. London: Kogan Page.

Busher, H. and Saran, R. (1995b) Managing with support staff. In Busher, H. and Saran, R. (eds.) *Managing Teachers as Professionals in Schools*. London: Kogan Page.

Busher, H. and Saran, R. (1995c) Working with support staff in some secondary schools. Unpublished report, University of Loughborough.

Cade, L. and Caffyn, R. (1995) Family planning for special needs: the role of a Nottinghamshire family special needs co-ordinator. *Support for Learning*, Vol. 10, no. 2, pp. 70–74.

Calderhead, J. (1993) The contribution of research on teachers' thinking to the professional development of teachers. In Day, C., Calderhead, J. and Denicolo, P. (eds.) *Research on Teacher Thinking: Understanding Professional Development*. London: Cassell.

Carr, W. (1993) Reconstructing the curriculum debate: an editorial introduction. *Curriculum Studies*, Vol. 1, no. 1 pp. 5–6.

Chamberlain, R. N. (1984) The comprehensive head of department. *Aspects of Education*, Vol. 33, pp. 18–25.

Chitty, C. (1993) *The National Curriculum – Is It working?* Harlow: Longman.

Clark, C., Dyson, A. and Millward, A. (eds.) (1995) *Towards Inclusive Schools?* London: David Fulton.

Clark, C., Dyson, A. and Millward, A. (1997) *New Directions in Special Needs: Innovations in Mainstream Schools*. London: Cassell.

Clark, C., Dyson, A., Millward, A. and Robson, S. (1999) Theories of inclusion, theories of schools: deconstructing and reconstructing the 'inclusive school'. *British Educational Research Journal*, Vol. 25, no. 2, pp. 157–78.

Claxton, G. (1988) *Teaching to Learn: A Direction for Education*. London: Cassell.

Clough, P. (1998) Introduction. In Clough, P. (ed.) *Managing Inclusive Education: From Policy to Experience*. London: Paul Chapman.

Coleman, M. (1999) The experience of women becoming headteachers. Unpublished PhD thesis, School of Education, University of Leicester.

Coleman, M. and Bush, T. (1994) Managing with teams. In Bush, T. and West-Burnham, J. (eds.) *Principles of Education Management*. Harlow: Longman.

Commission for Racial Equality (1997) *Exclusion from School and Racial Equality: A Good Practice Guide*. London: Commission for Racial Equality.

Cooper, H. (1989) Does reducing student to instructor ratios affect achievement? *Educational Psychologist*, Vol. 24, no. 1, pp. 78–98.

Creemers, B. (1994) *The Effective Classroom*. London: Cassell.

Crowther, F. (1993) How teachers view themselves. *Management in Education*, Vol. 7, no. 4, pp. 14–16.

Cubillo, L. (1998) Women and NPQH – an appropriate leadership model? Paper given at the British Educational Research Association Conference, Queen's University, Belfast, August.

Dalin, P. and Rust, V. D. (1996) *Towards Schooling for the Twenty First Century*. London: Cassell.

Darling-Hammond, L. (1990) Teacher professionalism. Why and how? In Lieberman, A. (ed.) *Schools as Collaborative Cultures: Creating the Future Now*. London: Falmer Press.

Day, C. (1985) Professional learning and the researcher intervention: an action research perspective. *British Educational Research Journal*, Vol. 11, No. 2, pp. 133–51.

Day, C. (1993) Reflection: a necessary but not sufficient condition for professional development. *British Educational Research Journal*, Vol. 19, no. 1, pp. 83–93.

Day, C. (1996) Professional learning and school development in action: a personal development planning project. In MacBride, R. (ed.) Teacher Education Policy. London: Falmer Press.

Day, C. (1999) *Developing Teachers: The Challenges of Lifelong Learning*. London: Falmer Press.

Day, C., Harris, A., Hadfield, M., Tolley, H. and Beresford, J. (2000) *Leading Schools in Times of Change*. Milton Keynes: Open University Press.

Day, C., Johnston, D. and Whitaker, P. (1985) *Managing Primary Schools: a Professional Development Approach*. London: Harper Row.

DES (1978) *Special Educational Needs: Report of the Committee of Enquiry into the Education of Handicapped Children and Young people (The Warnock Report)*. London: HMSO.

DES (1992) *Non-teaching Staff in Schools: A Review by HMI*. London: HMSO.

Dewey, J. (1916) *Democracy in Education*. New York: McMillan.

DfEE (1996) *Setting Targets to Raise Standards*. London: HMSO.

DfEE (1997) *Excellence in Schools*. London: HMSO.

DfEE (1998) *Teachers: Meeting the Challenge of Change*. London: HMSO.

Donnelly, J. (1990) *Middle Managers in Schools and Colleges*. London: Kogan Page.

Drummond, M., Rouse, D. and Pugh, G. (1992) *Making Assessment Work*. Nottingham: NES, Arnold and the National Children's Bureau.

Duignan, P. and Macpherson, R. (1992) *Educative leadership: Practical Theory for New Administrators and Managers*. London: Falmer Press.

Dunham, J. (1995) *Developing Effective School Management*. London: Routledge.

Dyson, A. (1990) Effective learning consultancy: a future role of special needs co-ordinators. *Support for Learning*, Vol. 5, no. 3, pp. 116–27.

Earley, P. and Fletcher-Campbell, F. (1989) *The Time to Manage: Department and Faculty Heads at Work*.Windsor: NFER/ Nelson.

Elliott, J. (1979) Implementing school based action research: some hypotheses. *Cambridge Journal of Education*, Vol. 9, no. 1, pp. 21–29.

Elliott, J. (1991) *Action Research for Educational Change*. Buckingham: Open University Press.

Elliott, J. and Adelman, C. (1976) Inquiry and discovery teaching. *New Era*, Vol. 54, no. 9, pp. 10–17.

English, T. and Harris, A. (1987) *An Evaluation Toolbox for Schools*. London: Longman.

Eraut, M. (1994) *Developing Professional Knowledge and Competence*. London: Falmer Press.

Esp, D. (1993) *Competencies for School Managers*. London: Kogan Page.

Everard, K. B. and Morris, G. (1996) *Effective School Management* (3rd edn). London: Paul Chapman.

Farrell, P., Balshaw, M. and Polat, F. (1999) *The Management, Role and Training of Learning Support Assistants. Research Brief 161*. London: DfEE.

Farrow, S., Tymms, P. and Henderson, B. (1999) Homework and attainment in primary schools. *British Educational Research Journal*, Vol. 25, no. 3, pp. 323–42.

Fidler, B. (1996) *Strategic Planning for School Improvement*. London: Pitman Publishing.

Fidler, B. (1997) Strategic management. In Fidler, B., Russell, S. and Simkins, T. (eds.) *Choices for Self-Managing Schools: Autonomy and Accountability*. London: Paul Chapman.

Fidler, B. and Bowles, G. with Hart, J. (1991) *Planning Your School's Strategy: ELMS Workbook*. Harlow: Longman.

Field, K., Holden, P. and Lawlor, H. (2000) *Effective Subject Leadership*. London: Routledge.

Fielding, M. (1999a) Target setting, policy pathology and student perspectives: learning to labour in new times. *Cambridge Journal of Education*, Vol. 29, no. 2, pp. 277–88.

Fielding, M. (1999b) Editorial. *Cambridge Journal of Education*, Vol. 29, no. 2, pp. 173–82.

Fink, D. (1999) Deadwood didn't kill itself: a pathology of failing schools. *Educational Management and Administration*, Vol. 27, no. 2, pp. 131–42.

Fish, J. and Evans, E. (1995) *Funding Special Education*. Buckingham: Open University Press.

Fitzgibbon, C. (1992) School effects at A level: genesis of an information system? In Reynolds, D. and Cuttance, P. (eds.) *School Effectiveness: Research, Policy and Practice*. London: Cassell.

Flanders, N. (1965) *Teacher Influence, Pupil Attitudes, and Achievement*. Washington: US Office of Education.

Fraze, L. and Hetzel, R. (1990) *School Management by Wandering Around*. Pennsylvania: Technomic Publishing Co.

French, J. and Raven, B. (1968) The bases of social power. In Cartwright, D. and Zander, A. (eds.) *Group Dynamics, Research and Theory*. London: Tavistock Press.

Fullan, M. (1991) *The Meaning of Educational Change*. London: Cassell.

Fullan, M. (1993) *The New Meaning of Educational Change.* London: Cassell.

Fullan, M. (1999) *Change Forces: The Sequel.* London: Falmer Press.

Fullan, M., Bennet, B. and Rolheiser-Bennett, C. (1990) Linking classroom and school improvement. *Educational Leadership,* Vol. 47, no. 8, pp. 13–19.

Galloway, S. and Morrison, M. (1994) *The Supply Story: Professional Substitutes in Education.* London: Falmer Press.

Gibb, C. (1947) The principles and traits of leadership. In Gibb, C. (ed.) (1969) *Leadership.* Harmondsworth: Penguin Books.

Gipps, C. (1992) *Developing Assessment for the National Curriculum.* London: Kogan Page.

Glatter, R. (1997) Context and capability in educational management. *Educational Management and Administration,* Vol. 25, no. 2, pp. 171–92.

Glover, D. (1994) *Ofsted and Middle Management: Research Report to Centre for Educational Policy and Management.* Milton Keynes: Open University Press.

Glover, D., Gleeson, D., Gough, G. and Johnson, M. (1998) The meaning of management: the development needs of middle managers in secondary schools. *Educational Management and Administration,* Vol. 26, no. 3, pp. 181–95.

Goodson, I. F. (1992) *Studying Teachers' Lives.* London: Routledge.

Goodson, I. and Hargreaves, A. (1996) *Teachers' Professional Lives.* London: Falmer Press.

Gray, J. (1990) The quality of schooling: frameworks for judgement. *British Journal of Educational Studies,* Vol. 38, no. 3, pp. 203–23.

Gray, J. and Wilcox, B. (1994) *Good School, Bad School: Evaluating Performance and Encouraging Improvement.* Buckingham: Open University Press.

Green, H. (1994) Strategies for management development: towards coherence? In Bennett, N., Crawford, M. and Riches, C. (eds.) *Managing Change in Education.* London: Paul Chapman.

Greenfield, T. and Ribbins, P. (1993) *Greenfield on Educational Administration.* London: Routledge.

Grundy, S. (1994) Action research at the school level. *Educational Action Research,* Vol. 2, no. 1, pp. 23–38.

Gunter, H. (1997) *Rethinking Education: The Consequences of Jurassic Management.* London: Cassell.

Gunter, H. (1999) Contracting headteachers as leaders: an analysis of the NPQH. *Cambridge Journal of Education,* Vol. 29, no. 2, pp. 251–64.

Hales, C. P. (1993) *Management Through Organisations: The Management Process, Forms of Organisation and the Work of Managers.* London: Routledge.

Hall, V. (1996) *Dancing on the Ceiling: A Study of Women Managers in Education.* London: Paul Chapman.

Hall, V. (1997) Managing staff. In Fidler, B., Russell, S. and Simkins, T. (eds.) *Choices for Self-managing Schools.* London: Paul Chapman.

Hamlin, B. (1990) The competent manager in secondary schools. *Educational Management and Administration,* Vol. 18, no. 3, pp. 3–10.

Handy, C. (1976) *The Gods of Management.* London: Pan.

Hannay, L. and Ross, J. (1999) Department heads as middle managers? Questioning the black box. *School Leadership and Management,* Vol. 19, no. 3, pp. 335–58.

Hannon, P. (2000) Rhetoric and research in family literacy. *British Educational Research Journal,* Vol. 26, no. 1, pp. 121–38.

Hardie, B. L. (1995) *Evaluating the Primary School.* Plymouth: Northcote House.

Hargreaves, A. (1991) Contrived collegiality: the micro-politics of teacher collaboration. In Blase, J. (ed.) *The Politics of Life in Schools: Power, Conflict and Cooperation*. London: Sage.

Hargreaves, A. (1994) *Changing Teachers, Changing Times: Teachers' Work and Culture in the Postmodern Age*. New York: Teachers College Press.

Hargreaves, D. (1995) School culture, school effectiveness and school improvement. *School Effectiveness and School Improvement*, Vol. 6, no. 1, pp. 23–46.

Hargreaves, D. and Hopkins, D. (1994) *Development Planning for School Improvement*. London: Cassell.

Hargreaves, D., Hopkins, D., Leask, M., Connolly, J. and Robinson, P. (1989) *Planning for School Development: Advice to Governors, Headteachers and Teachers*. London: DES.

Harris, A. (1998) Improving ineffective departments in secondary schools *Educational Management and Administration*, Vol. 26, no. 3, pp. 269–78.

Harris, A. (1999a) *Effective Subject Leadership: A Handbook of Staff Development Activities*. London: David Fulton.

Harris, A. (1999b) *Teaching and Learning in the Effective School*. London: Arena Press.

Harris, A. (2000) What works in school improvement? Lessons from the field and future directions. *Educational Research*, Vol. 42, no. 1, pp. 1–11.

Harris, A., Busher, H. and Wise, C. (2000) *Training Subject Leaders as Middle Managers: A Report to the Teacher Training Agency*. Nottingham: University of Nottingham, School of Education.

Harris, A. and Hopkins, D. (1999) Teaching and learning and the challenge of educational reform. *International Journal of School Effectiveness and School Improvement*, Vol. 10, no. 1, pp. 257–67.

Harris, A. and Hopkins, D. (2000) Introduction to special feature: alternative perspectives on school improvement. *School Leadership and Management*, Vol. 20, no. 1, pp. 9–14.

Harris, A., Jamieson, I. M. and Russ, J. (1995) A study of effective departments in secondary schools. *School Organisation*, Vol. 15, no. 3, pp. 283–99.

Harris, A., Jamieson, I. and Russ, J. (1996) What makes an effective department? *Management in Education*, Vol. 10, no. 1, pp. 7–9.

Hirst, P. H. (1974), *Knowledge and the Curriculum*. London: Routledge & Kegan Paul.

Hodgkinson, C. (1991) *Educational Leadership: The Moral Art*. Albany, NY: State University of New York Press.

Holly, P. (1987) Action research: a cautionary note. In Holly, P. and Whitehead, J. (eds.) *Action Research in Schools: Getting it into Perspective*. CARN Bulletin No. 7. Cambridge: Cambridge University Press.

Hopkins, D. (1984) Teacher research: back to basics. In Holly, P. and Whitehead, J. (eds.) *Action Research in Schools: Getting it into Perspective*. CARN Bulletin No. 6. Cambridge: Cambridge University Press.

Hopkins, D. (1985) *A Teacher's Guide to Classroom Research*. Milton Keynes: Open University Press.

Hopkins, D. (1986) Identifying INSET needs: a school improvement perspective. In McBride, R. (ed.) *The In-Service Training of Teachers*. Lewes: Falmer Press.

Hopkins, D. (1987) *Improving the Quality of Schooling: Lessons from the OECD International School Improvement Project*. London: Falmer Press.

Hopkins, D. (1993) *A Teacher's Guide to Classroom Research* (2nd edn). Milton Keynes: Open University Press.

Hopkins, D. (1997) *Powerful Learning, Powerful Teaching and Powerful Schools (an Inaugural Lecture)*. Nottingham: University of Nottingham, School of Education.

Hopkins, D., Ainscow, M. and West, M. (1994) *School Improvement in an Era of Change*. London: Cassell.

Hopkins, D., Ainscow, M. and West, M. (1997a) Unravelling the complexities of school improvement: a case study of the Improving the Quality of Education for All (IQEA) project. In Harris, A., Bennett, N. and Preedy, M. (eds.) *Organisational Effectiveness and Improvement*. Milton Keynes: Open University Press.

Hopkins, D. and Hargreaves, D. (1991) *The Empowered School*. London: Cassell.

Hopkins, D. and Harris, A. (1997) Improving the quality of education for all. *Support for Learning*, Vol. 12, no. 4, p. 2–4.

Hopkins, D., and Harris, A. (2000) *Creating the Conditions for Teaching and Learning*. London: David Fulton.

Hopkins, D. and MacGilchrist, B. (1998) Development planning for student achievement. Paper given at the 11th International Congress for School Effectiveness and School Improvement, Manchester, 7 January.

Hopkins, D., West, M. and Ainscow, M. (1996) *Improving the Quality of Education for All*. London: David Fulton.

Hopkins, D., West, M., Harris, A., Ainscow, M. and Beresford, J. (1997b) *Creating the Conditions for Classroom Improvement*. London: David Fulton.

Hoyle, E. (1980) Professional development of teachers. In Hoyle, E. and Megarry, J. (eds.) *World Year Book of Education*. London: Kogan Page.

Hoyle, E. (1981) Management and the school. In *Block 3, E323 Management Processes in Schools*. Milton Keynes: Open University Press.

Huberman, M. (1990) The model of the independent artisan in teachers' professional relations. Paper presented at the Annual Conference of the American Educational Research Association, Boston, MA.

Huberman, M. and Miles, M. (1984) *Innovation Up Close*. New York: Plenum Books.

Hughes, M. (1976) The professional-as-administrator: the case of the secondary head. In Peters, R. S. (ed.) *The Role of the Head*. London: Routledge & Kegan Paul.

Hughes, M. (1985) Leadership in professionally staffed organisations. In Hughes, M., Ribbins, P. and Thomas, H. (eds.) *Managing Education: The System and the Institution*. London: Holt Rinehart & Winston.

Hughes, M. (1990) Educational administration: international trends and issues. *International Journal of Educational Management*, Vol. 4, no. 1, pp. 22–30.

James, M., and Ebbutt, D. (1980) Problems of engaging in one's own school. In Nixon, J. (ed.) *A Teacher's Guide to Action Research*. London: Grant McIntyre.

Johnson, M. and Castelli, M. (1998) NPQH and Catholic needing something more. *Management in Education*, Vol. 12, no. 2, pp. 10–11.

Joyce, B. (1992) Co-operative learning and staff development: teaching the method with the method. *Co-operative Learning*, Vol. 12, no. 2, pp. 10–13.

Joyce, B., Calhoun, E. and Hopkins, D. (1997) *Models of Teaching Tools for Learning*. London: Open University Press.

Joyce, B. and Showers, B. (1980a) The coaching of teaching. *Educational Leadership*, Vol. 40, no. 2, pp. 4–10.

Joyce, B. and Showers, B. (1980b) Improving in-service training: the messages of research. *Educational Leadership*, Vol. 37, no. 5, pp. 379–85.

Joyce, B. and Showers, B. (1988) *Student Achievement through Staff Development*. New York: Longman.

Joyce, B. and Showers, B. (1991) *Information Processing Models of Teaching*. Aptos, Ca: Booksend Laboratories.

Joyce, B. and Weil, M. (1996) *Models of Teaching* (4th edn). Englewood Cliffs, NJ: Prentice-Hall.

Kakabadse, A. and Parker, C. (1984) *Power, Politics and Organisations: A Behavioural Science View*. New York: John Wiley.

Kemmis, S. and McTaggart, R. (1981) *The Action Research Planner*. Geelong, Victoria: Deakin University Press.

Kemp, R. and Nathan, M. (1989) *Middle Management in Schools: A Survival Guide*. Oxford: Blackwell.

Knight, B. (1993) *Financial Management for Schools*. London: Heinemann.

Kohn, M. N. and Kottocamp, R. B. (1993) *Teachers: The Missing Voice in Education*. Albany, NY: SUNY.

Kyriacou, C. (1986) *Effective Teaching in Schools*. Oxford: Blackwell.

Kyriacou, C. (1991) *Essential Teaching Skills*. Oxford: Blackwell.

Lambert, K. (1972) The role of the head of department in schools. Unpublished MA (Ed) thesis, University of Southampton.

Leask, M. and Terrell, I. (1997) *Development Planning and School Improvement for Middle Managers*. London: Kogan Page.

Leeds Education Department (1998) *Behaviour Management Support*. Leeds: Leeds City Council.

Leicestershire LEA (1989) *The Revised LEA Curriculum Statement*. Leicester: Leicestershire County Council.

Leithwood, K., Chapman, J., Corson, D., Hallinger, P. and Hart, A. (eds.) (1996) *International Handbook of Educational Leadership and Administration*. Dordrecht: Kluwer.

Leithwood, K. and Jantzi, D. (1990) Transformational leadership: how principals can help reform school cultures. *School Effectiveness and School Improvement*, Vol. 1, no. 4, pp. 312–31.

Leithwood, K., Jantzi, D. and Steinbach, R. (1999) *Changing Leadership for Changing Times*. Buckingham: Open University Press.

Levacic, R. (1995) *Local Management of Schools: Analysis and Practice*. Buckingham: Open University Press.

Levine, D. and Lezotte, L. (1990) *Unusually Effective Schools: A Review of Research and Practice*. Madison, Wi: National Center for Effective Schools Research and Development.

Levine, M. and Trachtman, R. (eds.) (1997) *Making Professional Development Schools Work*. New York: Falmer Press.

Lewin, K. (1948) *Resolving Social Conflicts*. New York: Harper & Row.

Lieberman, A. (1996) Practices that support teacher development: transforming conceptions of professional learning. In McLaughlin, M. W. and Oberman, I. (eds.) *Teacher Learning: New Policies, New Practices*. New York: Teachers CollegePress.

Literacy Task Force (1997) *The Implementation of the National Literacy Strategy*. London: DfEE.

Little, J. W. (1993) Teachers' professional development in a climate of educational reform. *Educational Evaluation and Policy Analysis*. Vol. 15, no. 2 pp. 129–51.

Lomax, P. (1990) *Managing Staff Development in School: An Action Research Approach*. Clevedon: Multilingual Matters.

Louden, W. (1991) *Understanding Teaching*. London: Cassell.

Louis, K. and Miles, M. (1990) *Improving the Urban High School: What Works and Why*. London: Cassell.

Lyons, G. and Stenning, R. (1986) *Managing Staff in Schools*. London: Hutchinson.

Macbeath, J. (1998) Introduction. In Macbeath, J. (ed.) *Effective Leadership: Responding to Change*. London: Paul Chapman.

Mahil, M. and Busher, H. (1998) *Leadership in education organisations in Saudi Arabia*. University of Leicester, School of Education, mimeo.

Marland, M. and Smith, S. (1981) *Departmental Management*. London: Heinemann Educational.

Marris, P. (1993) The management of change. In Mabey, C. and Mayon-White, B. (eds.) *Managing Change*. Milton Keynes: Open University Press.

Marsden, S. (1997) *Capital Fundraising for Schools*. London: Pitman.

Marsh, M. (1997) In conversation with Janet Ouston. In Ribbins, P. (ed.) *Leaders and Leadership in the School, College and University*. London: Cassell.

Mathematical Association (1988) *Managing Mathematics: a Handbook for Heads of Department*. Cheltenham: Mathematical Association and Stanley Thornes.

McIntyre, D. and Haggar, H. (1996) *Mentors in Schools: Developing the Profession of Teaching*. London: David Fulton.

McMahon, A. and Bolam, R. (1987) *School Management Development: A Handbook for LEAs*. Bristol: National Development Centre for School Management Training.

McNiff, J. (1988) *Action Research: Principles and Practice*. London: Collier-Macmillan.

Merchant, G. and Marsh, J. (1998) *Co-ordinating Primary Language and Literacy: The Subject Leader's Handbook*. London: Paul Chapman.

Miles, M., Saxl, E. and Lieberman, A. (1988) What skills do educational change agents need? An empirical view. *Curriculum Enquiry*, Vol. 18, no. 2, pp. 157–93.

Millet, A. (1996) Pedagogy – last corner of the secret garden. Lecture at King's College, University of London, 15 July (mimeo).

Millward, A. and Skidmore, D. (1998) LEA responses to the management of special education in the light of the code of practice. *Educational Management and Administration*, Vol. 26, no. 1, pp. 57–66.

Morris, T. and Dennison, W. F. (1982) The role of the comprehensive head of department analysed. *Research in Education*, Vo. 28, pp. 37–48.

Morrison, K. and Ridley, K. (1989) Ideological contexts for curriculum planning. In Preedy, M. (ed.) *Approaches to Curriculum Management*. Milton Keynes: Open University Press.

Mortimore, P. (1993) School effectiveness and the management of effective ilearning and teaching. *School Effectiveness and School Improvement*, Vol. 4, no. 4, pp. 290–310.

Mortimore, P. (ed.) (1999) *Understanding Pedagogy and its Impact upon Learning*. London: Paul Chapman.

Mortimore, P. and Mortimore, J. with Thomas, H. (1994) *Managing Associate Staff in Schools*. London: Paul Chapman.

Mortimore, P., Sammons, P., Stoll, L., Lewis, D. and Ecob, R. (1988) *School Matters: The Junior Years*. Wells: Open Books (reprinted in 1994 by Paul Chapman, London).

Mountfield, A. (1993) *School Fundraising: What You Need to Know*. London: Directory of Social Change.

Moyles, J. with Suschitsky, W. (1997) *Jills of All trades? Classroom Assistants in KS1 Classes*. London: Association of Teachers and Lecturers.

Moyles, J., Suschitsky, W. and Chapman, L. (1998) *Teaching Fledgings to Fly: Report on Mentoring in Primary Schools*. London: Association of Teachers and Lecturers.

Munn, P. and Drever, E. (1991) *Using Questionnaires in Small Scale Research: A Teachers' Guide*. Edinburgh: Scottish Council for Research in Education.

Murgatroyd, S. and Morgan, C. (1992) *Total Quality Management and the School.* Buckingham: Open University Press.

National Commission on Education (1995) *Learning to Succeed: The Way Ahead: A Report from the Paul Hamlyn Foundation.* London: National Commission on Education.

National Curriculum Council (1990) *The Whole Curriculum.* York: NCC.

Newsam, P. (1994) Last bastion of the mighty state: a governors' guide. *The Times Educational Supplement,* 30 September.

Nias, J. (1989) *Primary Teachers Talking: A Study of Teaching as Work.* London: Routledge.

Nias, J. (1999) Primary teaching as a culture of care. In Prosser J. (ed.) *School Culture.* London: Paul Chapman.

Nias, J., Southworth, G. and Campbell, P. (1992) *Whole School Curriculum Development in the Primary School.* London: Falmer Press.

Nutbrown, C. (1998) Managing to include? Rights, responsibilities and respect. In Clough, P. (ed.) *Managing Inclusive Education: From Policy to Experience.* London: Paul Chapman.

OFSTED (1995a) *Class Size and the Quality of Education: A Report.* London: HMSO.

OFSTED (1995b) *The OFSTED Framework: Framework for the Inspection of Nursery and Primary and Secondary Schools.* London: HMSO.

OFSTED (1998a) *An Evaluation of the First Two Years of the Working of the SEN Code of Practice.* London: HMSO.

OFSTED (1998b) *Secondary Education 1993–97: A Review of Secondary Schools in England.* London: HMSO.

OFSTED (1999) *Guidance on the Inspection of Secondary Schools: The OFSTED Handbook.* London: HMSO.

O'Neill, J. and Kitson, N. (eds.) (1996) *Effective Curriculum Management: Co-ordinating Learning in the Primary School.* London: Routledge.

Osler, A. (1997) *The Education and Careers of Black Teachers: Changing Identities, Changing Lives.* Buckingham: Open University Press.

Osler, A., Watling, R. and Busher, H. (2000) *Reasons for Exclusion from School: Report to the DfEE.* Leicester: Centre for Citizenship, School of Education, University of Leicester.

Ouston, J. (1997) Pathways to headship and principalship. In Ribbins, P. (ed.) *Leaders and Leadership in the School, College and University.* London: Cassell.

Ouston, J. (1998) Introduction. *School Leadership and Management,* Vol. 18, no. 3, pp. 317–20.

Ozga, J. (1988) Introduction. In Ozga, J. (ed) *School Work: Approaches to the Labour Process of Teaching.* Milton Keynes: Open University Press.

Plant, R. (1987) *Managing Change and Making it Stick.* London: Fontana.

Pollard, A. and Tan, S. (1993) *Reflective Teaching in the Primary School: A Handbook for the Classroom.* London: Cassell.

Poster, C. (1976) *School Decision-Making: Educational Management in Secondary Schools.* London: Heinemann.

Prosser, J. and Warburton, T. (1999) Visual sociology and school culture. In Prosser J. (ed.) *School Culture.* London: Paul Chapman.

Ransom, S. (1998) For citizenship and the remaking of civil society. Paper given at the University of Sheffield, Division of Education seminar, 'Education for new Times', January (mimeo).

Ribbins, P. (1992) What professionalism means to teachers. Paper given at the British Educational Management and Administration Society Fourth Research Conference, University of Nottingham.

Ribbins, P. (1995) Schools as organisations. In Hughes, M., Ribbins, P. and Thomas, H. (eds.) *Managing Education: The System and the Institution.* London: Holt, Rinehart & Winston.

Ribbins, P. (1997) *Leaders and Leadership in the School, College and University.* London: Cassell.

Riches, C. (1981) *Non-Teaching Staff in Primary and Secondary Schools. Block 6, Course E323.* Milton Keynes: Open University Press.

Riches, C. (1984) Management of non-teaching staff in a school. In Goulding, S. and Bell, J. (eds.) *Case Studies in Education Management.* London: Harper & Row.

Riches, C. (1988) *Managing Staff in Schools. Block 4, Course E325.* Milton Keynes: Open University Press.

Riley, K. (1994) *Managing for Quality in an Uncertain Environment.* Luton: Local Government Management Board.

Riley, K. and Rowles, D. (1997) Managing with governors. In Fidler, B., Russell, S. and Simkins, T. (eds.) *Choices for Self-managing Schools.* London: Paul Chapman.

Roaf, C. (1998) Inclusion, the Code of Practice and the role of the SENCO. In Clough, P. (ed.) *Managing Inclusive Education: From Policy to Experience.* London: Paul Chapman.

Rowland, S. (1984) *The Enquiring Classroom.* London: Falmer Press.

Rubin, L. (1985) *Artistry and Teaching.* New York: Random House.

Rudduck, J. (1985) Teacher research and research based teacher education. *Journal of Education for Teaching,* Vol. 11, no. 3, pp. 281–89.

Rudduck, J., Chaplain, R. and Wallace, G. (1997) *School Improvement – What can Students Tell Us?* London: David Fulton.

Rudduck, J. and Hopkins, D. (1995) Introduction. In Rudduck, J. and Hopkins, D. (eds.) *Research as a Basis for Teaching: Readings from the Work of Lawrence Stenhouse.* London: Heinemann.

Sallis, J. (1988) *Schools, Parents and Governors: A New Approach to Accountability.* London: Routledge.

Sammons, P., Hillman, J. and Mortimore, P. (1994) *Key Characteristics of Effective Schools: A Review of School Effectiveness Research.* London: OFSTED.

Sammons, P., Thomas, S. and Mortimore, P. (1997) *Forging Links: Effective Schools and Effective Departments.* London: Paul Chapman.

Scheerens, J. (1992) *Effective Schooling.* London: Cassell.

Schein, E. (1992) *Organisational Culture and Leadership* (2nd edn). San Francisco, Ca: Jossey Bass.

Schon, D. (1983) *The Reflective Practitioner: How Professionals Think and Learn.* New York: Basic Books.

Schon, D. (1987) *Educating the Reflective Practitioner: Towards a New Design for Teaching and Learning in the Professions.* San Francisco Ca: Jossey Bass.

School Teachers Review Body (STRB) (1995) *Fourth Report* (Cm 2765). London: HMSO.

School Teachers Review Body (STRB) (1996) *Fifth Report* (Cm 3095). London: HMSO.

Senge, P. (1990) *The Fifth Discipline.* New York: Doubleday Currency.

Sennett, R. (1995) Something in the city. *The Times Literary Supplement,* 22 September, pp. 13–15.

Sergiovanni, T. (1992) *Moral Leadership.* San Francisco, Ca: Jossey Bass.

Sergiovanni, T. (1994a) *Building Community in Schools*. San Francisco, Ca: Jossey Bass.

Sergiovanni, T. (1994) Changing our theory of schooling. *Management in Education*, Vol. 8, no. 1, pp. 9–11.

Sergiovanni, T. (1995) *The Principalship: A Reflective Perspective*, Boston, Ma: Allyn & Bacon.

Shulman, L. (1997) Knowledge and teaching: Foundations of the new reform. *Harvard Educational Review*, Vol. 57, no. 1, pp. 1–22.

Simkins, T. (1997) Managing resources. In Tomlinson, H. (ed.) *Managing Continual Professional Development in Schools*. London: Paul Chapman.

Simkins, T., Ellison, L. and Garrett, V. (1992) *Implementing Educational Reform: Early Lessons*. London: BEMAS/Longman.

Simons, H. (1978) Process evaluation in practice in schools. Curriculum Studies Department, University of London Institute of Education, mimeo.

Siskin, L. (1994) *Realms of Knowledge: Academic Departments in Secondary Schools*. London: Falmer Press.

Siskin, L. (1997) The challenge of leadership in comprehensive high schools: school vision and departmental divisions. *Education Administration Quarterly*, Vol. 33, no. 2, pp. 604–23.

Skinner B. F. (1938) *The Behavior of Organisms*. New York: Appleton Century Crofts.

Smyth, J. (1991) *Teachers as Collaborative Learners*. Milton Keynes: Open University Press.

Southworth, G. (1995) *Looking into Primary Headship: A Research Based Interpretation*. London: Falmer Press.

Southworth, G. (1998) *Leading Improving Primary Schools: The World of Headteachers and Deputy Heads*. London: Falmer Press.

Steadman, S., Eraut, M., Fielding, M. and Horton, A. (1995) *Making School Based INSET Effective. Research Report No. 2*. Brighton: University of Sussex, Institute of Education.

Stenhouse, L. (1975) *An Introduction to Curriculum Research and Development*. London: Heinemann.

Stenhouse, L. (1979) Research as a basis for teaching. In Rudduck, J. and Hopkins, D. (eds.) (1995) *Research as a Basis for Teaching: Readings from the Work of Lawrence Stenhouse*. London: Heinemann.

Stenhouse, L. (1981) Action research and the teacher's responsibility for the educational process. In Rudduck, J. and Hopkins, D. (eds.) (1995) *Research as a Basis for Teaching: Readings from the Work of Lawrence Stenhouse*. London: Heinemann.

Stoll, L. and Fink, D. (1996) *Changing Our Schools: Linking School Effectiveness and School Improvement*. Buckingham: Open University Press.

Stoll, L. and Fink, D. (1998) The cruising school: the unidentified ineffective school. In Stoll, L. and Myers, K. (eds.) *No Quick Fixes: Perspectives on Schools in Difficulty*. London: Falmer Press.

Strand, S. (1999) Ethnic group, sex and economic disadvantage: associations with pupils' educational progress from Baseline to the end of Key Stage One. *British Journal of Educational Research*, Vol. 25, no. 2, pp. 179–202.

Stringfield, S. and Teddlie, C. (1992) A hierarchical longitudinal model for elementary school effects. In Creemers, B. and Reezigt, G. (eds.) *Evaluation for Educational Effectiveness*. Groningen: ICO.

Tampoe, M. (1998) *Liberating Leadership*. London: The Industrial Society.

Tannenbaum, R. and Schmidt, W. (1973) How to choose a leadership pattern. *Harvard Business Review*, Vol. 51, no. 3, pp. 162–80.

Teacher Training Agency (TTA) (1998) *National Qualification for Subject Leaders.* London: HMSO.

Teddlie, C., Falowski, C., Stringfield, S., Deselle, S. and Garvue, R. (1984) *The Louisiana School Effectiveness Study Phase 2.* Louisiana: Louisiana State Department of Education.

TES (2000) Supply staff gain part-time rights. *Times Educational Supplement,* 12 May, p. 11.

Thomas, H. and Martin, J. (1996) *Managing Resources for School Improvement: Creating a Cost-Effective School.* London: Routledge.

Tomlinson, H. (ed.) (1997) *Managing Continuous Professional Development.* London: BEMAS/Paul Chapman.

Torrington, D. and Weightman, J. (1989) *The Reality of School Management.* Oxford: Blackwell.

UNESCO (1994) *Salamanca Statement and Framework for Action on Special Needs Education.* Paris: UNESCO.

Van Maanen, M. (1995) On the epistemology of reflective practice teachers and teaching. *Theory and Practice,* Vol. 1, no. 1, pp. 33–50.

Van Velzen, W., Miles, M., Elholm, M., Hameyer, U. and Robin, D. (1985) *Making School Improvement Work.* Leuven: Belgium ACCO.

Wallace, M. and Hall, V. (1994) *Inside the SMT: Team Approaches to Secondary School Management.* London: Paul Chapman.

Wallace, M. and Huckman, L. (1999) *Senior Management Teams in Primary Schools.* London: Routledge.

Wallace, R., Engel, D. and Mooney, J. (1997) *The Learning School: A Guide to Vision Based Leadership.* Thousand Oaks, Ca: Corwin Press.

Watson, L. (1969) Office and expertise in the secondary school. *Educational Research,* Vol. 11, no. 2, pp. 104–12.

Weber, S. and Mitchell, C. (1999) Teacher identity in popular culture. In Prosser, J. (ed.) *School Culture.* London: Paul Chapman.

Wenham, D. (1999) Civil liability of schools, teachers and pupils for careless behaviour. *Educational Management and Administration,* Vol. 27, no. 4, pp. 365–74.

West, N. (1995) *Middle Management in the Primary School: A Development Guide for Curriculum Leaders, Subject Managers and Senior Staff.* London: David Fulton.

West-Burnham, J. (1992) *Managing Quality in Schools: A TQM Approach.* Harlow: Longman.

Whitehead, J. (1986) Action research, educational theory and the politics of educational knowledge: an integrated approach to professional development. Unpublished paper, University of Bath.

Whitehead, J. and Lomax, P. (1997) Action research and the politics of educational knowledge. *British Educational Research Journal,* Vol. 13, no. 3, pp. 175–90.

Willis, P. (1977) *Learning to Labour: How Working Class Kids Get Working Class Jobs.* Farnborough: Saxon House.

Wise, C. S. (1999) The role of academic middle managers in secondary schools. Unpublished PhD thesis, University of Leicester.

Wolcott, H. (1977) *Teachers versus Technocrats.* Ann Arbor, Mi: University of Oregon.

Wood, D. (1988) *How Children Think and Learn.* London: Blackwell.

Index